ORGANIZING STRANGERS
Poor Families in Guatemala City

The Texas Pan American Series

Organizing Strangers
Poor Families in Guatemala City

BRYAN R. ROBERTS

UNIVERSITY OF TEXAS PRESS
AUSTIN & LONDON

The Texas Pan American Series is published with the assistance of a revolving publication fund established by the Pan American Sulphur Company.

Library of Congress Cataloging in Publication Data

Roberts, Bryan R.   1939-
    Organizing strangers.

    Bibliography: p.
    1. Guatemala (City)–Poor.   2. Community organ-
ization.   3. Sociology, Urban.   I. Title.
HN150.G8R6   301.44'1   72-3513
ISBN 0-292-76000-0

Manufactured in the United States of America

To my father and mother

CONTENTS

TABLES

PREFACE

This study of urban life in Guatemala did not result from a plan of investigation that predetermined the choice of Guatemala, its capital city, and specific neighborhoods. I was attracted by the idea of living in Latin America, and within this area the choice of Guatemala was, to some extent, accidental. While at Manchester, I was given the opportunity to join Richard Adams's research project on contemporary Guatemala. Given my own lack of experience, this seemed an excellent means to introduce myself to Latin American research. I was given every facility by the project and could make use of the excellent contacts that Adams had built up over the years in Guatemala. At the same time, I was in no way constrained in the choice of subject or in the manner of investigation.

In deciding to go to Guatemala, I did, however, have some specific questions that I wanted to explore. One of these concerned the nature of the social and political changes concomitant upon the rapid urbanization of much of the underdeveloped world. The reorganization of patterns of work, residence, and social relations implied in urbanization seemed to me at the time to promise dramatic changes in peoples' capacity to organize politically and economically. In Latin America the rapid urbanization that occured in the 1950s and 1960s promised to bring about changes in the social structure more basic than had any other factor since the period of Spanish and Portuguese conquest and consolidation. Given this starting

point, I decided on a study of migrants, especially those migrants whose shift to the urban area might be thought to be the
most dramatic: the rural poor living in the squalor and cramped
living conditions of the shantytowns and other urban slums. It
is clear to me now that by formulating my problem in this way
I placed too little importance on how the people involved in
these movements conceived of their situations. At first I tended
to overlook the social differentiation among them and the extent to which changes in location or style of work implied
meaningful changes in social context. Even the assumptions I
made about the nature of shantytowns and their inhabitants
proved to be mistaken.

In the course of the investigation I gave increasing emphasis
to the nature and genesis of individual perceptions of social situations, and it is fortunate that I did not so tightly define my
investigation that I was unable to recognize the need to change
my focus. I was able to feel my way slowly, using conversation
and observation to remedy my own inexperience of the local
culture. Partly because I chose to study people whose experiences had been so varied, I had to recognize that their perceptions of what to them also were often novel situations were
crucial variables in the investigation.

Both my wife and I greatly enjoyed living in Guatemala and
we have very good memories of both periods of field work. We
were delighted to be able to revisit Guatemala in 1972 on the
way to carry on field work in Peru. After an absence of almost
four years, I found little evidence of substantial change in the
conditions of life described in this book.

I revisited the neighborhoods that are the setting of this
study and could discern few social or physical differences. The
shantytown of San Lorenzo was still standing despite the firm
commitments of governments to remove it ever since I began
field work in 1966. Happily, the people I had interviewed were
still alive and persisting in their search to find better work; less
happily, several of them were finding increasing difficulties in
obtaining work as they grew older. Pepe, for example, was con-

stantly scouring the city in search of jobs since his shop had failed, and he was now too old to work on the urban buses. The cooperative to whose prospects I devote the whole of Chapter 6 had by now failed. I asked the reason why and the responses, like the situation, had not changed either: there was, they said, a lack of trust among the members. The streets of the shanty-town were still unpaved and drainage still ran through them; the number of shacks that had been improved had not noticeably increased. The organizations representing these poor families, the clubs and betterment committees, appeared as ineffective and as publicly distrusted as they had been when I left Guatemala in 1968.

I want to emphasize, however, that Guatemala is in many ways an exceptional case among Latin American countries. Conservative forces have, as is well known, been unusually successful in resisting an increase in the political or economic participation of the mass of its population. Also, it is by Latin American standards a very small country, and the presence of the United States is evident and dominant. The significance of these factors will be brought out in the book, but I mention them here because my research experience in Latin America since 1968 convinces me that Guatemala is an extreme case in these respects. Though a country like Peru may be a long way from solving its internal and external problems, I do not find there the acute feelings of frustration and helplessness that characterize so many of the urban poor in Guatemala.

ACKNOWLEDGMENTS

The early field work for this study was carried out while I was on leave of absence from the University of Manchester; it was financed in part by a postdoctoral fellowship from the Institute of Latin American Studies of The University of Texas at Austin. I also received a grant-in-aid from the Wenner Gren Foundation for Anthropological Research to enable me to complete the early stages of my work. The subsequent field work was facilitated by financial help from the University of Manchester, the Institute of Latin American Studies of The University of Texas, and from Teachers College, Columbia University.

I am indebted to Richard Adams, Max Gluckman, and Peter Worsley, whose encouragement and help enabled me to begin what has proved to be an enduring involvement in Latin America. I was particularly helped by being able to participate in the later stages of Adams's research in Guatemala, and his friendship and assistance throughout the period of research and writing have made possible the completion of this work. While in Guatemala, I was helped considerably by Flavio Rojas Lima of the Seminario de Integración Social Guatemalteca and through him made many of the contacts that shaped this study.

I cannot adequately express my personal and intellectual debt to the people I studied and worked with in Guatemala. They must unfortunately remain anonymous both in this acknowledgment and throughout the book. They taught me that underdevelopment is meaningful only as a description of structure and not of personal qualities. It is also difficult to do justice to the assistance I have received from my colleagues at Manchester. In providing a stimulating intellectual environment and in tolerating my leaves ·of absence, they too have made possible the completion of this study. Harley and Waldi Browning of the Population Research Center of The University of Texas at Austin have been constant sources of advice and encouragement, giving me every help and facility to analyze my data, reading and criticizing the manuscript as it evolved and, not least, by being good company. For their very useful criticisms and advice on the study, I would also like to thank Jorge and Shevy Balán, Bruce Kapferer, Chris Pickvance, and Gerald Suttles. My wife, Susan, was an invaluable companion during the research and a great help subsequently in reading parts of the manuscript and getting it ready for press.

ORGANIZING STRANGERS
Poor Families in Guatemala City

1. Social Change in City and Nation

The subject of this book is social change, particularly that change occurring as a result of rapid urban growth in under-developed countries. The material used here is drawn from a study of poor families living in Guatemala City. Their homes, their appearance, and their evident difficulties in meeting the necessities of daily life make me characterize them as poor. One group of families lives in a shantytown located near the center of the city; the other group lives in a legally established neighborhood on the outskirts. Both areas are well known in the city as the residences of poor families, and in this book they are given the pseudonyms "San Lorenzo" and "Planificada." Although these families include very few white-collar workers, they vary in income and other social characteristics and are, in most respects, similar to the majority of Guatemala City's population. In their own life careers, they have experienced the transition from villages and towns to a large, rapidly growing city, and it is through their life careers and present behavior that more general questions of social change are approached.

This study looks at the behavior of these families in terms of two distinct but interconnected perspectives. First is the analysis of the implications of rapid urban growth for the lives of poor people. During the lifetimes of our subjects, Guatemala City has considerably changed its social and economic organization, and these changes have affected the ways in which people interact with each other and cope with their environment. Some of these changes are necessary consequences of urban life, especially in a rapidly expanding city. Both migrants and city born have come to reside among strangers who are rarely related by familial or occupational ties. As position within a set of friends and kin has become less relevant to obtaining jobs, housing, and social standing, individual characteristics, such as education, age, and personal appearance, have become more relevant. However, to use the data only to illustrate change would be to ignore the importance that people's actions and perceptions have for directing change. It is in their attempts to cope with a series of problems and possibilities emerging from the rapid and unplanned growth of the city that the poor in Guatemala are themselves becoming further factors in social change. From this perspective, change is occurring in this city through the attempts of people with certain social characteristics to interpret and mold their urban environment so as to produce in it some degree of order and predictability.

These poor families are, then, active agents of change in urban life, but their activity is heavily conditioned by the links they have with urban organizations and with other urban social groups. Poor people do not form an isolated group in Guatemala City but are permeated by external influences. One of the defining characteristics of urban life is this openness of its residents to the diversity of influences present in a city. In studying the activity of poor families, the relevant context will be not only other poor people in their immediate vicinity, but also all the groups and organizations that intentionally or unintentionally relate to them.

The Significance of the Study of Marginal Groups

I will detail the actions and orientations of poor and ill-educated people who find themselves in a disturbing and often dangerous urban milieu. What is striking about their behavior is the extent to which they are active in shaping their own destinies. This is not to say that they are successful, either in their own terms or by some "objective" standard of economic and social development, but it is not for want of trying. We will see them using sophisticated strategies to manipulate their urban economic and political environment, calculations that are often surprisingly shrewd and rational. Their behavior is describable in terms that could be applied equally to people in the developed societies, and their own position appears to result not from their traditional practices or attitudes, but from more fundamental problems of the social and economic structure of their country. This book will show how external influences repeatedly condition and limit change within this environment. It is on this point that the present study and its conclusions differ from other studies of the poor in urban areas of Latin America. Here it is intended to demonstrate that whatever the reasons for the capacity or incapacity of the poor to organize, to get on with each other, or to improve their individual positions, these cannot be explained in terms of a "culture of poverty." Instead, this analysis emphasizes the importance of the outside influences that permeate these families. And for this reason the study also differs from analyses that emphasize the marginality of the poor as the obstacle to their urban adaption. On the contrary, the problem is precisely that these families are overly involved in urban life.[1]

[1] For the contrasting arguments, see Oscar Lewis, *La Vida*, pp. xliii-liii; and Charles Valentine, *Culture and Poverty*, pp. 48-77. For the marginality argument in a sophisticated form, see Torcuato di Tella, "Populism and Reform in Latin America," in Claudio Véliz, ed., *Obstacles to Change in Latin America*, pp. 47-75.

My aim is to provide documentary material to show that the analysis of the lives and prospects of the urban poor in underdeveloped countries cannot be relegated to a mere study of social and economic change. By showing the attempts of these people to construct a viable environment for themselves, it is intended to demonstrate that their actions are the important determinants for the direction of change in these countries. It is interesting to place the analysis of the politics of the shantytown, which occupies the last chapters, in the perspective of the total urban political structure. From observing the activities of inhabitants of one relatively small neighborhood, one gets a fairly complete picture of the dynamics of change in the urban political system. In addition to the local-level politics of the poor, ill-educated inhabitants of an urban slum, one also encounters in our field of analysis politicians and influentials who are prominent locally, throughout the city, and even nationally.

Though these families do not figure among the urban decision makers, it should be relatively obvious by the end of this book that their capacity or incapacity to organize themselves has been a vital influence on the policies and strategies of decision makers. For these reasons it is a mistake to neglect the importance of movements that are not immediately obvious to the casual urban observer, for such movements are a constant if not always explicit factor in the deliberations of those who do determine policy.

Growth and Order

The growth rate in Guatemala City is comparable to that of the fastest-growing cities in the developed or underdeveloped worlds.[2] It is also an unplanned growth; there is little attempt to control the inflow of migrants or to provide the surplus labor

---

[2] The particular statistics of the city's growth are given later. It is true that most cities in developing countries, particularly in Latin America, are growing more rapidly than did most cities of the industrial west at their comparative period of expansion. This comparison serves to illuminate the peculiar problems posed by the urbanization of developing countries. See L. Reissman, *The Urban Process*, pp. 158-166.

force with work and housing. The situation is similar to that posited by the early Chicago school as characterizing the urban process—a competition for jobs and available space. Under these conditions, we can expect an increasing differentiation in the urban area to serve groups with special characteristics such as age, income, and stage of the family cycle.[3] This process discourages the establishment of neighborhoods based on such stable relationships as kinship, friendship, and common workplace by lessening the importance of personal relationships as a means to recruit to residence and job. Such differentiation also separates home from work.

Heterogeneity is important because differences among the population in their socioeconomic characteristics are extended by differences in experiences. It is one consequence of rapid urban growth in developing countries that the people recruited to the city have diverse experiences. Even where evident differences in culture or ethnicity are not present, important differences are produced by the route through which people arrive at their urban destination.

To come straight from a rural village, to come via work on plantations or in the army, or to come in stages through smaller towns and villages implies a diversity of career experiences, and in these diverse situations individuals encounter new sets of people with a variety of normative expectations. These experiences mean that the urban population is not likely to share common attitudes toward work, the social categories thought relevant for purposes of interaction, and the desirability of actively participating in urban life.

Social heterogeneity and increasing differentiation are thus likely to be important conditions in the urban life of the poor in Guatemala City. In the subsequent pages we will be engaged

---

[3] This is to summarize an argument that will be detailed in subsequent chapters. A summary of the position of the Chicago school is provided by the introduction and the articles in the section on classical human ecology in George Theodorsen, ed., *Studies in Human Ecology*. There are important differences between this process in Guatemala and the one that occurred in early Chicago.

in documenting this diversity and looking at its consequences, especially as it affects the capacity of the poor to cooperate informally with each other in pursuit of common objectives.

We must ascertain how these families do maintain a degree of order in their environment and what are the consequences of their efforts for emerging social organization. The kind of order in which we will be interested is one that enables people to reduce the risks and uncertainties in their environment.[4] People neither can nor wish to avoid all risks and uncertainties in their daily life. Daily life inevitably presents many chance encounters with strange people or with strange situations; moreover, risk and uncertainty may also entail fresh opportunities. What is important, however, is the extent of information that an individual commands about the situations and people he is likely to encounter in daily life. It is this information that enables people to foresee the likely outcome of their actions and to recognize the opportunities that are presented to them. This focus on the importance of information is a familiar one in the study of economic transactions, and because the unstable conditions of Guatemala City make such a focus especially appropriate, it is extended here to analyze daily life. Moreover, a basic assumption of my analysis is that an individual's first priority is that of securing a degree of order in his personal environment; his success in achieving this is a precondition of his participation in a more extensive collective organization.

Adequate information about the characteristics and expected behavior of others allows people to differentiate the talents and capacities present in a group. It is the inability of these Guatemalans to agree upon such differentiation and their lack of information about each other that limits attempts at both formal and informal organization. When these families are

---

[4] The distinction I make between risk and uncertainty is that used by Bruce Kapferer (*Strategy and Transaction*, chap. 5, p. 25). Uncertainty refers to situations in which individuals have no prior knowledge of what costs or benefits their activity will entail, while in situations of risk past experiences and observations provide some idea at least of the costs and benefits likely to accrue to the individual.

brought together by concrete common interests, the quality of information available to them about each other is higher than at other times; for example, the expansion of common effort during the early years of the invasion of a shantytown or during the later stages of the formation of a consumer cooperative association.

The following types of personal information will be shown in the course of the study to increase the effectiveness of group organization: an intimate knowledge of the others with whom an individual interacts; a reliable knowledge of persons based on a variety of situations; an awareness of an individual's relationship to others with whom one has frequent contact. Further important sources of information that reduce risk and uncertainty in encounters are the presence of such visible credentials of status as a job, appearance, or speech, and the meaning of these to the relevant others. These latter sources of information were not readily available to the families in this study. We are dealing with interaction situations in which people are constantly attempting to establish for themselves and others a viable identity. By identity I mean the set of characteristics that define for oneself and others one's social position and expected behavior. The relative difficulty of recognizing the identities of others increases risk and uncertainty in encounters and underlines the peculiar position and experiences of families undergoing the experience of urbanization.

To further analyze the capacity of these people for organization, I will pay particular attention to the development of trust among them. Trust is crucial to effective organization not only because it integrates collectivities but also because it encourages individuals to give their time or resources to collective ends without requiring immediate returns.[5] It provides the "credit" that enables organization to extend its activities. Following

---

[5] Peter Blau, *Exchange and Power in Social Life*, pp. 91-114. My discussion follows that of Blau, both here and at later stages, to demonstrate how social transactions can be conceived as underlying the larger processes of social organization.

Blau, trust is analyzed as an emergent property of social transactions that is built up through the expanding exchange of
benefits of various sorts between individuals. The fulfillment of
small services encourages people to engage in transactions of
greater value that promote interdependence. This social bond
becomes fortified by normative constraints arising from the
interaction of the people involved, which stress a structure of
collective identities to ensure that cooperation is returned.
Certain social positions, such as professional occupations, have
attached to them identities that engender trust, and the
presence of people in such positions facilitates the extension of
trust within a group.

These families, however, live amid poverty and a mobile,
heterogeneous population, and these conditions limit their information about their encounters, particularly since the social
identities of the others with whom they interact are imprecise.
This means that, among families in Planificada and San Lorenzo, secure information about the identities of others is found
mainly when a group is small and interacts intensively. Trust
thus develops by first extending small favors and then greater
ones within a small group and by creating a bond within this
group that causes its members to recognize a common identity
separating them from others in their immediate environment.
Such categorization may not, however, allow for the flexibility
that facilitates cooperation over large groups. As Blau points
out, such practices produce segregating boundaries between the
solidary subgroups.[6] People cooperate with kin before friends,
with fellow Catholics before neighbors and so on, depending on
the amount of trust and information that is in the relationships.

This study of the conditions of information and trust among
these families has a more general significance for understanding
organization among the poor. The capacity of the poor to
organize themselves is often thought to be a question of their
being taught the relevant techniques and of their being brought

[6] Ibid., p. 280.

to a consciousness of their common situation. Such views are those of the professional organizers in Guatemala City whose activities are described in chapter 5. I argue, however, that a more fundamental handicap for the poor is the low quality of information about themselves and others that they are able to obtain. This is, of course, in part an educational problem, but to improve the information flow means that poor people must live in situations of sufficient stability to develop consistent identities in terms of each other. The likelihood of underprivileged people effectively intervening to change the prevailing social order depends on their living in an ordered situation and not, as is sometimes assumed, in a disordered one.

Apart from shared and evident interests, it is the quality of information that they possess about each other that enables professional and other high-status groups to combine effectively and extend their organization; it is this quality of information that underlies the often-noted differentiation in organizational capacity between other groups and the poor. This contrast is sharply and poignantly apparent in the dialogue between the professional cooperative organizers and the inhabitants of the shantytown reported in chapter 6.

Urbanism as a Way of Life

The use of these perspectives is intended to contribute case material to a theoretical dialogue that has long continued in studies of social change in cities. To a whole series of sociological theorists, one of the most important social changes is that which occurs when the basis for group organization shifts from stable face-to-face relationships to interdependence relationships where people fulfill specialized and related tasks. Interdependence through specialization permits the efficient but indirect cooperation of large numbers of people who need not know each other. Cities are the highest expression of the division of labor in society and the places where people are least bound by traditional practices and by ascribed personal relationships.[7] The potential of cities to foster economic and social innovation depends, however, on the emergence within them of ways of ordering social relationships that will convince their inhabitants of the mutual benefits of their interdependence. It is the individual's exposure to the complexities and inequalities of a society and not merely the size of his society that is crucial; in this respect it is misleading to make a sharp contrast between the cohesion of folk villages and the impersonality of city life, since in both societies people vary in the extent they are exposed to these complexities and inequalities.[8]

In his essay "Urbanism as a Way of Life," Louis Wirth summarized and extended this tradition of thought by linking the size, density, and social heterogeneity of cities to a distinctive style of life.[9] This life style emerges when people are brought into frequent and often dependent contact with others who are comparative strangers. It is a style reflecting both the relative anonymity of urban life and the need to cope with a variety of personal and material stimuli. Consequently, this style includes an emphasis on privacy, formal association with people of like interests, and the identification of others by their symbolic characteristics. Wirth thus posits a situation where urban dwellers are not encapsulated in stable relationships with kin and friends and are mobile both geographically and occupationally.

In this respect, he provides a model of the emerging tendencies in urban life rather than a description of any actual urban organization. In fact, his model best fits urban situations where city growth is uncontrolled and rapid, as is the case in Guatemala City. On the other hand, in some cities it is clear that the inhabitants are likely to continue to buffer themselves from the full impact of the city's density and heterogeneity by

---

[7] Emile Durkheim, *The Division of Labor in Society*, trans. George Simpson, pp. 256-296.

[8] Of particular relevance to the present context is Robert Redfield, *Tepoztlan: a Mexican Village, The Folk Culture of Yucatán*, and the criticisms by Oscar Lewis in *Life in a Mexican Village: Tepoztlan Restudied*, pp. 432-440.

[9] Louis Wirth, "Urbanism as a Way of Life," in P. K. Hatt and A. J. Reiss, eds., pp. 46-63.

relying on existing personal relationships and attributing personal significance to city space.[10] However, Wirth's model stresses what has often been neglected, the significance of the overall set of social interactions that occur within a city; for example, that the behavior of individuals and of groups needs to be understood in terms of the set of interactions occurring with others throughout the city. Though this emphasis is not fully developed by Wirth, it is the aspect of his work that will be developed in the subsequent chapters of this book, as it becomes apparent that the emergent patterns of organization among any social group are dependent not only on that group's assessment of the urban situation, but also on the needs and strategies of other social groups.

Wirth's model assumes, however, that individuals are necessarily exposed to the full complexity and heterogeneity of city life. His emphasis on the depersonalization and isolation of city life is thus at variance with my stress on the various ways individuals perceive and construct their social environment in Guatemala City. Perceptions frame the city and often provide local and community references that make the city anything but an impersonal or anonymous entity. As Gans has pointed out, few people are so physically or materially constrained that they cannot select their interactions; widely differing life styles thus emerge even among people living in the same area of the city.[11] The data on these Guatemalan families will show, as other studies have done, that urbanization does not entail the breakdown of either face-to-face relationships or the organization of the environment based on these, but that such relationships are often strengthened in the city. In this respect, my findings are similar to those of Lewis, who has observed that

[10] See the general discussion in Anseln Strauss, *Images of the American City*, and P. H. Chombart de Lauwe, et al., *Paris et l'agglomeration parisienne*, for the ways in which a city can be reduced in the minds and interactions of its inhabitants to sets of intersecting communities.

[11] Herbert Gans, "Urbanism and Suburbanism as Ways of Life: A Re-evaluation of Definitions," in Arnold Rose, ed., *Human Behavior and the Social Processes*, pp. 625-648.

among migrants to Mexico City such supposedly traditional customs as churchgoing, ritual parenthood, and kinship obligations were actually reinforced.[12]

A recurring theme of my analysis is thus the interaction between the "disorganizing" impact of the city's demographic and economic growth and the "reorganizing" activities of the urban population. This theme, an increasingly common one in recent studies of the urban process, may be clarified by comparison with recent studies by anthropologists of urban situations in Africa.[13] To these anthropologists the presence of face-to-face relationships in towns that allow individuals to cope with urban life is not problematic. Pons, working in the ethnically heterogeneous and rapidly growing colonial population of Stanleyville, stresses the numerous distinctions and combinations of residence, kinship, tribe, and degree of civilization as the basis on which associates are selected.[14] Even the uncertainity of not knowing what to expect from others in a mobile population means that individuals develop techniques for maintaining flexibility in their social relationships. Even the illiterate tribesman manages to learn the pattern of urban interaction and contributes to an overall, partially integrated set of urban norms. The fact that customary relationships persist alongside the new ones emerging from urban based work or residence does not reflect a problem of adaption to urban life; instead the migrant uses norms and relationships based on the familiar customary grounds, or on the more recent urban ex-

[12]Oscar Lewis, "Urbanization without Breakdown," *Scientific Monthly* 75, no. 1 (1952): 31-41. Similarly, in a study of Boston, Gans emphasizes the continuing significance of locality and face-to-face relationships between kin and friends (H. Gans, *The Urban Villagers*).

[13]This work is summarized and extended in J. Clyde Mitchell, "Theoretical Orientations in African Urban Studies," in Michael Banton, ed., *The Social Anthropology of Complex Societies*, pp. 37-68, and is given further theoretical content by the formal analysis of social networks. See J. Clyde Mitchell, ed., *Social Networks in Urban Situations*, in which, apart from Mitchell's introduction, there are a number of articles that show the importance of the emergent structure of interpersonal relationships for the way that people cope with the diverse situations of urban life.

[14]Valdo Pons, *Stanleyville*, pp. 257-274.

periences that are appropriate to the social situation in which he is placed. These anthropologists emphasize not the disorganization of urban life, but rather the manifold ways in which people organize their environment, and this becomes the dynamic of emerging urban organization. The social organization of Guatemala will also be described from this viewpoint, showing that it consists of networks of social relationships, more or less articulated with each other, through which individuals relate to their place of work, urban services and administration, and provide for their everyday and emergency needs. The impact of city life and mass media is thus filtered through the sets of relationships the new urban dweller makes available to himself from the particular situations to which he is exposed.

The degree of organization depicted by many of the African studies is, however, different from the one that will be described in this work; most of the African studies were carried out under colonial regimes, or at times or in cities where the incoming population was highly organized by industry or neighborhood. The significance of these external factors is clear in Epstein's study of local-level politics in a Zambian mining township, in which he stresses the emerging significance of work relationships as bases for solidary industrial action among tribal migrants.[15] The structure imposed by the working situation of the mine and the living conditions of the mine township are the crucial factors, as Epstein acknowledges, in leading such relationships and the norms associated with them to supersede other bases for organization. Tribe, religion, or family remain significant in appropriate situations but not in those dealing with opposition to the mine management.

The African mine workers described by Epstein can in certain respects be characterized as a provincial group in that their relationships with people in different social and economic positions outside the group are mediated by brokerage contacts,

[15] Epstein develops the perspective of situational selection outlined above to handle the process of change (A. L. Epstein, *Politics in an Urban African Community*, pp. 224-240).

and most activity relevant to the workers goes on within the group.[16] This concept of provincialism is used in subsequent chapters of this book to analyze the historical changes in social organization within Guatemala City. In a provincial group, people are more likely to know each other over a long period of time and to use their knowledge of an individual's particularities as the basis for interaction. In such a group, a morality emerges that takes account in appropriate situations of the circumstances under which people act.

In Guatemala City, a minimum degree of economic or adminstrative organization has been imposed upon the population. Consequently, there are numerous occasions when people of widely different backgrounds and social positions come into contact outside the framework of a clearly defined territorial or economic organization. Due to this diffusion, the bases on which individuals form relationships to cope with their environment are diverse and often badly integrated; it also means that most of an individual's personal contacts in daily life are with relative strangers. People may still have many face-to-face relationships, but most of their interactions are in situations in which they are guided and limited by a public morality that takes little account of their circumstances.

The aim of this analysis is, then, to identify those conditions that place low-income families in a situation where they are highly and individually linked with different groups outside their place of residence. It then explores the consequence of these linkages for the forms of organization that emerge among low-income families; the neighborhood is used as the focus of investigation.

The problem that we are to analyze is a difficult one, since we are looking at situations where there is no principle of

[16] This use of the term "provincial" is similar to that of Suttles in his description of the Italian section of a south-side Chicago slum (*The Social Order of the Slum*, pp. 4-6). A direct contrast with Suttles's material will be made in later chapters. Using the term "provincial" in reference to Epstein's study is a device, and his analysis of the differentiating factors within the mine-working population is a complex one.

organization inherent in the situation; neighborhood, socio-economic categories, ethnic groups, and age groups do not exist as available bases to organize the environment. No matter what type of analysis is conducted, its impact in most sociological studies is demonstrated in defined and relatively enclosed situations. It is ultimately this frame of reference that organizes the activities being described. In contrast, there are few studies that seek to apply the various theoretical perspectives to situations that are not already implicitly organized. One of the main points of this study is that it is as much the task of the sociologist to examine situations that are not defined or ordered, and to regard such situations as the problem and basis of the analysis, as it is to search, often endlessly, for implicit organizing principles that are thought to be present.

The kind of structural analysis beloved by the sociologist is not easily applicable here and, where most studies search for the underlying principle of order that "explains" the actions of individuals, this study starts from the assumption that the lack of any such principles is both the key to our analysis and the major factor in influencing the direction of change.[17]

Country and City

Present-day Guatemala is the remnant of the larger captaincy general of Guatemala founded by the Spanish conquerors. The effect of this institution was to establish a thin settlement of Europeans among a dense Indian population representing the fragments of the Mayan cultural empire. European settlement never increased to the degree that such immigrants constituted a large fraction of the population. The settlers established large farms, entered trade, or settled in one or two distinct areas of the country as small farmers.[18]

---

[17] Of the studies that have been influential in this analysis, Blau, *Exchange and Power in Social Life*, and Suttles, *The Social Order of the Slum* have elaborated their perspective in social situations where there are already implicit organizing principles, such as interacting work groups or the segmentary opposition of ethnic groups.

[18] This summary account is extracted from various sources, including Nathan Whetten, *Guatemala: The Land and the People*, and Mario Rodriguez, *Central*

The rest of the population was increasingly organized into nucleated settlements known as *municipios,* whose administrative center would be an urban area of one or two thousand people, but which would include smaller villages and some scattered homesteads. The center of each *municipio* became a link in an extensive network of administration that went through departmental capitals to the national capital in Guatemala City.

There also developed a religious network. The Spanish introduced Catholicism, and the missionary orders often provided the first stable contacts that many of the Indian settlements had with their conquerors. The conversion process was rapid, but never complete. Though the Indian groups accepted the framework of the Catholic faith, they filled it with much of their own tradition and adapted it to their own social and political organization. The church was still the most prominent and elaborate building in Guatemalan villages and small towns, but the religious life of the people was for the most part carried on outside the formal structure of the church. The sacraments were rarely taken, and many buildings had no resident priest but were visited only once a month, or yearly. The Catholic church and its ministers have never been a powerful organizing force in Guatemalan social life. The Catholic religion is observed in the daily activities and festivals that are organized and often created by the native population.

This feature of Guatemalan life is important to an understanding of urban Catholicism, where in the absence of small-scale and cohesive social organization that embodies religious

---

America. However, the recent study that provides the essential background to the events and processes to be described is Richard Adams, *Crucifixion by Power.* Adams's study is an attempt to analyze the entire social structure of Guatemala using an anthropological perspective. Apart from providing illuminating material on the various sectors of the population such as the military, the church, landowners, and others that are only alluded to in this study, its theoretical conclusions have many similarities with those arrived at here—notably the importance of external agencies for the development or rather underdevelopment of specific groups and even nations.

and political organization, the expression of Catholicism mainly occurs through its formal structure—the church and its priests rather than through an interacting congregation. Despite this aspect of its place in urban organization, the Catholic religion is another means whereby village, town, and city are joined in a common order.

The army and trade are the other factors that need to be mentioned as integrating forces in the society. For most of this century, the army has recruited most of its conscripts directly from the villages. The army is one means whereby illiterate peasants have received a modicum of education and traveled their country, often staying in or visiting the national capital. The trading networks that link the highlands, lowlands, and national capital are evidence that the various population clusters throughout the country depend to some extent on each other and are affected by fluctuations in the fortunes and production of each.[19]

Prices in the capital reflect conditions in the provinces, and the movement of goods and labor in the rural areas has long depended on what happens in the capital. Guatemala is a country that has relied on a few major export crops, first coffee, then bananas, and increasingly sugar and cotton. These exports have come to be handled through the national capital, but their fluctuations affect the conditions of life even in the remotest village. For example, subsistence farmers in Guatemala have used migration to coastal plantations to obtain extra wages to complement the produce of their own land. The failure of export crops affects this movement and the prosperity of even small, relatively enclosed villages.

The sensitivity of internal factors to the export market has meant that the effect of Guatemala's increasing dependence on the United States has been felt throughout the country. The legendary United Fruit Company is a less important part of the

[19] See Sol Tax, "Economy and Technology," in Sol Tax, ed., *Heritage of Conquest*, pp. 43-65.

country's economy than it once was, but it and its subsidiaries remain significant and have been complemented by heavy U.S. investment in commercial agriculture and industrial development. The fluctuations of American foreign policy and the relation of Guatemalan governments to them become important to the peasant too. Many of the families whose careers we trace have been employed in American plantations or have been dislodged from their villages and farms by the vicissitudes of Guatemalan–U.S. relations.[20]

The important thing to remember about rural social organization in Guatemala is that it is, and has been, permeated by influences radiating from the capital and, ultimately, from foreign lands. Few of the villages from which many of those questioned in this study migrated are so enclosed as not to have been affected by, or to have been aware of, events elsewhere in Guatemala and, in particular, those in the capital.

Accompanying this interdependence has been an increasing mixture of ethnic groups in Guatemala. At the time of the conquest, all but a few thousand of the inhabitants of Guatemala were Indian; by 1921, 64.8 percent were classed as Indian; by 1950, 53.5 percent of the population were so classed; and in 1964, 43.4 percent.[21] The reduction in the proportion of the Indian population was not produced by a higher birth rate among the non-Indian group, the Ladinos, nor by immigration from abroad. Rather, it resulted from linked processes—the intermarriage of Indians and Ladinos, the classification of their children as Ladino, and the movement away from their village homes by Indians who adopt the Spanish language and dress and, in a strange place, became identified as Ladino.

[20] This argument is spelled out in great detail by Adams, from whose work these and subsequent comments in this section are largely derived (*Crucifixion by Power*, pp. 124-238).

[21] The 1921 figure is from Jorge Arias B., "Aspectos demográficos de la población indígena de Guatemala," *Boletín Estadístico*, nos. 1-2 (1959), pp. 18-38, and the latter two are census figures. There is a problem of comparability, but it does not affect the general trend.

An important element in the relation of ethnic groups in Guatemala is that, although in small communities the relations between them resemble caste relationships with no inter-marriage or social mixing, away from home, especially in urban areas, it is relatively easy for Indians to become accepted as Ladinos.[22] The census definition, for example, pertains only to whether the respondent habitually speaks an Indian tongue and wears Indian dress.

This loose definition, however, appears to reflect the real situation in the large urban places where people rarely question the public face that families present with respect to their ethnic allegiance. In the life histories that I taped of both Ladino and Indian migrants to the city, it is striking that, while in every case they stressed the differences between Indian and Ladino that existed in their home villages, they denied that such differences existed in the town. When pressed, urban Ladinos will identify other families as Indian, but they do so only when these families wear Indian dress and speak an Indian tongue.

The Political Background

Guatemala is also a country that has been dramatically affected by national and international politics. Though the basic structure of power in the country, centering on the large landowners, financiers, and industrialists of local and foreign origin, has changed little through the years, events have produced upheavals in city and countryside.[23] The continuing theme is that of palace revolutions, with coups d'etat replacing one set of military officers or civilians with another of similar ideology.

Since recent political events play an important part in the analysis of the life careers that will be covered in Chapters 2 and 3, a survey of the most significant developments is necessary. The man that figures prominently in the recollections of the families studied here is a military dictator—Jorge Ubico (presi-

[22] See Melvin M. Tumin, *Caste in a Peasant Society*.

[23] The continuity in the structure of power is Adams's basic thesis (*Crucifixion by Power*, pp. 318-353).

dent 1936-1944), who treated his country very much as a personal plantation. He constantly drove about to inspect its outlying parts and ruled through a system of local officials appointed by him and removable by him. Migration was forbidden without explicit permission, and those found wandering in the roads without a pass were liable for conscription in the labor gangs that were constructing a road system in the countryside.

Forced labor obtained from the rural areas and the army provided most of the labor for the road and public-works programs undertaken by Ubico. During his regime, foreign investment was protected and encouraged; this period represented the height of the United Fruit Company's influence. However, the expansion of export crops and improved communications began to make the country more externally visible and more internally integrated. The United States became increasingly involved in Guatemala during the war years and forced Ubico to confiscate the plantations of the large number of German plantation owners in the countryside. In these years, Guatemala's sphere of orientation changed from Europe to the United States; the export markets in Europe were lost and replaced by those in the United States.

Along with American influence came American personnel, military and civilian, and an increasing American interest in the development of the country. At the end of the war, the United States encouraged reform elements in Guatemala and withdrew its support from Ubico. Ubico fell not only because he had alienated sections of the rural and urban populations by his repressive policies, but also because of the gradual expansion of the Guatemalan economy and the improvements in communication, both internally and externally, which were making his traditional conservative regime appear anachronistic to his own officers as well as to his civilian opponents.

These events were affecting migration into the city also—the rate of migration had been low during the prewar period, but during the war the confiscation of the German plantations and the changes in the economy produced dislocations in the rural areas.

After the fall of Ubico in 1944, the civilian government of José Arévalo undertook gradual reforms, one of which was the increasing articulation of the rural areas, the departmental capitals, and the national capital. For the first time office-holding in local communities was subject to the electoral process, and party politics increasingly entered the local village. These years, however, were prosperous, and the civilian reform government generated confidence in internal investment. The period also coincided with favorable conditions in world trade, and Guatemala's exports fetched high prices. During these years, both in the rural areas and in the capital, low-income groups were organized for the first time in labor unions and rural syndicates. Agrarian reform was promulagated and a labor code drawn up.

The Arévalo government was succeeded in 1951 by that of Jacobo Arbenz, under conditions of rising tension. Arbenz was suspected of coming under the influence of the Communist party and of being partly responsible for the assassination of his major rival and fellow hero of the 1944 Revolution—Fransisco Arana. In both city and rural areas, communists and rival political parties became active in attempting to enroll members. The various factions used whatever influence they had with the government to get their own members appointed to key posts and to tie the distrubution of land and other favors to political support. The communists, for example, were quite successful in obtaining such posts and expanding their influence.

These various events were effectively disturbing the traditional relations of rural and urban areas—even traditional Indian organization was becoming permeated by the conflicts of political interests.[24] In contrast with previous years when villages and towns had always been sensitive to political issues

[24] See, for example, Manning Nash's account of political troubles in a highland Indian village affected by industrialization in *Machine Age Maya: The Industrialization of a Guatemalan Community*, pp. 102-106.

and to the political demands of the government, the various parties were now operating independently of the established social structure, contacting members directly and creating new bases of local power. The turmoil into which much of the country was being thrown was accentuated by a period of economic difficulty as world trade turned against Guatemala. During those years, the increasing migration toward the city was thus accelerated by political difficulties; in the movements of people of this time, political incidents figure prominently as occasions for their moving.

The United States, in coordination with landed interests in Guatemala, was becoming increasingly disturbed by the turn of events and moved to displace Arbenz. The counterrevolution of Carlos Castillo Armas in 1954 is well known as one of the recent incidents of U.S. intervention in Latin America. During that time, two events occurred that affect our study. One is that the reforms of previous years came to a halt and, in some cases, such as in the redistribution of land, the reforms were even revoked. Labor unions were banned except under stringent conditions. The counterrevolution provided ample opportunity for the settlement of old scores. Again, and for different reasons, the provinces became unstable, and further occasions for migration arose.

The second event was the increasing influence of the United States in planning and development. To justify their intervention, the United States heavily backed the Castillo Armas government with loans and assistance. It is from this period on that Guatemalan policy became increasingly articulated in a direct manner with that of the United States. The American embassy and development agencies increased their personnel in Guatemala and, in city and country, assisted in programs of development. Even the poorest peasant became aware of the presence of the United States as it surfaced as an apparent and important element in his world view.

Toward the end of the Castillo Armas regime, the country's economy, fortified by American aid, began to improve; this improvement was not sustained and by the time of the assassination of Castillo Armas in 1957, it had entered upon a major recession. A conservative military officer, Miguel Ydígoras Fuentes, eventually replaced Castillo Armas. From this regime onward, there was little attempt to control movement within the country. The rural areas settled down to some degree of peace, but with increased government supervision of local administration. The city expanded apace and evolved an elaborate administrative bureaucracy.

The last important regime in power before our account proper begins was that of a military junta headed by Colonel Peralta, which deposed Ydígoras in 1963 on the grounds of laxity and corruption. A major motive for the takeover was the belief that Ydígoras would be unable to cope with the increasing challenge from left-wing revolutionary forces that had become active during and after the Cuban Revolution.[25] This junta received tacit support from the United States and continued a policy of very cautious development which involved distribution of some national lands to peasants, slow industrialization, and building schools and roads.

Finally in 1966, when field work for this study commenced, a civilian government won the national election that the junta had agreed to hold. The winning party was the most reform oriented of the three parties that had stood for election. The other two were conservative parties heavily dominated by the military, and the victory of the Partido Revolucionario was hailed as signifying the possibility of a fundamental change in Guatemala's politics and social structure. The votes that won the election for the party came from the urban or rapidly urbanizing areas of Guatemala.[26] The election was thus hailed as showing that the increasing urbanization of the country

[25] Adams links the capacity of the military to take over at this time with its unprecedented equipment in skills and material by the United States in the years immediately preceding (*Crucifixion by Power*, p. 262).

[26] Kenneth F. Johnson, *The Guatemalan Presidential Election, 1966*.

provided a base for the political strength of left-wing reform governments.

This book is, in one way, an account of the reasons for the failure of this prediction. Throughout the field work, more time was spent under martial law than under constitutional government. States of siege and alarm were constantly being declared and often made field work difficult. The wave of political assassinations and kidnappings that put Guatemala in world headlines was occurring in the city during this period, and these events were often reported to me by my informants in the neighborhood.

Though this political violence is an important background to the events described here, it did not directly affect the lives of the families in this study. It was a violence directed against people of middle and upper social status, and poor families in the city were spectators rather than participants in these events. Such violence increased the uncertainties associated with urban life and was an additional factor in the distrust these families showed for any form of organization. In this respect, the degree of political activity and organization reported in subsequent chapters is the more remarkable. At the end of the field work, the evident failure of the civilian reform government to achieve reform or to free itself from military influence was being remarked upon internationally and, as we will see, locally by the people whose activities we are to study. In 1970 the national election was won by a conservative political party headed by a military officer explicitly following the tradition of Castillo Armas.

The events to be described are interwoven with the major political events, and not only do they provide the context of the following analysis but often enough are concretely embodied in the careers and present activities of the subjects. Historical events in a country like Guatemala are themselves independent factors in any analysis of contemporary behavior and in the following account they will be treated as such.

The background to this study is thus that of a country

experiencing an uneasy passage into the international politics and economics of the last half of the twentieth century. Like many developing countries, Guatemala has become increasingly dependent on one of the two major world-power blocs, and its internal development is heavily conditioned by this circumstance. Since 1944, the social and economic organization of the country has been disturbed on several occasions and, though control remains with the same interests, the manner of control has changed. The small and isolated villages, with their own form of political and religious organization, have been increasingly articulated with the national capital through development agents, political party officials, military commanders, and the like. Social, medical, and educational services increasingly appear throughout the country and are the further means by which village, town, and city are linked. Above all, the rapid rise of the urban population to some 35 percent of the country's population represents an important social transformation.

The City

The population of Guatemala City at the beginning of this field work was in the region of 600,000. The city's expansion to its present size appears to have occurred disproportionately in the last twenty-five years. Unfortunately the censuses prior to 1950 do not have a high reliability, so the figures given are only suggestive of a possible trend.[27]

The figures below indicate that the rate of growth of the city has substantially increased in recent years and that <u>between 1940 and 1964 the city apparently tripled its size.</u> This growth, though high by world standards, is not unusual for Latin America. Indeed, the growth rate of Guatemala's urban sector

---

[27] These are all census figures. The first four are taken from Theodore Caplow, "The Social Ecology of Guatemala City," *Social Forces* 28(December 1949): 113-135. The figures for the 1950 and 1964 censuses are from Deanne Termini, "Socio-Economic and Demographic Characteristics of the Population of Guatemala City with Special Reference to Migrant-Non-Migrant Differences," p. 6, which is based on data from the Dirección General de Estadística of Guatemala.

Census	Guatemala City	Total	Percentage in City
1880	58,000	1,225,000	4.7
1893	72,000	1,365,000	5.3
1921	121,000	2,005,000	6.0
1940	186,000	3,283,000	5.7
1950	284,276	2,790,869	10.2
1964	572,937	4,284,473	13.4

(defined as a place with two thousand or more inhabitants), an annual average of 5.64 percent between 1950 and 1964, ranks fifth in the overall Latin American urban growth rates, being exceeded only by such countries as the Dominican Republic, Costa Rica, Venezuela, and Brazil.[28]

The city's growth is produced by two processes—natural increase within the city and migration into the city. There is little evidence to suggest that the rate of natural increase within the city is substantially different from that of the country as a whole, and assuming the rate to be that of the country as a whole—3.28 percent annually—approximately 40 percent of the growth of population of the city in the period from 1950 to 1964 was due to immigration.[29]

Though the proportion of growth due to immigration may appear surprisingly low if urban growth in developing countries is seen as primarily a problem of migrants, the importance of the migrant contribution to growth is greater than these figures suggest. Migrants who come to the city are not a random sample of the total population, and their characteristics make them an active element in changing city life.

The migrant population is the more interesting because it

[28] Lowdon Wingo, "Recent Patterns of Urbanization among Latin American Countries," *Urban Affairs Quarterly* 2, no. 3 (March 1967), Table 2.

[29] Termini, "Socio-Economic and Demographic Characteristics," p. 7. Though it is likely that the urban birth rate is somewhat lower than the provincial one, the social characteristics of urban dwellers in Guatemala do not lead to substantial reductions, and any reduction may be compensated by better medical facilities in the city.

Table 1. Distribution of the Economically Active Male Population According
to Occupation by Migration Status (Percentages)

Occupation	Nonmigrants	Migrants
Professional	7.8	7.8
Administrators	5.7	5.3
Office workers	8.3	8.6
Sales persons	7.6	7.3
Agricultural workers	4.8	5.6
Miners	0.2	0.3
Transportation workers	7.9	10.1
Craftsmen	46.2	33.2
Manual workers	5.5	8.4
Service workers	1.9	10.7
Unknown	4.2	2.6
Total	100.1	99.9

Source: Deanne Termini, "Socioeconomic and Demographic Characteristics of the
Population of Guatemala City," Table 23.

appears that their occupations show a similar range to that of
people born in the city (Table 1). The implications of this distribution are explored in the course of the next two chapters;
but we can note that migrants are somewhat overrepresented in
the service and manual work categories of the occupational
structure. Among women migrants the proportion of service
workers is extremely high—63.7 percent as compared with 28.3
percent of nonmigrant women.

The disproportionate entry of migrants into the service
occupations is indicative of the availability of such occupations
in the city. Guatemala City has not developed industrially at a
rate similar to the expansion of its potential labor force. The
city has never been industrial in the sense that it possessed
large-scale industry, and recent years have seen few additions to
the number of its large-scale enterprises.

In the city there are some fourteen hundred industrial
establishments employing an average of twenty-seven people,
with very few firms employing more than one hundred
workers.[30] The government and its dependencies are both the

[30] Adams, *Crucifixion by Power*, p. 172, reports figures collected for the whole
country by Bruce E. Bechtol, Institute of International Studies, University of

largest single employers of labor and the largest single employers within any occupational category. The municipality, the police force, and the public works are the largest sources of employment in manual, craft, and service occupations.

The industrial activity that does take place in the city is for the most part limited to small-scale production in such areas as shoemaking, carpentry, tailoring, metal working, and the like. There are few factories using sophisticated heavy machinery to produce mass consumer goods, and the levels of skill and literacy required for most manual work are low. To take one indicator of the slow rate of technical improvement in Guatemalan industry, Guatemala's annual growth rate of labor productivity in industry from 1950-1963 was 1.8 percent, which was the lowest of all the Central American countries. Yet Guatemala's rate of urbanization is one of the highest.[3][1]

In Table 2 the percentage of the labor force employed in the various sectors of the urban economy is compared with the percentages of those so employed in Monterrey, Mexico, a rapidly expanding and rapidly industrializing city.

In Guatemala City, a much higher percentage of the labor is employed in the service sectors of the economy and a lower percentage in industry. There is also some evidence that the concentration in the service and commercial sectors of the economy has been increasing in recent years.[3][2] When it is remembered that industry in Guatemala mainly includes craft workshops, the contrast with Monterrey—a city with heavy industry—is heightened. The contrast is also brought out by

---

Oregon, manuscript. It is interesting to observe that the average number of employees in establishments in the department of Guatemala (basically the city and a few small villages) is lower than that reported for some of the provincial departments such as Escuintla. There is certainly no suggestion that heavy industry is located in the capital or its environs.

[3][1] Bank of London and Montreal, *The Central American Common Market*, p. 46.

[3][2] Between the censuses of 1950 and 1964, the proportion of the city's labor force engaged in manufacturing appears to have decreased from 31 to 28 percent. See Dirección General de Estadística, *Sexto censo de población, 1950*, Table 49; and Dirección General de Estadística, *Censos 1964*, Table 12.

Table 2. Percentage Distribution of the Economically Active Population in Guatemala City and Monterrey, Mexico, According to Industry (Both Sexes)

Industry	Guatemala City	Monterrey
Agriculture	2.9	1.2
Mining	0.1	0.7
Manufacturing	26.7	40.3
Construction	7.3	7.6
Commerce	15.1	17.0
Transportation	6.1	6.7
Services	38.9	24.7
Unknown	2.8	1.9

Sources: Guatemala: Deanne Termini, "Socioeconomic and Demographic Characteristics of the Population of Guatemala City," p. 91. Monterrey: Jorge Balán, "The Process of Stratification in an Industrialising Society: The Case of Monterrey, Mexico," p. 49.

comparing the percentage who are owners of enterprises or self-employed; in Guatemala this percentage is 27.3%—over a quarter of the male labor force. In Monterrey the equivalent figure is 11 percent.

The structure of Guatemala City's economy is affected by its position as a metropolitan capital. In such cities it can be expected that a high proportion of the labor force will be engaged in such service activities as administration. However, the high percentage of self-employment indicates that the concentration in the services and commercial sector is not solely the product of the capital's formal position as the organizing center of the country. A casual city observer notes the profusion of street vendors, shoeshine boys, small shopkeepers, and the like, whose presence has less to do with the capital's organizing role in the economy than with the difficulty people experience of finding stable and remunerative work in industrial and other enterprises.

The relative informality of the economy is accompanied by an informal urban administration and settlement pattern. The administrative boundaries of the city are almost coterminous with those of the administrative department of Guatemala, and the relative jurisdictions of the departmental governor, the mayor, and indeed the national government, whose seat is in the city, are not precisely defined.[33]

These competing jurisdictions are further complicated because Guatemala City is functionally related to a much larger area than is included within the city limits. Throughout the period of field work, a major water project vital to the city's continued water supply was being held up because the municipality and the army were competing to undertake it. The army claimed the project lay outside the capital and within the army's provincial jurisdiction; whereas the mayor claimed that, since the project was to serve the city, it was he who should plan it.

In the absence of a professionalized administrative career service, the competing jurisdictions of the various urban authorities are complicated by the desires of their staff members to expand the work so as to provide jobs for kin and friends.

Poor families have also been concretely affected by the relative inability of urban administrations to find the resources to provide adequate welfare services, cheap housing, or indeed even such rudimentary services as drainage, water, and paved streets. The municipality collects a tax on property and a head tax of one dollar for which it issues an identity card. The revenues from these sources and from licensing powers are relatively low, and the work of properly installing urban services has been slow.

The city still has the appearance of a small provincial town despite its large size. Once out of the main thoroughfares and the center of the city, one often finds unpaved streets, which are little more than dirt or mud tracks, and most buildings are only one story tall. Even in the center of the city, despite recent developments such as modern shops and administrative buildings, the streets are lined with a series of small, varied edifices, mostly shops, offices, houses, restaurants, and small

---

[33]The department of Guatemala is one of twenty-two administrative units into which the nation is divided. The department's population is 778,000, approximately 73 percent of whom reside within the municipal limits of Guatemala City.

workshops. The streets are narrow and accommodate only one-way traffic and, even so, the rattling, antiquated buses that roar along belching oil fumes constitute a hazard to pedestrians on the sidewalk.

The expansion of the city has not been planned and has depended on the availability of land and commercial developers' estimates of the profit that could be made from different types of housing. The new neighborhoods of mass-produced housing springing up on the outskirts of the city have catered mainly to the middle- and upper-income groups. The needs of the lower-income groups have been accommodated by splitting up houses into apartments in the central zone, and subletting houses at the periphery. Also, on vacant lots of land throughout the city, small shacks have sprung up, legally or illegally, to accommodate other low-income families. The ravines that cut up the city and extend into its center have been used similarly, and those which once served as urban rubbish dumps now accommodate shantytowns of the type described in this book.

For people living and working in it, Guatemala City is an informal place. Superficially the informality is noted in the relative absence of formal attire in the city streets or in its restaurants. More seriously, it is indicated by the relative absence of formal administrative and welfare services. In the activities of daily urban life there is little that requires urban dwellers to behave in a formal way. There are few forms to fill out or qualifications to establish, because what little there is to administer and to give out is as likely to be done by personal contact as by surveying the qualifications of candidates.

In the daytime the city is a bustling and active place. People crowd onto the sidewalks and into the small business establishments. What distinguishes this city is the great range of social types to be observed in the city center and other zones. Hours of work are not so formalized nor zones so ecologically specialized that people are segregated by occupational function. The high proportion of self-employment makes for a variety of types, ranging from shantytown dwellers to owners of respectable businesses, all bustling about the center and elsewhere in search of profit. This is not only a city that is informal in its economic and administrative organization, but also one where the opportunities for the interaction of people of many social positions is maximized. Such interaction is an important factor in the social organization of the urban poor.

The Neighborhoods

This study is mainly located in two urban neighborhoods, which throughout this book will be called San Lorenzo and Planificada. The use of these names simplifies the discussion, since the particular names reflect something of the contrasting character of the two neighborhoods. San Lorenzo is a shanty-town that was actually named by its inhabitants, who desired to name their home after a saint; Planificada, in contrast, is a formally established and laid out neighborhood that has evidenced less sense of its own identity.

In the absence of large-scale industry or of work-based or other organizations that include significant sections of the urban poor, a local neighborhood is the one place which the poor have in common. It is only here where one can observe low-income families attempting to organize themselves to achieve common objectives; it is also a location that poses peculiar problems for their joint action. The choice of these two neighborhoods was made by selecting two low-income neighborhoods that had contrasting legal origins. In many underdeveloped countries, the scarcity of urban housing and the press of incoming population have resulted in the mushrooming of illegal urban settlements. In these, groups of people squat on private or governmental land, erecting first insubstantial dwellings of paper, board, or straw and replacing them over time with more substantial edifices. These shantytowns have been shown to have peculiar properties that affect the ways in which the poor cope with city life.[34] The act of occupying illegal land

[34] William P. Mangin, "Latin American Squatter Settlements," *Latin American Research Review* 2, no. 3 (October 1967): 65-98.

and the manner in which it is done—through the gradual and dense settlement of the area, involves interaction and cooperation among the settlers. There are present, therefore, the occasions for interaction that are not present in more formally established neighborhoods.

Since illegal settlements are pervasive in developing countries, it is wise to include them as one important variable in describing urban organization. In Guatemala, it is estimated the 15 percent of the city's population live in illegal settlements of the type to be described. This percentage is often higher elsewhere in Latin America. In Peru, for example, it is estimated as 18 percent of Lima's population and in Venezuela as 25 percent of the population of Caracas.[35]

However, despite the recent interest in such settlements, shantytowns are not the only modes of residence that the poor have in cities in developing countries. Consequently, since shantytowns have peculiar properties, another neighborhood was selected that was legally settled and whose families, though poor, live in rented and owned accommodations that are common among the urban poor of developing cities—single rooms opening into a courtyard or a small dwelling of rudimentary structure with open space for washing and cooking.

Naturally, in choosing the neighborhoods on this basis many other possible ecological contrasts have been ignored. Both neighborhoods have different ecological positions with respect to the center of the city. The shantytown occupies a branch of a large ravine that cuts off the center of the city from the residential zones to the west. By cutting across this ravine, residents of the shantytown can arrive in the center after about a ten to fifteen minute walk. Otherwise, they can catch a bus at the top of the shantytown and arrive at the center in about ten minutes. By contrast, the legally settled neighborhood is located some six miles from the center of the city at its southernmost periphery.

[35] José Matos Mar, *Urbanización y barriadas en América del Sur*, p. 212.

We can thus expect that the ecology of both neighborhoods is significant for the patterns of social organization we are likely to find within them. This consideration also implies that caution is needed before generalizing too readily about other low-income families. Since low-income neighborhoods differ on a series of ecological variables, it is likely that they create contexts with special effects on social organization. However, we will investigate some of these ecological effects and, by identifying them, attempt to add to our understanding of the situation of poor people in a rapidly developing city.

The need for caution is reinforced because it proved impossible to work intensively in more than one of the neighborhoods. Although the survey and the informal interviews were carried out in both neighborhoods and I spent much time attending meetings and visiting families in the legal neighborhood, the bulk of the intensive observation was conducted in the shantytown.

Because of this circumstance, the two neighborhoods do not receive equal attention throughout the book. Indeed the material on which Chapters 6 and 7 are based is drawn exclusively from events within and around San Lorenzo. This means that the later chapters contain less comparative material; instead they present case studies of particular types of social process. I do not claim that this arrangement is necessarily a desirable one, but it was the one forced on me by pressures of time and resources.

Despite these various caveats, it is the intention of this study to emphasize the general implications of the patterns of behavior to be described, and consequently it is necessary to have some idea of the extent to which these neighborhoods differ from each other in the characteristics of their inhabitants and differ from the urban population as a whole.

Both neighborhoods contain the same proportion of migrants, which is higher than is the case for the urban male adult population (75 percent as compared with 58 percent of urban males). But in both areas, migrants have been, on the average,

Table 3. Length of Residence in City According to Neighborhood of Heads of Household: Males and Females (Percentages)

| Neighborhood | Born in City | Resident | | | | Total |
		1-10 Years	11-20 Years	21-30 Years	31 Years and Over	
San Lorenzo[a] N (127)	26	8	22	23	21	100
Planificada N (125)	25	17	24	14	20	100

[a]The survey sample is based on a total of 252 cases. The nature of the sample is detailed in the section on methodology later in the chapter.

long-term residents of the city.[36] It is clear from Table 3 that we are dealing with a sample that has had considerable experience.

The occupational distribution of San Lorenzo and Planificada is not comparable with the city distribution reported earlier since the census categories are distinct, including within the category of craftsmen many of those described here as workers in large-scale enterprises (Table 4). However, the two neighborhoods have a higher proportion of self-employed males than is true of the city (34 percent compared with 18.2 percent in the city).

In neither neighborhood is there a significant proportion of white collar workers; both have disproportionate numbers of their employed males in service and trade occupations. Though it is not indicated by the occupational distribution, the workers of Planificada are more likely than those of Lorenzo to have relatively skilled jobs and to work in more formally established companies.

Despite these differences, perhaps one of the surprising things about these figures is that they do not deviate more from each

___

[36] Comparing the neighborhood figures with the city figures is not strictly correct, since the neighborhood sample is of male heads of household, not all adult males. The city figure is calculated from the data given in Termini, "Socio-Economic and Demographic Characteristics," pp. 131-132.

Table 4. Occupations of Heads of Household in the Two Neighborhoods:
Males and Females (Percentages)

Occupation	San Lorenzo		Planificada	
	Males	Females	Males	Females
Workers in established enter-prises (factories, bus companies)	19	3	20	
Construction workers	18		20	
Craftsmen (shoemakers, tailors, dressmakers)	20	11	19	
Service workers (police, domes-tic service, waiters, barbers)	23	51	18	57
Traders	16	32	13	36
White-collar workers	4		5	
Agriculture			5	
Unspecified[a]		3		7
Total percentage	100	100	100	100
Number	(90)	(37)	(110)	(15)

[a]Unemployed are given their previous occupation. In both neighborhoods unemployment is about 4 percent (underemployment is more frequent).

other. After all, we are dealing with neighborhoods which were selected to represent the residential areas of some of the poorest families in the city, and certainly the shantytown presents conditions that are often thought to attract only the most destitute of people or the most recent of urban arrivals. Instead, we find that in terms of migrant status and occupation, the distribution in each neighborhood is not greatly different from the other.

This assertion is reinforced by the similar distribution of educational attainment in the two neighborhoods. Although in neither neighborhood has a significant proportion of the adult population attained a secondary school education or more, in both the large majority of adult males are literate, and the percentage that have not attended school is similar to that of the city as a whole (23 percent as compared with 17 percent of city males over twenty-five).

Table 5. Incomes of Male and Female Heads of Household in
the Two Neighborhoods (Percentages)

Income	San Lorenzo	Planificada
Earn less than 30 dollars a month	34	23
30-49 dollars	34	28
50-69 dollars	16	22
70-89 dollars	8	10
90 dollars and over	8	17
Total percentage	100	100
Number	(117)	(110)
No answer	(10)	(15)

In income distribution, the neighborhoods differ more radically from each other (Table 5). There is evidently a significant section of the shantytown dwellers living there from pure necessity since their incomes fall below thirty dollars a month, barely enough for subsistence. Other families in the shantytown, however, earn incomes that would permit them to easily rent accommodations elsewhere, and we will explore some of the reasons why such families should wish to remain rather than settle elsewhere. The range of incomes in the two neighborhoods is probably representative of the range of incomes found among some 80 percent of Guatemala's urban population. This is a city in which a primary-school teacher earns some eighty dollars a month, and one hundred dollars a month is considered a good wage for an ordinary office worker. The minimum wage is one and a quarter dollars a day, or approximately forty dollars a month. Though the families we are dealing with are poor, their poverty is similar to that of a large section of the urban population.

One factor clearly differentiating the two neighborhoods is apparent in Table 4; that is the higher proportion of women who are heads of household in San Lorenzo. This factor will also be explored more fully later when we look at possible explanations for their pattern of settlement. In the majority of cases these women have dependent children to maintain and are separated from their spouses. There is also a higher proportion of couples united by <u>consensual union</u> in San Lorenzo. Of couples living together, forty-two percent are legally married in San Lorenzo as compared with 54 percent in Planificada. Since the city-wide figures are based on all males and females above the age of fourteen, including those who are single, no accurate comparisons can be given. In the city, 21.5 percent of males and 16.0 percent of females are consensually united; it is thus likely that both neighborhoods have unusually high proportions of consensually united families. We can also note at this stage that the mean number of children per family in the neighborhoods is approximately the same as that of children per family in the city (between three and four). The age of heads of households in both neighborhoods is shown to be older than that of adults in the city. Approximately 56 percent of the neighborhood heads of household are aged forty-four and under, compared with 70 percent of the urban population who are between twenty and forty-four. The selection of household heads as the basis for my samples does mean, however, that their age distribution can be expected to be older than that of all urban adults.

The above survey of socioeconomic characteristics of residents in the two neighborhoods is intended to provide a general outline of their position with respect to the rest of the city. The difference between the two neighborhoods needs to be kept in mind for the subsequent analysis that will be presented later and can be briefly characterized by noting that the residents of San Lorenzo are the more underprivileged. The important point is that the characteristics that emerge from the survey indicate populations that are poor, with traits such as "marginal" occupations, migrant status, consensual union, and low educational levels that have often been found to accompany poverty.

Yet the characteristics do not suggest a population that is so deviant from the urban distribution as to make it likely that it is unrepresentative of low-income people in Guatemala City. The similarities between the shantytown and the legal neighborhood further indicate that, although their ecological differences are reflected in the social characteristics of residents, these differences are not so important as to completely differentiate the range of people that settle.

We are thus studying neighborhoods that are not isolated from or marginal to urban social organization, and their residents have characteristics that are shared by many others living under different residential conditions.

Methodology

This study was carried out on two field trips over a period of three years, from April 1966 to September 1968; a total of fourteen months was spent in the field. The strategy of research was to spend the first, longer period in choosing the neighborhood locations and in familiarizing myself with the social environment and the variables that appeared important within it. A period of four months was spent in selecting the two neighborhoods. This was accomplished by traveling about the city and making contact with the various government and foreign agencies that participated in health and welfare work in poor neighborhoods. Planificada was ultimately selected because of an offer of cooperation from the local health clinic, which was run jointly by the municipality and the university. The shantytown, San Lorenzo, was selected because it had been the recipient of a grant from a United States welfare association and was well known to the urban administration and social welfare administration. Using contacts from all three sources, I introduced myself into the neighborhood.

The selection of neighborhoods, then, did not occur according to any formal or objective plan, and this should be remembered throughout the account to follow. However, the initial contacts with the neighborhood influenced much of the subsequent work, and certainly the emphasis of this book on the articulation of poor families with the rest of the city was first made apparent by the way I entered these neighborhoods.

Although I did not make my residence in either San Lorenzo or Planificada, I did spend almost every day and much of the night there, as I interviewed various persons and made observations. In the initial period, I familiarized myself with the ways these families perceived their urban environment and interacted within it. I also began to accumulate data on their attempts to organize themselves. I used the observations of the initial period to formulate a series of propositions about the nature of the social interaction of these families within and without the neighborhood and about the relation of these patterns to their participation in organization.

Interviews

In the first field period (1966), I personally interviewed 109 families in San Lorenzo and 127 families in Planificada. These interviews consisted of a semistructured session, which lasted about an hour. I would ask a set number of questions and wait until I left the house to record the answers. Respondents were encouraged to elaborate on the themes, and I deliberately avoided writing in their presence to encourage free response. The sample was interviewed twice, with an intervening space of about three months; the first interview elicited basic census-type data, and the second explored attitudes and the extent of social activity. The second interview was always carried out with the head of the family, but the first interview, which was also a means of getting to know the families, was occasionally conducted with the wife.

The sample in San Lorenzo was drawn from a list of families that the neighbors themselves had composed in order to organize their drainage project. To check the accuracy of this list, I mapped each shack in the neighborhood and established the total number of families. The correspondence between the map and the list, with one or two exceptions, was an exact one—a factor attesting to the organizational capacity of these families. This list then served as a sampling frame for the interviews and for the later survey conducted in 1968, sampling one family in three.

In these interviews, approximately 80 to 85 percent of the

sample was interviewed. Those not interviewed were mainly families that I was unable to contact because of limited time. There was no case of a refusal, but undoubtedly some of the families that could not be contacted had occupations or characteristics that made them unavailable at normal times.[37]

In Planificada, I obtained a map of the housing lots in the neighborhood, and I used this as a sampling frame. In the first field period, I interviewed all families within one sector of the map, but for the survey in the second field period I used random numbers to sample a quota of 125 families from housing lots drawn from the whole neighborhood. This change was made because the choice of a sector of the neighborhood proved a biased one in that, when compared with the health center's data on a neighborhood—wide sample, it appeared to contain a higher proportion of wealthier families and long-term residents of the neighborhood. In the second interview of the first period, the initial selection of 127 families in the map sector had to be cut down to 66 families, for lack of time. In the survey the interviewers interviewed each family found on the housing lot, even when there was more than one family, until the quota was filled, noting as refusals or absences the families that could not be contacted after three return visits.

In the second field period (1968), a formal questionnaire was designed and administered with the help of six interviewers. It was designed to cover deficiencies in the earlier data, especially with respect to life histories and kinship networks, and made extensive use of a questionnaire designed by a team from the University of Texas at Austin that had recently been working in Monterrey, Mexico.[38] I personally introduced the interviewers to the families in the shantytown, since these were, in most cases, the same families I had interviewed earlier; thus I was able

[37] Some of these families were probably not residing in the shacks appearing on the list, and for this reason I cannot accurately cite the percentage responding.

[38] See Jorge Balan, et al., "A Computerized Approach to the Processing and Analysis of Life Histories Obtained in Sample Surveys," *Behavioral Science* 14, no. 2 (March 1969).

to check the interview schedules with my own data and knowledge of the families. This procedure enabled me to correct
early mistakes and to insist on return interviews where there
seemed evidence of serious deficiencies.

I was unable to check the survey data with my earlier interview data in Planificada, since I was using a different sample,
but the interviewers, the neighborhood social worker and his
two assistants, were known and liked in the neighborhood, and
I had a high degree of trust in their work. Undoubtedly, their
position in the neighborhood may have influenced some of the
replies they received—especially the replies to the attitudinal
questions, but this was compensated for by the confidence that
appeared to exist between them and the respondents.

In the course of the following chapters, I will use data from
both my own interviews and the survey, thus the sample sizes
will vary. When the data used are from the semistructured interviews of the first field trip, this will be specified and will consist
of a total either of 236 families or of 175 families, if the data are
from the reduced sample of the second visit. Most data are,
however, based on the survey, which consists in a total of 252
families, representing approximately a 90 percent response rate.
The 1964 census estimate of the population of the shantytown
is approximately 2,000, that of Planificada 12,000.

In comparing the data I am struck by the extent the information they obtain is of different utility. The interview data,
though suffering from my own deficiencies in recording, is
much richer with respect to attitudinal issues. In the informal
setting, families explored the meaning of their social situation
more amply than was permitted by the survey. While observing
the interviewers, I noted that they restricted replies more than I
had done and that the respondents felt inhibited by their
presence. It seemed people found it easier to express their
attitudes to me as a foreigner, than to the middle-class interviewers of their own nationality.

This means that with respect to some of the questions on
social relationships, my own data are more relevant than are the

survey data. The survey questions were often interpreted so literally that they did not capture the sense of many relationships; for example, the analysis of friendship has to be dealt with using the interview data rather than survey data.

The survey did, however, provide consistent and quantifiable data of considerable range, and I found both the life history and kinship network data not only to be useful but also to have a high degree of accuracy when checked against the concrete cases I obtained by talking with others, by observation, and by repeated interviews.

Observation and Life Histories

During the first field trip, and throughout the second, I was collecting as complete data as possible on the various public incidents of organization or attempted organization in the shantytown. I participated fully in these events, following participants not only inside but outside the neighborhood. The events increased my range of contacts outside the neighborhood, and in the second field trip a great deal of my time was spent in observing people and organizations that lay beyond the boundary of the neighborhood. It is evidence of the articulation of these families with other urban groups and organizations that the mere act of tracing their daily non-work social relationships often took me throughout the city and even into the countryside. To locate a number of people during their leisure time, I frequently had to follow them to different zones of the city.

I also decided to collect tape-recorded life histories of a select sample of shantytown dwellers. I did this to obtain a record of their perceptions of their own careers so I could use them to complement the survey life-history data and my own observations. I only recorded the histories of people with whom I had developed relationships of some degree of trust and about whose lives I had some prior knowledge. In addition, I selected individuals that I thought represented distinct types of resident. Thus among those interviewed are neighborhood activists, both migrants and city born; religious leaders of the neighborhood;

men involved in national politics; and people distinguished by nothing except the fact that they represent the "silent majority" of neighborhood inhabitants. This sample of ten life histories is in no sense representative, but it will illustrate many of the points that can be made from the survey and observational data. Also, hearing and reflecting on the tapes helped me to rethink my analysis of events by alerting me to some of the significant ways in which the people themselves responded to their environment.

The reader should beware of relying on the empirical data too heavily, and, indeed, if my argument is to be acceptable it must be acceptable because it is reasonable rather than because it is "proved" by empirical analysis. Of course, the various types of data that I bring to the analysis will, hopefully, build confidence in the argument; but this argument, ultimately, has derived from the sense I developed of the field situation. The field work was an enjoyable and involving experience, and in choosing and assessing the empirical data I am constantly guided by that experience. For these reasons, the argument to follow is as much my reconstruction of events as it is the presentation of data fixed by the formal methodology of the study.

2. The Experience of Migration

Since the majority of adults in the city and in the two neighbor-hoods are migrants, we need to determine the differences their experiences and characteristics make in their participation in urban life. The particular perspective of this and subsequent chapters is that the social organization of the city is made up of changing sets of relationships and orientations, and that one of the most important elements of change when the city is growing rapidly is the constant influx of migrants. Migrants are thus not adapting to any fixed pattern of urban life, but are themselves helping to create new patterns of association.

The analysis of migration is crucial to understanding the social changes resulting from rapid urban growth, because migration entails a special problem for the maintenance of order in the city. The influx of migrants disrupts existing social and economic relationships in the city by adding a population of all age levels whose skills, personal commitments, and perspectives often have been shaped prior to their arrival in the city. Thus, migration adds to the social heterogeneity of the city and makes it more likely that city dwellers interact with others with whom they do not have common understandings and with whom they are not linked by social relationships. The extent to which migration leads city people to reorder their personal environment and becomes a factor in increasing the urban activity of both migrants and city born is the focus of the present analysis.

The impact of migration depends on the extent to which migrants are able to enter the various spheres of urban social and economic life and to compete for the resources there. An additional factor is the extent to which migrants are seen by themselves and others to form categorical and interactional groups within the city.

People categorize others in terms of ethnicity or moral attributes to simplify their social environment by attributing a degree of predictability to the behavior of relative strangers. Conversely, the better a person knows someone the less likely he is to use categories to describe him. It is often in the most unstable urban situations where individuals are confronted by a very heterogeneous population that categorization is used as a means of imposing order.[1]

Where migration entails the arrival in the city of people who belong to distinct and relatively solidary cultural groups, both members and nonmembers can use the appropriate categories to simplify their social environment and to predict the behavior of those around them. The way such preurban experiences affect group formation is a recurring theme in this chapter, and this theme will be extended in the next chapter by considering the urban careers of both migrants and city born.

---

[1] J. C. Mitchell, *The Kalela Dance*, analyzes the emergence of tribal categories among the heterogeneous and mobile populations of the towns of the Zambian copperbelt. He shows that the use of categories, including associated joking relationships, is an important means for recent tribal migrants to cope with their urban environment.

Perceptions of Provincial Life

Migrants originate and often spend their formative years in places where the pattern of life is different from that of the city. During these years they work, form opinions, enter into relationships with others, and adopt a pattern of behavior appropriate to the conditions of their home. When they enter the city these experiences are continuing reference points whose implications we need to investigate. They are likely to be as important as the migrant characteristics, which are detailed later, in determining whether migrants compete directly with the city born or are channeled into certain occupations or places of residence; these experiences are certainly important factors in the migrants' tendency to form groups and to be recognized by others as forming distinctive groups.

It should be made clear from the outset that the intention here is not to contrast people from the "traditional" village with those from the "modern" city. This would be a dubious contrast to make in Guatemala and would not serve our present purpose, in any event. Although differences in the norms and consequent attitudes of provincials and of city-bred people often appear as the most dramatic feature of urbanization, they are misleading guides to the urban behavior of migrants, because norms appropriate to provincial places are based on the circumstances and necessities of life in those places. Those norms do not survive in the city unless reinforced by a similar social context. Thus, a peasant in town behaves like a peasant so long as he interacts with fellow villagers and works and lives under conditions similar to those he experienced in his home. Moreover, as an individual moves from one urban situation to another his behavior, and even his norms, are likely to change depending on the conditions he faces there. From the range of norms and attitudes that an individual has developed through his experiences, he selects those appropriate to the constraints of the situation at hand. This is the principle of "situational selection" explored in the analysis of urbanization in Africa, where various studies have shown tribal Africans operating as tribesmen in some contexts and as factory workers or working-class Africans in others.[2]

In this respect, Guatemala City is no different from other urban milieus where, as studies have shown, people move from small, relatively enclosed rural villages to a large city or town and have little difficulty in adjusting to work in factories or in participating in national politics. It would be wrong to assume, however, that the change from one social environment to another has no effect on the way people react to the present. A villager, for example, may shift from working alone in the fields of a quiet, remote mountain farm to living in a crowded, noisy shantytown and working with machines in an ill-lighted factory without showing evident signs of maladjustment; but undoubtedly the transition has meant something and colors his expectations of what is to come. The significance of these points of comparison depends, of course, on the nature of an individual's urban career and, along with identifying the traits of the comparisons that are made, their significance for different urban careers is also explored.

The one aspect of provincial life that migrants constantly refer to more than any other, favorably and unfavorably, is the slow tempo of life in the villages and small towns from which they come. In responding to a survey question about the possibility of returning to the provinces, the reason most frequently cited in favor of returning was the peace and quiet of the countryside. This is a quality of rural life that would be emphasized by city dwellers almost everywhere, and there is nothing exceptional in the emphasis that Guatemalans give to it. It is, however, a longing that is a constant theme of their conversations, and it affects their recreational activities. To go to the countryside with the family is the preferred recreation of this sample. Many choose to take vacations there, fishing or

---

[2] See J. C. Mitchell, "Theoretical Orientations in African Urban Studies," in Michael Banton, ed., *The Social Anthropology of Complex Societies*, pp. 37-38. A study that reaches similar conclusions for a textile mill in rural Guatemala is Manning Nash's *Machine Age Maya*.

visiting relatives, as well as going on shorter day trips from the capital. In the tape-recorded life histories, the respondents were most nostalgic about the leisure activities of rural life, about the picnics, the fishing, playing by the rivers, or dancing to a small band on the balcony of the village hall. There is an evocation of tranquility and relaxation that undoubtedly does not reflect the reality of every rural day, but which is an evocation that brings up common memories among a group of men and women chatting in the street of a city neighborhood.

Most adults in the city have experienced a transition from the slower tempo of this rural life to the noise, frequent interactions, and pace of city life, and this contrast is a recurring one that is used to evaluate the choice of urban residence and the style of urban occupation. The most frequent reason given by respondents in Planificada for their decision to move there was its tranquility, that it reminded them of the countryside.

Notwithstanding the densely crowded conditions of the shantytown, several inhabitants in a public meeting hotly attacked a government project for multifamily houses on the grounds that it did not provide space for chickens, pigs, and other domestic animals. Similarly, jobs are evaluated by the freedom of control the employee will have over the pace of work, and migrants cite the advantages of employment in the provinces where the worker, if he is an independent farmer or craftsman, sets his own pace. In this sense, migration does involve a "ruralization" of the city, but only because it is aided and abetted by the structure of the urban economy and administration. The slow tempo of rural life is a point of comparison that influences choice in the city because it is not entirely inappropriate to urban living conditions.

However, these perceptions of provincial life depend on the place of origin of the migrant and the position he occupied there. Those migrants who were small independent farmers emphasize aspects different from those who were day laborers or craftsmen. Likewise, women emphasize different aspects than men. Farmers and day laborers often perceive tranquillity as being purchased by a monotonous and enslaving routine. In contrast, women, provided they had not sought employment in the countryside, and some independent farmers and craftsmen defined tranquillity as the ability to produce one's own food and freedom from dependency on the employment or the goodwill of others. The qualities valued by some migrants connote a negative image to others. What is perceived as "peaceful" in one migrant's account is said to be "sad" in another's.

These variations result both from differences in the migrants' provincial lives and in their subsequent careers. Older migrants who take a less active part in city life are likely to evaluate more positively the peace and quiet of the countryside, while men in their prime are more likely to comment on the lack of activities in small villages and towns. In the first period of field work, I asked respondents in both neighborhoods about their attitude toward life in the countryside and whether they would return there. In the informal interview situation, a range of replies was given that expanded on the themes mentioned above, and there were also comments about such positive advantages of city life as employment and health and educational facilities. The data did not facilitate the grouping of respondents according to provincial occupation, but differences did emerge between replies in terms of respondents' sex, age, and income. Wives were more favorable to the countryside than husbands, but single women maintaining a family were more unfavorable to the countryside than men. Older men were more favorable to the countryside than younger men, and lower-income people more favorable than higher-income people. The only grouping in which the majority wished to return to the countryside, as distinct from those being simply favorable to it, was made up of people earning less than thirty dollars a month.

These differences in perception are compounded by those migrants who come from villages or towns already subject to heavy outmigration; the peacefulness of rural life there often is due to the decline of the society they remember. One migrant, for example, who still prefers agriculture as an occupation, reported feeling depressed on a recent return to his village because so many people had left and many of the old social activities had ceased. Another migrant, Angel, reflected on the changes in his village; he remembered the times when the village held weekly dances with music provided by its own local band; the dances subsequently came to an end as the members of the band migrated in search of work. They left their instruments behind, but there was no one who could play them. These are reminders that the shift in population from provinces to capital is accompanied by an increasing disappearance of many services and activities in the smaller centers as the city becomes increasingly the center of marketing, retailing, and recreation.

Turning now to migrant perceptions of social relationships in the provinces, we find agreement on the nature of the contrast between capital and provinces, but the meaning attached to provincial organization depends on the position and experiences of the individual. To take the agreed contrast first: it is common for migrants to talk about how people in their home villages or towns know each other and overlook each other's behavior. This was put most succinctly by a city-born inhabitant of the shantytown, José, who recollected his own migrations through small provincial towns:

In San Raimundo the life of that town is, well better to say *was*, because now the situation of all those towns has changed, but formerly life was an agreement of all, everyone knew each other. In San Raimundo it happens that the town was made up of about five families, five types of surnames. The person who wasn't an uncle was a son-in-law; he who wasn't a cousin was a . . . . But that was formerly, now the situation has already changed. People there always were expected to be a little more brotherly, that was how it was there; while here in the capital it is very different, for there are people from all over; like there are good people, bad people here. But there, someone who had a vice, or something of the sort, then he was immediately subject to control.

Several migrants in the two neighborhoods originate from this small town, but the description has general significance as a reasonably typical perception of the different bases of rural and urban life.

Closeness of relationships does not imply cohesion or harmony within a community; what does emerge from migrant perceptions is a sense of provincial society as fragmented and differentiated. Indeed, where social and economic differences exist, knowing everybody only emphasizes these differences. True, the more differentiated the social organization of a migrant's place of origin, the more likely he is to emphasize the divisions in his home community. Conversely, those from relatively isolated villages make few social and economic distinctions. Such differences in perception are documented by Mendez in his study of three types of provincial places in Guatemala—a small isolated village, a small town, and a departmental capital whose population was a little over six thousand.[3] He asked a panel of local respondents in each place to list the characteristics they thought were the most important in differentiating inhabitants of their place. In the isolated village, the only distinctions made were those of caste (Indian-Ladino) and whether the individual could accumulate resources or not. In the small town, seven distinctions were made and in the departmental capital ten distinctions, each detailing type of occupation, wealth, power, social behavior, and so on. As size increases and the economic structure of the town changes, then a greater perception of differentiation and of social inequality emerges. Since migrants to the city come from a range of places, they are thus likely to have a range of perceptions of the meaning of the close social relationships in the places from which they originate.

Two descriptions of provincial relationships are set out below, one by a Ladino migrant from a small but economically and socially differentiated town of some two thousand inhabi-

[3] Alfredo Mendez, *Zaragoza*, pp. 179-196.

tants, the other by a migrant of Indian background who had worked as a plantation laborer. The first is by Angel, whose case is considered in more detail later. He had helped his father and other relatives in agriculture and in crafts, but also migrated to the coffee plantations of neighboring San Salvador to supplement the low wages of his home:

But within families there are those who are poor, and the rich—I don't know why—don't help the other families so that they can improve themselves. For that reason it is an effort for the poor man to improve himself there [in his home town]. Within the same family—for in Concepción we are all the same, almost all the people is Rodríguez, is almost one family, but is by groups—there is a distance in the way each one lives. Let's say that the rich is one group of the same family but there is a distance between them and another group which is of the same family but which lives apart and who are poor. The rich look down on us, for the simple reason that for instance our clothing—that we go about badly dressed. This is always the case in my home that there the rich man dresses better and the poor not, although of the same family.

Angel, like José, emphasizes the importance of kin as an organizing principle of life in his small town, but it is clear that the closeness of relationships aggravates the sense of social inequality. Angel described his migrant career subsequent to leaving the town as an experience in which an individual, whether in the countryside or city, is constantly beset with social inequalities that frustrate the attempts of a poor individual to improve his own position. Angel represents a type of migrant for whom the provinces are perceived as places of social inequality and places where it is difficult to improve one's position, but his experiences give him similar perceptions of urban life.

The case of Félix is different, partly because of his perception of rural life and his emphasis on the Indian-Ladino distinction, but also because his subsequent career and urban life have been different than those of Angel, involving fewer moves and less disturbing experiences. Félix claims to have enjoyed the life of an agricultural laborer, but complains of the low wages in the rural areas and of the large landholders' refusal to help their tenants improve their farming with chemical fertilizers and loans of equipment. His perception of social relationships adds an interesting dimension to that of Angel:

In the countryside the rich man shares in the life of the city—he lives here and he lives there: he has a greater reach. In contrast, the person whose participation is that of being an Indian, then he does not have "reach"; he works and works, and he isn't participating in anything. He becomes accustomed to working from five or six in the morning until six in the evening, and he has to work so, because that is rural life. Now the situation here is different; one has one's hours; one works from seven to four and the work day is finished. So there is participation here, but in the countryside there is not.

[The relationship between Indians and Ladinos] in the city becomes more alike. For the one who is an Indian and the one who is a Ladino, well, they are now sharing life together, now they are becoming mixed together, facing life together. Let's take the example of moneyed people, people like rich government officials: well, if one works, then they know how to treat you. One now has one's position and knows how to look after oneself in matters of work and things like that. Now there are not those kinds of groups in which exist Indians and Ladinos and the kinds of relations they have between them. Now there is not the situation where the rich man who has money looks down on the poor man; for here it's more like a mixing, all united.

Félix, like Angel, emphasizes the social divisions of the countryside, but to him the city is seen as a place where he is relatively free of these inequalities. This illustrates an earlier contention that peoples' perceptions of their social environments are likely to interpret only a fragment of urban life and are heavily influenced by the nature of their actual interactions. Félix arrived in the city and found a room with friends from his home village, and the next day with their advice took a job as an unskilled construction worker—a job he has never left except for periods of short temporary unemployment. For nine of his eleven urban years, he has lived in the shantytown, maintaining relationships with his neighbors, his kin now resident in the city, and some of his workmates. The only social and economic superiors he has ever encountered are friendly ones like the engineers who give him work, the social workers, and myself. His urban experiences have thus been relatively continuous, and, in comparison with his experiences in the countryside, ones in which he has been impressed by the helpfulness of others. It is thus not surprising that he should feel social distinctions less in the city than in the rural area, and for those migrants who, like Félix, have had continuous urban careers, it is likely that in comparison with the felt and evident inequalities of the countryside, the city, because it is larger and more impersonal, involves less social friction.

Félix's account also shows that, even for the inhabitants of villages and towns, the city is an important element in their local evaluations of a person's standing. The social stratification of the provinces consists both in differences of wealth or caste and in the degree that an individual maintains contact with the city. This illustrates the meaning that the concept of a "part society" has for its members who are not only tied economically, politically, and culturally to the capital, but themselves conceive of their own location as being only a part of the wider, urban-dominated society. Observe the way in which another migrant who, as a police officer, traveled throughout the provinces before settling in the city, recounts his stay in a remote mountain village:

I went to San Diego—a remote place deep in a mountain where all there is to be seen is the birds flying and the people are not acquainted with the capital—they have little breadth and this [type of] rural laborer on seeing someone who is from the capital, they worship him, as if he came from a foreign land. . . . I tried to get hold of the best friendships in the town— that's to say to become a friend to the mayor, the secretary of the municipality, and the telegraphist.

We can now bring together these various perceptions of rural life and organization and look at them as an ongoing frame of reference that migrants employ in their urban activities. What emerges from migrants' accounts is a picture of a provincial society that is small-scale, but divided by ethnic and socioeconomic differences. People know each other but do not act together or seek a common welfare. The positive sides of rural society that are stressed are always the individual advantages— the peace, the independence, and control over one's working day. This group of migrants has little perception of provincial life as including participating with others in a range of activities beyond the immediate family. They perceive provincial and urban society as interdependent and changing, and the city as embodying the most economic and social prestige. Thus, in making the move from provinces to city, many of the migrants perceive themselves as abandoning a rural society that is anyway disintegrating and moving to the city, which at the least brings them to the center of affairs. They are both socially and geographically mobile, and their mobility has taken place individually or with the help of a few kin or friends.

The interconnections of city and provinces and the economic differentiation of the latter show that migrants are not characterized by a distinctive or homogeneous culture. Nor are they likely to be shocked by evidence of social inequality or impersonality in the city. Likewise, their experiences are not such as to orientate them to radically different ways of acting than those of the city born. Before coming to the city most of these migrants have had experiences of manipulating personal relationships, have been manipulated by others, and have competed for scarce resources. By their own perceptions, their move to the city is not one to a strange place, but to a position where they can better utilize the resources of their society.

The Social Characteristics of Migrants

Migration is often depicted in economic analysis as explicable in terms of calculable costs and benefits in which the rate of migration is represented as some function of earnings and employment opportunities in place of origin and place of destination.[4] Analysis of the migration process in Guatemala

---

[4] A summary of these views and a partial application of them to Chile is given in Bruce Herrick, *Urban Migration and Economic Development in Chile*, pp. 10-23.

clearly indicates it to be a more complicated phenomenon than can be usefully subsumed for the present purposes within a cost and benefits model. Apart from the difficulty of estimating costs and benefits in the informal economic conditions of Guatemala, there is the more fundamental consideration that migrants' estimates of costs and benefits are influenced by differences in the flows of information to which they are exposed, in their cultural priorities, and in their social relationships. The influence of these factors is outlined in the pages below to emphasize that migration takes place within a social as well as an economic context and is affected both in its rate and incidence by the political and social relations that exist between city and provinces. Also, to assess the impact of migration on city life means that the actual move must be analyzed within the context of a set of career decisions influenced by changes in life cycle, by the accumulation of skills and other commit- ments, and by the actions of others, such as fellow villagers who have already moved to the capital. All these factors "refract" the perception of economic opportunities so that migration is not likely to be experienced as a closely calculated or planned event.

Some of the factors influencing the pattern of migration in Guatemala are commonly reported for Latin America; but the small size of its territory, rural underdevelopment, and the low level of industrialization in the capital, among other factors, mean that the pattern of migration reported here is in many respects a special case.[5] In this respect, the present analysis differs from other studies that have attempted to identify those

[5] Despite considerable differences in the national and economic context, the Monterrey migration study (Jorge Balán et al., "The Lives of Men") indicates some similarities in migrant characteristics: the first job before arrival is non-farm; most migrants come directly from place of origin; their educational qualifications are superior to those of the population in their communities of origin; and short-distance migrants predominate over long-distance ones. A general overview of findings in the literature on Latin American migration is given by Morse, in which it is apparent that there is considerable variation between and within countries. See Richard Morse, "Trends and Issues in Latin American Urban Research, 1965-1970, Part One," *Latin American Research Review* 6, no. 1 (February 1971): 3-33.

variables in the structure of cities, towns, and villages that need to be distinguished in order to begin a comparative study of migration.[6] The pattern of migration in Guatemala is analyzed as an important contextual variable for understanding the status and behavior of migrants in the capital.

The major economic factor affecting migration from the provinces to the city has already been outlined in the previous chapter: a high rural population density relative to the distribution of easily cultivatable land. Although Guatemala has rich agricultural resources, they are mainly concentrated in the hands of a few large landholders. In 1950, 2.1 percent of farm operators were holding 72.2 percent of the total farm land, and 88.4 percent of farmers operated farms below 17.2 acres.[7] It is thus difficult to accomodate the increasing rural population by further subdividing farms to sustain adult children and their families. In recent years, food production in the countryside has barely kept abreast of population increase, and increases in production are mainly produced by the large, commercially organized plantations. Under these conditions the diet of the average rural family is simple and often inadequate, consisting of corn meal, beans, and local vegetables. It is only on special occasions that food is varied and abundant.

Under these conditions it is not surprising that considerable numbers of people leave the land in search of work elsewhere. However, one of the most striking characteristics of Guatemala's urban population is that it is overwhelmingly Ladino. In a national population that was classified as 43.3 percent Indian in the 1964 census, Indians comprised an estimated 5.4 percent of migrants living in the city (Termini, p. 35.). Approximately 5 percent of the population of the two neighborhoods is Indian.

The contrasting types of rural social organization are thus important variables affecting urban migration. Indians, as noted

---

[6] Placing Guatemala City within a typology of migration is done by Balán; see his "Migrant-Native Socioeconomic Differences in Latin American Cities: A Structural Analysis," *Latin American Research Review* 4, no. 1 (February 1969): 3-29.

[7] See Nathan Whetten, *Guatemala*, pp. 92-94.

in the preceding chapter, have been exploited members of the Guatemalan population. Experience of exploitation and the peculiar nature of their social organization have made the Indian population wary of dealings with Ladinos. Their contacts within the national political system, for example, are often mediated by indigenous office holders who act as brokers for national political parties. When an Indian leaves his village, he is thus leaving a location to which he has strong social ties and entering a world in which he is potentially exposed to hostility and exploitation.

Though Indians are likely to migrate to supplement their subsistence agriculture; their migration is likely to be short-term and circulatory, involving return to their home village.[8] This is, in fact, one outstanding trait of Guatemala's internal migrations. Indian migrations are usually for a period of three to four months when workers leave for the coffee or other cash-crop harvest on the coast and return to cultivate their land for the rest of the year.

In contrast to the Indian population, rural Ladinos, whether poor or rich, are members of Guatemala's dominant culture, and even in the capital they are not faced by the sharp contrasts confronting an Indian who makes this move. Ladinos in town and country wear the same style of dress, speak Spanish, and accept traditional forms of Spanish Catholicism. Divisions among Ladinos in rural areas are based, as in the city, on differences in economic and social status. The range of wealth among rural Ladinos is considerable, and some areas of the country, notably to the east and south are predominantly Ladino. The numbers of Ladino migrants are, however, swelled by Indians who, because of family quarrels, illegitimacy, difficulties with their landholdings, and other reasons, become marginal to the organization of their home village.[9]

[8] This contrast between Ladino and Indian migrations is partially documented from census evidence in Alvan O. Zárate, "Principales patrones de migración interna en Guatemala, 1964," *Estudios Centroamericanos No. 3.*

[9] See R. N. Adams, "La Ladinzación en Guatemala," in J. L. Arriola, ed., *Integración Social en Guatemala*, where he outlines the process of "Ladinization"

The migration of this category of Indian is usually part of a larger migration process wherein, after leaving his place of origin, he moves around the provinces and gradually abandons Indian characteristics of speech and dress. There are no statistics of the percentage of these Ladinized Indians among the urban population, but in the two neighborhoods some 15 percent of the migrants had one or both parents who they said were of Indian origin.

Apart from the Indian-Ladino distinction, other socio-economic distinctions within the provincial population are likely to be related to cityward migration. Occupation makes people available for migration by endowing them with skills that are transferable to urban occupations and by making available work relationships that are not locally based. Though Guatemala is basically an agricultural country, crafts such as weaving, tailoring, shoemaking, carpentry, and pottery have long flourished in villages and small towns and have traditionally encouraged itinerant work. Construction labor, trade, and the maintenance of machinery are also important provincial occupations, and even in the least urbanized departments of the country, 15 to 20 percent of employed males are in non-agricultural occupations.[10]

Census figures are not available for the occupations of migrants prior to their arrival in the city, but Table 6 lists the range of occupations that migrants in the two neighborhoods held before arriving in the city. These migrants are predominantly drawn from nonagricultural occupations. Even those employed in agriculture come from those groups least tied to the land—agricultural laborers and family workers. Only a small

---

and attributes to it the decline in the proportion of the population categorized as Indian in the last century.

[10] The appropriate figures are given in the 1964 Census of Population. The department of Totonicapan, which is mainly Indian, has over 80 percent of its population defined by the census as rural, while less than 30 percent of its economically active population is engaged in agriculture. This department is an extreme case, but in most provincial departments commerce and craft industry flourish.

Table 6. Last Occupation of Male Migrants before Arrival in City

Occupation	Percentage
Craftsman (tailor, weaver, shoemaker, carpenter, etc.)	13
Operative (mechanic, factory worker)	3
Construction laborer	7
Trader/shopkeeper	4
Service worker (custodian, barber, servant, etc.)	5
Transport driver or helper	4
Office worker	1
Police or long-service soldier	4
Farm laborer	12
Helper on family farm	14
Farm owner	8
No job before arrival in city (arrived in city when child or young adult)	24
Total	99
Number of cases	148

percentage of migrants actually owned their own farms before coming to the city.[11]

Education is also associated with migration: migrants are better educated than the provincial population that does not migrate but have less education than the city born (Table 7). School facilities are poor in the provinces and it is only in the last few years that serious attempts have been made to improve schools in the provinces relative to those in the capital. Often a rural school contains only one class in which children of all ages and different school grades are taught together. To enter more advanced grades of primary or secondary school means traveling to a departmental capital or nearby large town. Under these conditions, and also because child labor is useful in agriculture, provincial children are less well educated than their city counterparts.

Among this provincial population, migration appears to skim off the educationally better qualified. The differences are quite

[11] This pattern is almost identical with that reported for San Salvador by Alistair White in "The Social Structure of the Lower Classes in San Salvador, Central America," Ph. D. dissertation.

Table 7. Educational Levels of Migrants, City-Born and Provincial Population,
(Males) 7 Years of Age and Over (Percentages)

Level of Education	Ladino Provincial Population*	Migrant Population in City	City-Born Population
None	57.5	21.5	17.8
Completed One through Six Years	39.6	58.5	62.3
Completed Seven through Nine Years	1.7	10.0	10.5
Completed Ten through Twelve Years	.9	5.7	5.4
Completed Thirteen Years and Over (University)	.3	4.3	4.1
Total	100.0	100.0	100.1

Source: Deanne Termini, "Socio-Economic and Demographic Characteristics of the Population of Guatemala City," M.A. Thesis, University of Texas at Austin, 1968, Table 18, adapted. *Censo de Poblacion, 1964*, Department of Cenos y Encuestas, Ministerio de Economia, 1966, Table 7, adapted.
*The provincial population tabulated here is the provincial male Ladino population of age seven and over. Restricting the comparison to the Ladino population makes the statistics more comparable with the city population, which is overwhelmingly Ladino. Provincial Indians have lower levels of education.

considerable; especially notable are those in the levels of secondary and university education. Though they are not the subject of the analysis, urban white-collar occupations are heavily recruited from people of provincial origin. In this sense, migration to the capital in Guatemala is as much a middle-class as a lower-class phenomenon, involving professionals, established merchants, and middle and large landowners. As the city becomes increasingly urbanized and organized from the national capital, so the wealthier and better-educated provincials have been coming to the capital where they are closer to, and in more effective control of, the sources of jobs and financial credit. Relative to the population of educated provincial families, this middle-class migration to the capital probably has more dramatic effects on provincial social life than does the migration of rural workers.[12] It represents one important effect of the concentration of resources and population in the cities of Latin America, but it is also a regular feature of the process of urbanization, since with increasing interdependence there is no longer the local basis for much retailing, trading, and other services. At the national level interdependence occurs between as well as within regions, with consequent redistribution of professional, managerial, and other occupational groups. The best-educated provincial people migrate to the city, intensifying the competition there for professional and office jobs. Thus, when we compared the occupational distribution of migrants and city born in the last chapter, we found few differences in the occupational categories that they enter.

Naturally, it is possible that some of the differences between migrants and those who do not migrate are produced by migrants receiving education in the city; for example, a migrant starts out with the same education as everyone else in the village, but makes use of the superior educational facilities in the city to improve himself. However, since most migrants come to the city after the age of 14, when formal education ceases and can be made up through night school only with difficulty, all the educational differences between migrants and non-migrants cannot be explained in this way. This can be documented by looking at the educational levels of migrants in the two neighborhoods. Migrants who came to the city at an age when they could effectively profit from city schools are better educated than those who came when too old for formal education; but this latter group, although a low-income sample, is still

---

[12] This phenomenon of disproportionate "middle-class" migration from provinces to the city is reported for other Latin American countries also; see Bruce Herrick, *Urban Migration*, pp. 71-100. For its effects on the structure of rural society, see Julio Cotler, "Actuales pautas de cambio en la sociedad rural del Perú," in J. Matos Mar, ed., *Dominación y Cambios en el Perú Rural*, pp. 60-79.

Table 8. Migration and Education of Heads of Household
(Males and Females) in Percentages

Years of Schooling	Born and Educated outside the City	Born outside the City and Educated in the City	Born and Educated in the City
None	27	27	17
1-2	47	29	31
3-5	13	23	25
Primary school and above	13	21	27
Total	100	100	100
Number	(120)	(65)	(62)

Note: Age does not appear to affect the relative distribution of education between these three classes. Older people, however, are less educated than younger people.

considerably better educated than the comparable provincial population (Table 8).

Age and marital status are also associated with migration and, like occupation and education, make certain categories of people more available for migration and reduce the costs of the move. The age structure in 1964 of the migrants to the city shows large groupings in the ages fifteen through thirty-four, suggesting that migrants are most likely to come to the city as young adults (Termini, pp. 19-20). Since the data from the two neighborhoods include age at arrival in the city, this suggestion can be directly examined (Table 9). Also, of those who arrived in the city when over the age of 14, 65 percent arrived between the ages of 15 and 29. Most came as single males or females.

The census data indicate one further outstanding demographic characteristic of these migrations: more women than men migrate and women arrive at an earlier age. This predominance of females is not unusual in citywards migration in Latin America. Similar imbalances have been reported, for example, for neighboring San Salvador and Santiago in Chile. This high proportion of females, however, is not always found in Latin American urbanization and is unusual when compared

Table 9. Age at First Arrival in the City of Migrants from
Neighborhood Sample (Males and Females) in Percentages

Age	Males (Heads of Household)	Females (Heads of Household)	Age of the Guatemalan Population (National Census)
0-9 years	22	13	33
10-19 years	29	49	23
20-29 years	26	15	15
30-39 years	12	10	12
40-49 years	7	5	7
50-59 years	3	5	5
60-and over	1	3	5
Total	100	100	100
Number	(147)	(39)	

Source: Neighborhood Survey. Census 1964 de Población, Table 3, adapted.

with African and some Asian migration and needs some comment.[13]

One of the major reasons for differences between countries appears to be the ease with which rural systems of landholding accommodate returning migrants and single females by giving absent people rights to which they can return and which females can "protect" for them. In Guatemala, there are, however, few alternative employment possibilities open to women in the provinces; they cannot find employment as itinerant laborers or plantation workers to the extent that male migrants can. For women, the city is the surest and most available source of employment. Also, the considerable male outmigration from villages and towns creates a potentially difficult marriage market. Males often do not return to their home villages, and rarely is there communal property in which they are interested in retaining rights. So, in contrast with many parts of Africa,

[13] Both Bruce Herrick reporting on Santiago, Chile (*Urban Migration*, p. 73) and Alistair White ("The Social Structure of the Lower Classes in San Salvador," p. 33) note such imbalances for these capital cities. Examples from Africa and Asia of cities with predominantly male migration are given in K. C. Zachariah, "Bombay Migration Study," *Demography* 3, no. 2 (1966): 378-392; and Valdo Pons, *Stanleyville*, pp. 43-46.

women in Guatemalan villages have little economic or social inducement to await the return of the males, and, once in a city, they have few claims on their home village that make their return worthwhile.

Also, the relative ease of female employment in metropolitan areas is important. In Latin America an urban middle class located in capitals and other large cities is a substantial source of employment for females who, as single individuals, have little place or prospects of employment in the rural areas. Female labor in service occupations is cheaper than male labor, and middle-class families in Guatemala often have contacts in villages and small towns who find likely girls for service. The city employer also visits a village to talk with parents or relatives about the possibilities of employing an available member of their family.

The changing commitments that make potential migrants of these various categories of people within provincial society are mediated by the system of communication within the country. Thus, a person may have all the characteristics that make him available for migration, but his decision to migrate is also dependent on his perceiving the capital as a feasible destination: the flow of information and the existence of possible help to find work and housing are independent and continuing factors in migration movements significantly altering the evaluation of costs and benefits.[14] Since Guatemala is a small country with an adequate network of roads, distance is not the basic problem. Though villages and towns differ in their accessibility to the capital, almost all areas of the capital are within a day's bus journey. More important is the extent of information available in villages and towns as a consequence of the interdependence of capital and provinces. This information flow results from interconnections of trade, from being on major transport routes, and from the existing movement of people between capital and provinces. Prior migration to the capital

[14] See Philip Nelson, "Migration, Real Income and Information," *Regional Science* 1, no. 2 (1959): 43-74.

provides sources of information and help in the city, thereby encouraging the movement of fellow villagers or townsmen. Since some of these migrants are likely to be more prosperous members of their community, their migration to the city both provides influential contacts there and removes sources of work from the home village or town.

However, the marketing and communication system in Guatemala is still quite localized. Apart from some of the bigger departmental capitals on major roads, the capital is a marketing and communication center mainly for the contiguous departments and the larger urban places. People in such places have frequent contact with the capital and often use it to purchase clothes or obtain medical services. One respondent, for example, reported coming to the city for the first time at age fifteen to buy clothes and food and then coming two or three times a year subsequent to that before making his final decision to migrate when he was twenty-two.

Because of the above considerations, we can expect that migrants to the capital should come from the larger urban places, be predominantly short-distance migrants, and should originate in a variety of places. The social insecurity of moving longer distances or from small places balances the relative difference in economic opportunities in city and provinces. Yet, within these limits the communication net of the city includes a variety of places tied to it by trade, roads, and population movement; from these, people with the appropriate characteristics are "selected" for migration. In the two neighborhoods, 60 percent of male migrants originate in towns of more than two thousand people, as compared with the 25 percent of Guatemala's population that was in areas so populous in 1950.[15]

Migrants are also disproportionately drawn from the areas nearest the city. Fifty-four percent of the sample originated in

[15] This figure is based on the 1950 Guatemalan Census, because the 1964 Census has changed its system of classification from one of size of urban place to one of administrative definition.

the departments contiguous to the city which contain 25 percent of Guatemala's population. Since one of the neighborhoods is located at the city's edge, on a communications route with populous departments, it contributes a disproportionate number of short-distance migrants. However, in the city-wide census of 1964, the percentage of migrants originating in contiguous departments (47 percent) was still higher than the proportion of the national population in these departments. The range of places from which migrants originated was considerable; the 252 people in the neighborhood samples of heads of household came from over one hundred different places.

The characteristics of migrants to the city have been sketched in general form to emphasize that there are structural factors underlying the patterns of migration. The economic and social organization of provinces and city are important influences on the nature of migration, and any future changes in Indian-Ladino relations, in the communications between city and provinces, in employment opportunities in town and countryside, and in the pool of provincial people with different occupational skills will affect both the rate and content of migration.

Migrants who come to the city have characteristics that are likely to enable them to cope with the various requirements of urban life, since Guatemala City's economy and administration are highly informal. Migrants are consequently competitive with city born for urban jobs and services. The impact of migrants on city life is the more considerable because they enter at a variety of points in the urban social and economic organization, affecting the established relationships between city dwellers and their jobs, residences, and administration throughout the city.

The type of migration that is being described here contrasts with one in which migrants do not have the characteristics that make them competitive with the city born. This second type of migration has been described in the growth of cities in the United States of America and elsewhere when immigrants come from either foreign countries or underdeveloped rural areas to industrial cities. It has indeed been a recent criticism of the early work done on characterizing urban life—work that mainly originated with the "Chicago" school of Robert Park, Ernest Burgess and Louis Wirth among others—that they took this type of migration that characterized the particular urban growth of Chicago and generalized its consequences to urban life everywhere.[16] These migrants were of low socioeconomic status and were confronted by industrial cities whose rapid growth was molded by an entrepreneurial capitalism and in which the organization of work, residence, and government was relatively unfamiliar. The process of their assimilation is one in which migrants of similar ethnic or cultural background group together, often in urban ghettoes at the center of the city, use brokers to obtain work or other favors from the dominant social groups, and maintain relatively cohesive social relationships among themselves. With time, successive waves of migrants, provided their color is correct, prosper and gradually move from the inner city to more distant outer locations. The form of migrant assimilation is, thus, to enter near the bottom of the urban stratification system and gradually, through group and individual mobility, to attain higher socioeconomic positions.

This is the familiar process of migrant assimilation that predominates in the literature on rapid urban growth, but it depends both on the city being culturally strange to migrants and on an expanding pool of urban jobs that accommodates both new migrants and the ambitions of the old. Any competition that migrants offer the city born is buffered according to this model, because the entering groups are not competing for the same class of jobs, housing, or services. The contrast between this type of migration and that being described in this

---

[16] There is an extensive literature on this topic, many examples of which are found in George Theodersen, ed., *Studies in Human Ecology*; for criticism see Leonard Reissman, *The Urban Process*, Jorge Balán takes account of both these migration patterns in reference to the status of migrants in Buenos Aires; see his "Migrant-Native Socioeconomic Differences," *Latin American Research Review* 4, no. 1 (February 1969): 13-14.

book is thus considerable, indicating not only differences in the historical periods of migration, but also in the characteristics of migrants and of the city to which they are migrating. In Guatemala City the influx of migrants with the characteristics described conditions the relationships between and within social groups and creates a competitive climate that affects the marriages, jobs, and social relationships of all city dwellers.

Contextual Parameters: Provincial Instability

The emphasis on the characteristics of migrants and their meaning in terms of the factors that make certain groups of people more likely to move than others should not obscure the importance of the actual migration. Migration is potentially a disturbing personal event, and the experiences involved are variables affecting the sensitivity of migrants to the problems and possibilities of their urban environment. Whatever the underlying reasons for migration, the timing of the move is often affected by incidents disruptive of the normal pattern of life.

Some of these incidents—such, for example, as a family quarrel—are not examined in detail, but they enter into migration and are factors in the discontinuities involved. Thus, of the nine migrants whose life histories are tape-recorded, all but two report the breakup of their families through the death or separation of parents as being the occasion for their leaving their home villages. Rural poverty, migration, and high birth rates are some of the factors that weaken the stability of family life in the provinces and create a pool of "marginal" people with low attachment to their place of origin. The incidence of family disorganization is fairly evenly spread throughout the provinces and thus is considered here as an occasion of migration. A family quarrel can provide the final stimulus to move to people who, by reason of poverty, occupation, or education, are always available for migration. This distinction is to some extent arbitrary, but it enables us to distinguish the structural reasons for migration—the continuing factors that make a certain rate for migration likely—from the individual reasons that account for the incidence and variability in migration.[17]

Historical events, including political and economic changes, influence peoples' perception of the relative advantages of city and countryside and are decisive factors in the decision to migrate. Exploring the impact of political and economic events on fluctuations in migration thus shows how informed migrants are of conditions in town and provinces and how sensitive they are to changes in these conditions. This perspective provides us with a further dimension for differentiating the impact of migration in countries such as Guatemala by linking the amount of discontinuity that people experience as a result of migration to the particular historical process of urbanization.[18]

In Guatemala, both city and countryside have experienced considerable recent political and economic upheavals as a result of the social and economic changes that have been outlined in the introductory chapter. People in both neighborhoods report that these changes have directly affected their migration movement. Thus, Félix talks about his movement to the city:

> Arévalo came [to power] and all was fine. Then came the change to this. . .this. . .I don't remember. Then there was a kind of disturbance, let's say: politics. Then they took away the land they had given us. In short, since I had my land and did not join the party, I lost my land. So I came and spent two months in the city in jail, I don't remember the year, since they forced one to join the party. We left prison and I took to the road and that was my adventure until I came to rest here in the capital.

Félix's account is confused and he could not remember at all clearly either the year or the president in power. It was certain-

---

[17] See J. C. Mitchell, "Labour Migration in Africa South of the Sahara," *Bulletin of the Inter-African Labour Institute*, no. 1 (1959): 12-46.

[18] Fluctuations in the rate of rural-urban migration is an indication both of changing political and economic conditions—of instability—and of the extent of communication between city and provinces. Fluctuations can be expected in countries whose economy or polity is changing and whose communication system enables migrants to perceive such changes. For an example of this, see K. C. Zachariah, "Bombay Migration Study," *Demography* 3, no. 2 (1966): 378-392.

ly the time from 1951 to 1954 when Arbenz and Castillo Armas
were in power and when rival factions of left and right were
alternatively seeking support and vengeance in the provinces. To
Félix, the names of the parties or personalities are not important, and he is unable to discriminate, even when asked
directly, which faction had caused his troubles. His experience
was quoted to me by several people in the neighborhood, some
saying that it had been Arbenz and the communists that had
jailed him, while others blamed Castillo Armas and his conservative allies. The important point however, is that political and
economic events are having a direct effect on an individual's
decision to move, and that consequently the move involves the
experience of considerable discontinuities.

These historical changes are reflected in the incidence of
migration to the city. Had political upheavals not affected
migration we would expect the proportions of migrants arriving
in different years not to show marked fluctuations but to
remain constant or increase or decrease in a consistent
direction.[19] The data are not available to examine the flow of
migrants on a city-wide basis, but the neighborhood samples
contain the relevant information and serve our purpose by
enabling us to further add to our information about the sources
of heterogeneity among the people whose particular behavior is
the subject of later analyses. Also, although the sample is in no
sense representative of all migrants who have arrived in the city,
the sources of bias—that, for example, the sample is predominantly of married couples and that the neighborhoods are relatively recently founded—are not likely to intervene to explain
the particular fluctuations.[20]

We can match the fluctuations in the volume of migration to

[19] Contrast the smooth flow of migration reported by Herrick in *Urban Migration*,
pp. 54-55.

[20] The data on the settlement of the two neighborhoods in chapter 3 indicate that
neither was settled by recent migrants to the city and, taking account of migrant
characteristics at the date of settlement (late 1950s), does not explain the fluctuations.

Table 10. Historical Period and Frequency of Migration to the City (Neighborhood Sample of Male and Female Heads of Household)

Period	Average Rate of Migration (Number of Persons a Year)
1	1.2
2	3.0
③	1.0
4	3.7
5	5.2
6	8.0
7	2.5
8	5.0

eight historical periods that involved important, distinct, political and economic changes (Table 10).[21]

1. The years prior to 1940, the period of relatively stable military dictatorship.

2. 1941-1943. The last years of Ubico and the loosening of his control over city and countryside.

3. 1944-1949. The stable period of the Guatemalan revolution, with a degree of economic prosperity in both city and countryside.

4. 1950-1953. The unsettled years preceding the overthrow of Arbenz and a worsening economic situation.

5. 1954-1957. The counterrevolution to the assassination of Castillo Armas; repression and some turmoil in the countryside, but city beginning to prosper with foreign aid.

6. 1958. Economic recession.

7. 1959-1962. Gradual economic recovery and increased stability with first years of Ydígoras Fuentes.

8. 1963-1964. Political and economic instability; overthrow of Ydígoras Fuentes.

[21] In order to collapse the table, it is assumed that the average life span of these people is sixty years, and, since we are looking only at those who came to the city aged fourteen years and over, the earliest time of arrival will be taken as 1922. This provides us with eighteen years prior to 1940. The frequency with which the table starts is thus an average frequency for those eighteen years. In effect this means we are neglecting possible sources of variation before 1940 to concentrate on those

The number of people involved is small, but what is convincing is the fit between the fluctuations and the historical periods. In periods of relative stability and prosperity in both city and provinces, the rate of migration is lower than in those periods marked by high degrees of rural instability. In these periods the situation in the provinces was aggravated by felt insecurity of land tenure, by direct political repression and by the closure or slowing down of many commercial agricultural ventures. In contrast, the city in these periods continues to prosper as the channel through which foreign funds pass and as the center of events: its size also makes political and economic vendettas more difficult to pursue.

There is another possible means of estimating the significance of historical events for migration decisions—by considering the return migration of this sample. Some 25 percent of migrants returned to the provinces for a period of one year or more subsequent to their arrival in the city. Their return was often occasioned by employment in the police or in some other government department that works throughout the country; but for many it was a deliberate decision to try their luck once again outside the city.

In these cases the decision to return reflects perceived changes in the relative advantages of city and provinces. Unfortunately, however the character of the sample severely restricts the conclusions we can draw, since the sample is not one of all migrants who have returned to the provinces but one where the return migrant comes back again.

There are thirty-two migrants in the sample that returned to the provinces for more than a year and were not in government employ. If we take account of the numbers of the sample who were present in the city at the different time periods and thus "available" for return migration, we can make some estimates of the fluctuations in the timing of return. These are consider-

---

occurring subsequently. The table ends in 1964, since in subsequent years the figures are biased by the lack of opportunity for migrants to the city to "reach" the two neighborhoods.

ably less than those for first arrival in the city, and indeed it is only in one period, the period of sharpest provincial dislocation from 1954 to 1957, that the average number of people returning to the provinces is sharply reduced, so that only two return in that four-year period. Return migrants in the sample spend, on the average, some four years in the provinces, and thus it is unlikely that the reduced migration of this period results from it being too recent to have a full complement of return migrants who come back to the city. Other periods of provincial instability—notably the Arbenz period of 1950-1953—do not, however, appear to discourage return migration. Indeed, along with the economic and political dislocation of the provinces, land was being offered in this period to urban and rural poor through land reform.

The timing of these migrants' arrival back in the city is affected by considerations similar to those affecting first arrival. Thus, only one return migrant comes back to the city in the period 1944-1949, the period of economic and political stability, even though some ten had returned to the provinces before or during this period and could have returned then. In contrast, half of the return migrants came back in the period 1950 to 1957 or the period of political and economic dislocation.

The fluctuation of migration in different historical periods indicates the type of historical discontinuities that migrants have experienced and that affect their orientations within the city. Instability in the provinces appears to be a powerful motive force in encouraging migration, suggesting that the consequences of political and economic instability are more directly felt and less easy to escape there than in a city. However, these historical discontinuities are only some of the possible discontinuities involved in the process of moving to the city.

Pathway to the City

One vital factor in a migrant's decision has so far received only passing attention: the degree to which he can expect to receive help when he first enters a city. However much an individual's skills and experiences fit him for city life, he will be deterred from undertaking the move unless he has some reasonable guarantee from friends, a sure job, or kin that he can find some means of subsisting in the city. Conversely, such contacts can represent commitments that encourage the move to the city. Most migrants are thus likely to have some contact in the city prior to migrating there. This is certainly the case for migrants in the two neighborhoods, and of the male migrants only 13 percent had no kin, fellow villager, or friend in the city before their first arrival. If an individual has no such guarantee of easy reception into the city and finds it difficult to subsist in his provincial home, then instead of migrating to the city he is likely to seek known and available employment in large commercial plantations or with the military or police force.

Migrants describe the care they take to ensure that they would be helped over their initial period in the city by the aid of friends or relatives. Often the husband or wife would make preliminary visits to the city to discuss with their contacts means of settling in the city. Migrants already established in the city would often provide temporary accommodations to relatives and their families while these sought housing and jobs nearby. Sometimes an established migrant would secure a nearby hut or room and then send news to the countryside that a relative could now come to the city with his family. These moves often involved quite close calculations of costs and benefits both for the migrant and for the person receiving him. Angel, for example, described how his wife's brother had come from the home village, where he had been earning twenty cents a day, to stay with them and to take a job for three or four days a week in a liquor factory at one hundred cents a day:

> But he was happy with three quetzales a week. But I, seeing that the three quetzales was not much, came and said to him that if he really paid for all he ate the money would not be enough for him, since he had his food with us and I said nothing. But I started to think about him, that when I could not help him, he would have to pay for his food, lodging, and everything. So I thought about all this and tried to call his attention to the

possibility of learning to be a barber. He told me that he would be de-lighted if I would help him to do it. I did, and in three months . . . he learned to be a barber.

Examples of this process of the settling in of new migrants could be multiplied. One migrant told of how he had been working and playing the marimba in Quetzaltenango, the second largest city of Guatemala, and had finally been per-suaded to move to the capital by a friend who had preceded him; the friend had played the marimba with him in Quetzalte-nango and after settling into the capital had sent word of a definite job and accommodations. Visiting families in both neighborhoods I often encountered a relative or friend who had just arrived to stay in the city, or I would be told about the projected visits of kinsmen or fellow villagers. However, it is part of the process of migration in Guatemala that the move to the city does not always proceed smoothly; there are some people who are forced from their village of origin and have little choice but to come to the city with or without contacts. Apart from economic necessity, two factors make it likely that a large number of migrants arrive in the city without the safeguard of adequate contacts.

Political instability is one factor that forces people to move to the city even where calculations of cost and benefit would argue otherwise. Secondly, in a highly centralized country many provincial jobs ultimately lead to the capital. A migrant who starts out by joining the police and army finds himself assigned to different parts of the country, but each new assignment involves a journey to the city and a sojourn there of days, weeks, or months. To petition for a new job or for improved conditions also involves a journey to the city. Many migrants who began their migrant careers outside the city find themselves being brought into contact with urban life, and when they lose their jobs or can continue them no longer it is usually in the city that they will be left without employment. This migration is clearly a career process and not a simple response to eco-nomic opportunities.

People who arrive in the city because of the sudden pressure of events or as the last in the series of migration steps are not as likely to have useful contacts in the city as those who have come directly through the careful balancing of costs and benefits. Not only is their career before arrival in the city more likely to be discontinuous when compared with those others, but this discontinuity is also likely to be increased by having to find their own way in a new environment.

Angel's account of his first days in the city without contacts of any kind illustrates the difficulty faced by this kind of migrant:

I did not know the city, but asking I arrived. Once in Guatemala seeing that the situation—in terms of work, for example—I saw that it was very difficult because a lot of people were arriving, and so I said how will I get work and where are the factories? So I decided to join the army. After three days of being in Guatemala, seeking work, I saw a lot of people but did not see how to ask. I slept in a pension called the Pension Popular. . . because it was near the station.

For such migrants the first weeks and months involve much worry and often a bewildering process of constantly moving around the city in search of accommodations and jobs, without contacts or the knowledge of how to set about it. In the course of their search, they are likely to learn more directly and more painfully about the social and economic structure of Guatemala City than those who are helped by friends or relatives. Consider Angel's description of his and his wife's attempts to find accommodations when they finally settle in the city, after he has served in the army and worked in the provinces with a government department:

We rented a house in. . .Zone 12. There was a relative living near that area, I felt a little protected by him, although he was very poor, but I felt protected. I went searching in all of Zone 12 and there would be a sign saying this room is for rent. When I asked "How much is the apartment, ma'am?" She says to me, "it's only seventy-five quetzales a month." I was astonished, then I went back and not to shame myself I said to the lady that I would come back. We continued looking for humbler little houses. We would ask how much is the rent of this little house. "More than thirty-five quetzales young man. . ." "Ah, in that case I will be back," I would say. We asked how much is the rent of this room. "This is worth twenty-five quetzales," she says to me. I did not think that this one was the one for me either, since I was going to earn forty-five quetzales and to pay twenty-five quetzales did not suit me. Eventually we came to a little house, a shack like the one we are living in now and I asked the lady, "How much is the little room?" "Eight quetzales," she says, "do you have children?" "Yes," says I, "I have four." "Ah, we don't want anyone with children."

The lady eventually rented to Angel, but his experience is similar to that of many who come to the city without contacts. The search for a job is likewise a difficult and dismaying enterprise. The best available manual jobs are filled by people recommended by friends or kin already working, and those who search on their own must often make do with ill-paying and unpleasant work that no one else will undertake.

The importance of different types of migration for the ease of an individual's reception into the city can be illustrated by looking at the range of contacts that migrants from the two neighborhoods had on arrival in the city. Respondents from the survey were asked if they had been preceded by a member of their immediate family, whether they had any relatives or friends in the city prior to their first arrival, and whether there were any people from their home town or village living in the neighborhood to which they first came in the city. They were also asked if these relatives or friends helped them to settle in in any way and whether their first city job was obtained through such help. To compare groups with different migration experiences, the sample of migrants is divided into three: those who came as young children (under fourteen), those who came as adults straight from their homes to the city, and those who came by way of other provincial places or through the army or police force. A simple scoring procedure assigns one point for each affirmative response made by respondents and, in the question concerning being preceded by their immediate family, assigns an additional point if migrants were preceded by two or more family members. To facilitate the analysis, the table categorizes respondents by whether they score two or less points or

Table 11. Contacts of Migrants on First Coming to the City
(Male Heads of Household) in Percentages

Contacts	Migrated to City as a Child (under 14)	First Adult (14+) Migration Direct to City[a]	Arrived in City as Adult (14+) after Prior Provincial Migration or as Members of Police or Army
Three or more sources of contact and assistance	45	39	16
Two or less sources of contact and assistance	55	61	84
Total	100	100	100
Number	(42)	(61)	(43)

[a]Categorizing in this way underestimates the amount of step migration, and of this category 23 percent had migrated around the provinces while small children.

three or more points. The latter category is likely to represent the group that is most easily received into the city through a range of contacts and assistance (Table 11).

Those who arrived as children report more contacts on arrival, but the significance of this is not clear. Arriving as children, their memories of their first days and weeks are not likely to accurately reflect the conditions of their reception; it was after all their parents or relatives who had the responsibility for making the way in the city. However, though the data do not permit an exploration of this point, it is likely that migrants who migrate as family groups will move only when they have sufficient contacts in the city. The difficulties and costs involved for a family in finding accommodations and a job are considerably higher than for a single person, and their move to the city is in this sense more risky. Those who arrive as children may well have remembered their easy reception because the way had been paved for them by the earlier migration of siblings, parents, or relatives.

Those who migrate directly to the city as adults have more contacts than those who come via other places or through army or police. Thus, those whose arrival in the city is the least buffered by prior contacts are also those whose previous careers have involved the widest range of preurban experiences. Any discontinuities in immigrants' previous careers are thus reinforced by the manner of their reception into the city, and whatever the contrasts between city born and migrants, the process of urbanization ensures that migrants are themselves differentiated by their life experiences.

The way a migrant enters the city has consequences beyond the immediate problems of transition. To enter through kin or friends is to enter into sets of relationships that endure and lead a migrant to commence his urban career in ways that influence his subsequent career. One important condition of this type of entry is that starting through the help of kin and friends is likely to mean that a subsequent career occurs within a close circle of acquaintances. From the beginning, services are exchanged with people of similar social background, and the commitments thus established constrain the subsequent paths of migrants, making it likely that they continue in a particular job or neighborhood.

In contrast, those who enter without adequate contacts are more likely to rely on the help of a range of social contacts, including those with social and economic superiors. This is, in part, a consequence of their preurban careers. Those who move around the country are brought into contact with superiors who can help in the transitions from one social setting to another. These movements prevent peer relationships from effectively aiding the transition. The influence of superiors, however, has a wider geographical reach; a letter of recommendation, a personal call, or the actual movement of the chief make it easier for his subordinate to find a secure place in a new environment. Whether or not they are personally in favor of cultivating relationships with superiors, those migrants in the sample who had frequently moved found it necessary to cultivate relations with superiors as a means of easing their transitions. Policemen or soldiers cultivate relations with army and police officers to enable them to obtain transfers or recommendations for civilian jobs. Cultivating such relations becomes for some a way of life as well as a necessity that influences their perception of their society. When migrants enter the city without adequate contacts, they are likely to use and to cultivate whatever relations with superiors they have developed in their previous careers. These relationships, once entered into, influence their future urban careers lessen their dependence on their peers, and lead them into those occupations where contacts with superiors are likely to be of most value. The transition of such migrants is thus a complex one in which the discontinuities of the immediate transition are added to by the increasing range of urban social relationships into which they enter.

The Significance of Discontinuity

The term "discontinuity" has been frequently used in the preceding discussion and it is now time to give to it a precise definition, so that its importance as a variable in the urban behavior of migrants and city born can be better understood. I am using discontinuity to refer to the degree to which the life situations through which individuals pass expose them to different experiences and different expectations of behavior. A person may undertake many different jobs in his lifetime and meet many different people, but these experiences are discontinuous only if they require him to act in ways to which he is not accustomed.

Usually an individual moves by stages from one family and occupational role to another, from son to father or from apprentice to master of his trade. The transition is gradual and is prepared by an awareness of what is to happen and by prior acquaintance with a future role. For some people there is no such smooth transition, and they must unexpectedly undertake roles of which they have little prior experience or are faced by situations with which their previous experiences or personal relationships do not help them to cope. In such a career, an individual's expectations are constantly subject to question, and he must actively adapt his behavior to meet new conditions. No longer present are the common understandings that allow an individual to enter situations and to perform in them with the assurance that both he and the others attribute the same meaning to his actions.

Migrants with discontinuous careers must actively seek to establish a perception of themselves and others that allows them to engage in uneventful or rewarding urban interaction. In the quotation above, Angel discovers through the process of encountering landlords that any dialogue concerning housing must be based on recognizing a far greater economic and social range than was the case in the countryside. In his discussion of his frequent moves in the countryside, housing never occurs as problematic, but with his transition to the city he encounters situations that lead him to include it as an important part of his understanding of his urban environment.

Migrants whose transition to the city is eased by the help of friends and relatives are not as likely to be forced to recognize the sharpness of this aspect of their transition. This is not to say that such migrants are not aware of differences in housing or of the problems people face in obtaining housing, but that their awareness is not based on a personal experience that makes them include such problems as a lasting part of their perceptions of their urban environment.

Migrants whose transition to the city is eased by friends and kin are not likely to encounter many situations leading them to reformulate their understandings of their environment. From the day of their arrival, they deal with people with whom they already share experiences and understandings. These people help them to get jobs and accommodations and provide most of their recreational contacts. Whatever additional understandings of urban life are gained in the course of residence are added through the mediation of kin and friends. The way, for example, that the very recent migrants from a small village, San

Antonio de la Paz, encountered the relatively novel (to them) organization of a consumers' cooperative was through the explanations and canvassing of kinsmen or fellow villagers who had already joined and who acted for them in meetings and transactions. To them, the cooperative was not an innovation but an extension of the relations and common understandings that people like themselves had always had. The continuity-discontinuity dimension is thus thought to relate to the nature of migrants' participation in urban life, indicating why some become active participants, aware of social and economic differences within the city, while others take little active part and define their objectives in terms of their immediate interests and needs. The dimension refers both to personal relationships and to orientations. Thus, an individual who has a continuous career is encapsulated in a relatively stable set of relationships through time and through various activities; also, his orientation to life is likely to be stable and to accord with these relationships. This orientation, in turn, makes it unlikely that he will choose to venture outside of his set of relationships. In contrast, a discontinuous career involves an individual in changing his friends, workmates and neighbors and developing different orientations to meet the new situations. The readiness to change orientations becomes then a factor leading individuals to make new personal relationships and forsake old ones.

We are identifying an additional dimension of social change associated with urban growth: a change in the characteristics of individual life careers. Lack of change in a society is partly definable by the extent that the life cycle entails similar patterns of behavior from generation to generation. The stages of family life are experienced by the individual within a context where the norms of behavior and even his personal relationships remain fairly stable. Migration contributes to basing social organization on life careers that are no longer truly cyclical, because passage through life exposes individuals to new relationships and new experiences of behavior for which there are no precedents. This means that traditional patterns of behavior are not reinforced, and the individual is "available" to participate in economic and social innovations. It also means that a basis for relating to people must be found to replace that offered by shared experiences and mutual social relationships. The succeeding chapters are, in part, an account of the attempts of individuals to identify those others with whom they can enter into profitable association even in situations of high personal mobility. The success they have in finding such a basis determines whether individuals take advantage of the changes around them and whether, as a group, they have the social flexibility suited to continuous and unpredictable change.

Two Migrant Careers

The data presented so far suggest that discontinuity in life careers is a useful means both to distinguish among groups of migrants and to characterize the overall pattern of migration. Guatemala's particular political and economic conditions entail that migration is a relatively discontinuous experience even for those who migrate directly to the city with the help of kin; this is one key to understanding these migrants' participation in urban life. To illustrate the differences in migration pattern, I present two migrants' accounts of their experiences until final settlement in the city. The synopsis of Prudencio's migrant career is deliberately short, but this does reflect the length of his recorded life history and his own perception of the uneventfulness of his life. It provides an example of a relatively continuous career. In contrast, Angel's fuller account reflects the attempts of one migrant to cope with rapid and disconcerting changes.

Prudencio

Prudencio was born in San Antonio de la Paz in 1943, a municipality of some four thousand inhabitants located in the ill-named province of El Progreso, some twenty-five miles from the capital. His father is a small farmer who rents land from another, and Prudencio is the eldest of four children. The municipality is predominantly Ladino and for many years has been a source of outmigration to the capital and neighboring departments, since scarcity of water makes agriculture a difficult enterprise. Prudencio did not go to school, but from the age of twelve began to help his father in the fields. They have many relatives in the township and visit frequently, but there seems to have been little cooperative farming. Prudencio describes in detail the procedures of farming and the crops they cultivate, recounting a routine starting at 5:30 A. M. and carrying on to late in the afternoon, with a day of relative rest on Sunday.

Prudencio's parents attend the Protestant church in the town, and their religious difference results in a certain apartness from their other relatives. From the age of about fifteen Prudencio remembers visits to the capital to buy material for the farm and for domestic use. He also played on the football team of the town, making trips to neighboring villages. He claims that there is little difference of rich and poor in the home town, saying that the rich are only moderately so and gain their money through hard work and are, in any case, often related to the poorer families. He remembers little of these years except the occasional fiesta and the routine of farm work. Then, at the age of twenty-one, he received news of a construction job in the capital from a friend who had gone to settle there. Prudencio got the job, and he lived with a relative in the shantytown for a month and a half.

He then received word from home that an influential contact—a local man whose family are small to middling farmers, but who had become a colonel in the military police— had secured him a job in the force. Prudencio spent three months traveling with the police through various departments, and he recounts the places he has seen and the satisfaction of the regulated and intimate life. His patron was killed in a confrontation with guerrilla forces operating in the mountains, and Prudencio was not happy to stay on with other chiefs. He sought an honorable discharge, and in 1965 he returned to the city, to the shantytown, and stayed with relatives from home. He says that there was a little coolness in their relationship, due probably to religion, but that they got him a job helping with a pickup truck and got him a shack in the shantytown. He spends most of his free time sitting in his shack, occasionally visiting with his relatives, and he has begun to go to night school to obtain his first year of education. He does not regret that he is settled in the city. He makes little attempt, however, to analyze the people around him, categorizing them simply as "good" or "bad." He interacts with few people apart from his relatives, except to increasingly join in the activities of the local Protestant church, of which he has become a devoted member.

Prudencio does not lack aspirations, and he appears able to cope with the urban life of Guatemala, but he is encapsulated, both in orientations and relationships, from the social and economic complexity of the city. He is not an active participant in neighborhood affairs and rarely initiates a relationship. He professes himself satisfied and impressed by the improvements made to the shantytown. However, it is worth noting that even in such a relatively uneventful career as Prudencio's, there are discontinuities, items that make him and his family somewhat marginal to the ordinary run of affairs: their Protestantism and the fact that they rent their farm.

However, in contrast to the career to which we now turn, Prudencio's career takes place in the context of kin and friends, and he reports only one relationship with a social superior.

Angel

The following account consists of Angel's own description of his life, which is sometimes summarized for convenience and other times presented in his own words to convey a particularly interesting perception.

Angel was born in 1925 in a municipality of approximately six thousand, almost all of whom were scattered in small hamlets around a tiny market center. It lies close to the border with El Salvador, approximately 150 miles from the capital. His mother died when he was a child and, because his father drank heavily, the family of four barely subsisted on the produce of the few acres his father rented. Angel worked in the fields and learned from his grandfather and uncle something of the trades of barber and tailor.

His education was rudimentary, and, though nominally attending school for four years, he received only one proper year of schooling, since he spent most of the time playing with other children. It was only when the school authorities drew his father's attention to what was happening that he regularly attended school. At the age of fourteen, he learned from passing workers that there was work in the neighboring coffee plantations of San Salvador, and he migrated to work there. When he returned home with money saved, the family gladly received him, using some of the money to provide a large homecoming supper, the first adequate food his father had eaten for some time.

Angel clearly remembers his father's reply to his own first greeting: "How's life with you, father?" "Just as you see me, son, still collecting wild bananas." The wild banana is a common source of earning extra money, but the work is laborious and the price paid extremely low, so that it constitutes an extreme resort of those in need of money.

Though his father has remarried, Angel speaks well of his stepmother. However, work at home brings in little money and involves long hours compared to those of San Salvador; so, overhearing pilgrims passing to the nearby national shrine, talking about job opportunities in Guatemala City, he caught a bus to the departmental capital. The next day he continued on to the national capital, lodging in a boarding house near the bus station. Bewildered at the difficulty of finding a job and without contacts, he entered the army after three days.

His description of army life stresses two things: that he did not find army life difficult and that he was able to establish good relations with his superiors. Army life in those days, he says, was different to what it is now; there was an emphasis on basic drill and marching and, in short, it was not very different from the games he had played as a child. He became a valet attached to the minister of war and made many contacts with staff officers. Serving in the presidential palace, he was an eyewitness to the Guatemalan revolution of 1944. His account of the revolution indicates that he had no clear idea either of what was happening or of where his loyalties were.

As we were on staff duties we had nothing to do with going out and restoring order.... Our work was that of an assistant, to polish shoes ... and we had to clean his uniforms.... When the revolution of the twentieth of October occurred, we were within the palace and we realized it when an explosion was heard in the tower of San José and they began attacking the barracks, and when we too were being attacked.... We did not know where the shooting was coming from, the only thing we knew was that it was the people. But suddenly we realized that it was our own comrades from the Guard of Honor that were attacking.... Then they officially told us that the people had won the revolution along with the Guard of Honor. We were almost without leaders. The general had sought refuge in the embassy, and all the old commanders had taken refuge. So I came and said to a friend, look, I believe that we belong to the Guard of Honor, and the most important thing for us is to go to the Guard, for who can we rely on here—the general has gone—all the generals have gone .... So then and there we collected our belongings in a bag—there were no suitcases then—and left by the main door—it was [closed]—and we were all standing there with our bags ... some fifty soldiers but dressed in civilian clothes and all of us somewhat ignorant and when one is ignorant one does not know what to do.... Then, suddenly they opened and we came out with our bags and went by foot, with shooting in the streets—we went and presented ourselves to the Guard of Honor ... because we belonged there and then came Colonel Arana [revolutionary leader later assassinated], and he ordered us to go out and patrol the streets since we too, so to speak, were of the revolution, we went with machine guns. . . But the revolution was almost over. Afterwards, they came and decorated us with the medal of the Guatemalan woman of the Guard of Honor, but. . .I lost it."

This is the account of the man who was to become one of the neighborhood leaders of the political party that sees itself as the one representing the revolution described above. In this period, however, he was encapsulated in army life without contact with the people living in the city outside.

After the revolution he did not stay long in the army and transfered to the police to work in the customs near his home town. The next eight years were taken up with a succession of moves from one police post to another as, for one reason or another, he quarreled with his superiors or did not like the working conditions. Each time he had to return to the capital to obtain a new post.

During this period he took up with a woman who bore him two children, but, finding her too jealous, he abandoned her with money to set up in petty trade. Then, in a small village, he fell in love with a young girl—his present wife—and told of the secret meetings necessitated by her parents' opposition to the match. Angel was regarded as unsuitable because of his previous marriage, and anyway, says the girl's father, he would prefer his daughter to marry a dog than a policeman. Angel and the girl eloped together, but to avoid trouble he transferred to a post in another village.

Once again he was in the midst of dramatic political events—the beginnings of the counterrevolution of 1954. While the situation in the provinces became increasingly disturbed, he seized the opportunity to become a police barber, and, as the rumors of revolution fluctuated, he changed back and forth from barber to policeman. The counterrevolution arrived, and he describes it:

When Colonel Castillo Armas entered Guatemala, some of the police deserted, others had some quarrels or other, and the head of the department also deserted. But . . . it did not affect us directly because the areas that were in my concern were not his areas, and when he became president and there were changes it did not affect me. So there I was seeing myself as a barber and remained until the end. There was a new head of department and he asked me saying that any police who wanted to continue could. Since I needed to and wanted to, I tried to keep working as a barber. But I was demobilized . . . and decided to work in agriculture.

His attempt at agriculture was a failure because the crop did not fetch good prices, and they were mainly sustained by his wife's work of making bread and engaging in petty trade. The only alternative was another return to the city to petition for another police job; as he said, the only thing he knew how to do in the city was to enter the police. His work with the police finally came to an end when he met an old police friend who had a job with the anti-malaria branch of the Health Ministry. They exchanged comparisons of pay and working conditions, and Angel decided he would be better off in that job. The friend provided him with a letter for an influential person in the city, and, armed with this and a letter of recommendation from his police superior, Angel took up the contact. The contact secured him a personal interview with the director of the anti-malaria branch, and he got the job.

He traveled all over the country with his work. His wife and growing family accompanied him from village to village; he went ahead and rented rooms for them. He worked in a small team, and relations among them appeared good, but he said little about his companions. After about a year, there was trouble in the work, since some of the insecticide began to poison the workers. Angel described the development of the symptoms of poisoning over the period of their work. However, their foreman did not believe them, and Angel talked with his fellow workers:

"I came and said that it was absolutely necessary that we go to the Justice of the Peace and depose that we were victims of poisoning—through fault of the place and not ourselves—so that afterwards they would [not] dismiss us for carelessness, since in malaria [Health Ministry] they ordered to fulfill all the rules of putting on gloves, masks, etc. We made the deposition, but then another workmate fell ill . . . and we said to the foreman that we must send him to Guatemala, but he did not wish to do it. Consequently, since he didn't want to send him, we ourselves went along so that the director would give the order for us to be cured. We arrived and found that in the office there were some eighty with symptoms of poisoning. The director asked us on what authority we had come. We said we were ill. . . . We began being examined in the institute. Then seeing that they said that we had been careless, the doctor came and said we should be dismissed since they are ill. So we began to take action, we went to the street and to the press to publicize our protest. So the director summoned us and said that [although] we had complained of unjust dismissal, we had been dismissed through our own fault, of having left our work. . . . Yes, we replied, we left our work since we are ill . . . as always seeking your help. He said that he would help us on condition that we would only receive half pay while we were being cured. After two months of treatment all the men tried to talk to him to say that we were fine . . . and they went away to work again, some to the same locale. Now it appears that the director took a special liking for me . . . and said that I should remain to repair the apparatus.

This excerpt is the first time in recounting his life history that Angel talked at any length about relationships with his peers or workmates. Previously, in recounting his movements, the relationships he stressed were those with superiors, and, indeed, given his mobility and job, it is reasonable that superiors should figure prominently in his memory of past events. Even in this excerpt, which describes a situation in which his own interests and those of his workmates were clearly opposed to those of his superiors, his final interpretation of events (how he came to remain in the city) was based on his personal relationship with the superior. Angel continued working for the anti-malaria branch for about a year in the city, and after hours he took on an extra job as a barber. In his first year in the city, working at two jobs, he saved some five hundred dollars, which allowed him to set up in his present barber shop. The contacts he made working part-time as a barber helped him get information about the best place to set up his own shop and where to get good equipment.

The story of Angel's migrations before settling in the city illustrates many of the points that we have discussed in this chapter. The centralization of administration made him constantly return to the city to seek a new post and ultimately he remained there as a result of illness and a desire to settle in one place with his family.

This migrant career also led him to frequently redefine his social image of himself. Remember that his account is basically his present interpretation of what happened to him in the past and is in this sense an attempt to make sense of the past in light of present circumstances. Angel strongly emphasizes his personal progress and his aspirations for improving his social and economic position. This view of himself is related to his past and as he says: "I only think in progress, or better what I think of most is my children, what I most desire is that the day I die my children should have a roof over their heads, their own house. . . . I have faith; more than faith in God, I also have faith in my plans."

His view of his past is of a constant endeavor to make his way in life and to preserve an independence of action. Each of his many movements is presented as being for the best given the low pay of a job, unpleasant working conditions, a bad superior, and the like. Yet it is also possible to see that many of his moves have resulted from forces beyond his own control and that some—for example, his move into agriculture—were unsuccessful. His present position—seven children and living in bad housing conditions in a shantytown—is also hard to relate consistently to the image he has of himself. In terms of his life history the problem becomes clearer. He has moved through a series of social and historical situations that have often been different from each other, and he has had few continuing social relationships to buffer the transition from situation to situation. A recurrent theme of his descriptions is the social innocence with which he enters each new situation: the migration to San Salvador, his first encounter with the city, the army, and the revolution, his relations as a policeman with people in the provinces, and his work as an employee in a large government enterprise. As he moves into the new situations he has to redefine his image of himself and others. Note, for example, his surprise at the difficulty of finding work in the city and his

rapid enlistment in the army; and this contrasts with the ease
with which he finds work in his previous migration to San
Salvador. Likewise, encapsulated in the ordered relationships of
the army, he has suddenly to confront the situation of a revolution without the aid of social relationships that allow an easy
transition. He serves his superiors in the police and Health
Ministry loyally, and yet he loses his job.

These series of encounters have led Angel to actively seek a
social identity that allows him to attribute meaning to his past
and to his present. He cannot rely on a set of established and
continuing relationships that give him a definite social position
and enable him, through a process of mutual understandings, to
make sense of unfamiliar situations. Consequently, in the
present, Angel has constantly to initiate action as a means of
establishing a social identity. The circle is a vicious one, since
through initiating action he enters new situations and disrupts
old ties. Yet, desiring to demonstrate his progress through
concrete achievements, initiating relationships with superiors
and helping to organize in the neighborhood, Angel is one of
the most publicly active people in the neighborhood.

Angel's is just one case that illustrates a more general contention that the careers of many migrants are likely both to
expose them to diverse situations and to deprive them of
continuing social interactions that enable them to assimilate
change. They are spurred to activity, but that activity is
directed to the fulfilment of individual needs confused by the
pattern of their past experiences, toward reliance on superiors
but also toward identification with the social problems of their
country. The point is not merely that certain migrant careers
encourage public activity while others do not, but that a life
career involves a set of social interactions that continue to
constrain the paths that migrants follow. Discontinuity in past
experiences prejudges the relationships that migrants both can
and will mobilize in pursuit of their goals. Within the city there
is a group of people both more likely to be active than others
and whose mode of acting is conditioned by a set of prior
constraints.

3. Urban Careers

The background for the discussion of urban careers is the rapid population increase of the city. The increasing size and density of the city affects both the job and residential mobility of poor people and is an important factor in the changes in social environment experienced by city dwellers. Among these changes are the decline of personal or family reputation as a basis for knowing and interacting with others and its replacement by the more impersonal means of evaluation given by an individual's social and economic characteristics. We will thus be analyzing a process often linked to economic development; but we will see that these changes have a particular significance within an economic and administrative structure where socioeconomic characteristics are rarely stable or readily identifiable. In this respect, one of the crucial arguments to keep in mind is that economic development proceeds with a change in the structure of relationships that facilitates the participation of urban dwellers in a modern industrial organization, requiring a labor force unconstrained by extended local obligations, operating on the basis of reward for performance rather than for status.[1]

These processes are described through the urban careers of our sample, and indeed the social changes occurring with urban development are changes in careers and not just changes in social relationships. Life careers cease to be pursued within a stable context of locality, fixed occupation, friends, and kin, and increasingly involve individuals in different experiences and different sets of relationships. These changes have happened during the lives of the sample, and many careers span these different patterns of urban life. Life careers constitute experiences that condition an individual's evaluation of the present and make the past a continuing factor in present behavior. Indeed, using a life career perspective demonstrates that the social field influencing individual action has a historical as well as a contemporary dimension.

We will examine the extent that urban careers have the characteristics of social paths where each step conditions but does not determine the next, and where the influence of earlier stages on later stages is mainly indirect.[2] A path thus describes a life career taking place outside a closed system of relationships and traditions, whose characteristics are no longer truly cyclical but evolutionary; for, instead of reinforcing an established organization, it constantly adds new experiences and new relationships. The paths of people with similar backgrounds may thus significantly differ where there are, for example,

---

[1] A full discussion of these issues is found in Arnold S. Feldman and Wilbert E. Moore, eds., *Labor Commitment and Social Change in Developing Areas*. Particularly relevant to assessing the argument in this and subsequent chapters is the theoretical scheme of Feldman and Moore and the qualifications made of them by Hoselitz (ibid., pp. 46-77 220-232).

[2] Robert C. Hanson and Ozzie G. Simmons, "The Role Path: A Conceptual Procedure for Studying Migration in Urban Communities " *Human Organization* 27, no. 2 (Summer 1968): 152-158. In this study of the movements of migrants in Denver, the authors indicate the importance of the articulation of different sectors of the urban economy for the urban careers of migrants starting at different points.

differences among areas of the city and among occupations in their rates of mobility, in their economic fortunes, and in their links with other areas and other occupations. These differences become important sources of horizontal differentiation within low-income groups, and, in this chapter, are used to show how locality—in this case represented by the two neighborhoods—ceases to be an important basis for maintaining urban order because it merely represents a convergence of different urban paths. These paths guide future behavior, influence people's perceptions of the city, and differentiate their expectations of urban life. They also inhibit the development of a locally based community of people with shared sentiments and a readiness to cooperate for the mutual welfare.

The Traditional Basis of Urban Life

Until 1945, the population increase of Guatemala City had been a slow and gradual process that could be absorbed within a relatively stable social and economic structure. It appears that, at least for low-income people, the city prior to 1945 was composed of small, relatively well-defined neighborhoods in which the inhabitants knew each other well enough to have a sense of neighborhood identity and within which people carried on their occupations and social relationships.

José describes his own youth in one of these neighborhoods in the years prior to 1945:

At that time the city was quite small; there was not any [names several modern zones of the city]. No one wanted to go and live in La Reformita [the present Zone 12], because it was like another nation for the people. Everyone wanted to be in the center.

Every president used to leave land as a keepsake, and the land bore his name, at least his surname. In that period almost all the people treated each other like kinsfolk. It was almost as if, on feeling the grief of one, it became the grief of all. Since there were few, everyone liked each other, respected each other and, as everyone had enough, no one quarreled. Today it's different, since the one fights with the other because the one needs something and wants to take it from the other.

But from one barrio to another, that was different. Those of one district could not go to another, since both young and old used to fight. The old used to exchange insults and went about with knives, and the kids had stone fights from the area that belonged to them, one group on one side, the other on the other. I remember us gathering stones and making piles of them. At that time all the streets of the city were cobbled—there wasn't asphalt then—and so when they were repairing them we used to go to the heaps of stones and take them in our leather bags and have them ready for the fights.

I do not present José's account to suggest that neighborhoods within Guatemala City were formerly cohesive and conflict free. Recollections are colored by the difficulties of the present and the distance of the past. In retrospect, close-knit relationships often have an attraction that obscures the conflicts and unpleasantness that are often fostered by such relationships. What is important is José's emphasis on compact relatively stable neighborhoods. It is a description repeated in other accounts of the city prior to 1945, and it also fits other evidence about the changes in Guatemala City's organization that will be discussed in the following sections of this chapter.

It is likely that in the years prior to 1945, such important career events as taking a job, getting married, or setting up house occurred within the framework of the neighborhood and through the mediation of family and friendship relations. José, for example, speaks of his father placing himself and his brothers in various trades and describes the associations based on the local church, which were an important source of social activity for the youth of the neighborhood. A similar reconstruction of previous patterns of urban organization is made by Redfield in discussing the changing importance of barrios as inclusive bases for lower-class urban life in Mérida.[3] Making such a comparison underlines the nonindustrial nature of Guatemala City's past and is a reminder that in the case of many Latin American cities their contemporary growth can be as disconcerting for those born in them as it is for those who arrive from villages and small towns.

[3] Robert Redfield, *The Folk Culture of Yucàtan*, pp. 26-32.

Prior to 1945, then, we can conceive of the social and economic life of the urban poor as being largely based on ascriptive criteria; that people's capabilities were evaluated on the basis of who they were in terms of the reputation of their families, employers, or neighborhoods, and not on the basis of what they had achieved in terms of learned skills or qualifications. Employers, who were mostly owners of small workshops, recruited new workers on the basis of the reputation of an applicant's family or on that of his previous employer. Employment itself was often locally based, and the products were sold to a local clientele. This is especially apparent in the accounts given by craftsmen such as tailors, shoemakers, and carpenters of their work during this early period. The proximity of workplace and residence meant that most of the activities important to life were carried out within a neighborhood and people could pass through the stages of the life cycle within its confines. It is this characteristic that endowed the neighborhood in which José lived with its especial quality; it was the place of work, of family, and of friends.

This description is not an exact one even for the years prior to 1945, and in that period there undoubtedly was movement from one area to another occasioned by changing jobs, by marriage, or by other personal or public events. Yet, it is a description that is given by present-day city dwellers when they remember their urban past and contrast it with the present. It also fits the literary descriptions of the city in this period, most notably Miguel Angel Asturias's account of city life in *El Presidente.*

Residential Mobility

The growth and economic development of cities is associated with their increasing spatial differentiation.[4] As cities grow, their sub-areas grow increasingly homogeneous in respect to the social and economic use to which they are put. Some areas

[4] The following argument is that commonly used in the writings on urban ecology, but it is an argument that best applies, as in the case of Guatemala, to unplanned urban growth in capitalist societies.

specialize in industrial activity, others in commerce, and others in housing for people of similar income range. In the modern industrial cities of Europe and the United States, whose growth has been unplanned, the mechanism through which differentiation takes place is the competition of different economic and social uses for preferred locations in the city. The external economies of locating similar business, industries or housing type together are sufficient to ensure that most industrial cities become increasingly differentiated with time. There is some reason to expect, then, that urban growth and particularly rapid urban growth results in city areas becoming more specialized, and the available evidence suggests that the growth of many Latin American cities has been accompanied by such specialization.[5] In the Latin American case this process has been more dramatic because it contrasts with traditional urban ecology in which the central areas have been the location of government and the residence of the urban elite. There has traditionally been little specialization by economic function in the center, and the poorer sections of the urban population have lived on the periphery of the city.

It is this pattern that Theodore Caplow describes when he analyzed the spatial organization of Guatemala City in 1948.[6] His study serves as a useful base line against which to compare subsequent changes. In 1948 he described a city whose spatial pattern had not radically changed for fifty years or more. Indeed, Caplow was able to show that many of the city's principal families resided in the same areas as their ancestors fifty and even a hundred years previously. Those principal families whose wealth was more recent or who had recently come to Guatemala (German immigrants) were more likely to live outside the central urban area and in the newly emerging

[5] Leo F. Schnore, "On the Spatial Structure of Cities in the Two Americas," in *The Study of Urbanization*, edited by Philip M. Hauser and Leo F. Schnore, pp. 347-398.

[6] Theodore Caplow, "The Social Ecology of Guatemala City," *Social Forces* 28(December 1949): 113-135.

suburbs. The description Caplow gives of the center of the city emphasizes its low economic and social differentiation:

Stores, ranging from small, well-stocked department stores down to the one-room *tienda* with its open doorway on the street, are scattered throughout the urban area proper, as are schools, textile factories, printing plants, churches, government buildings and motorcycle agencies. A fairly typical block more than a mile from the center includes: a barber shop, a dressmaker's shop, the office of an accessories firm, five extremely modern duplexes occupied by middle class families, a 22-room private residence about forty years old, and two slightly smaller houses occupied by upper-class families. Across the street is a row of old subdivided dwellings rented one room at a time to impoverished families, a plant nursery, a small woodworking plant, a large grocery store, a doctor's office, and several homes of moderate size.

He attributes the absence of substantial change in the spatial pattern to a slow population growth that has enabled the existing urban spatial pattern to absorb the increase. The migrant population, housed at the periphery in burgeoning slums, did not disrupt the existing organization by its influx. Also, the economic fortunes of the city were in the hands of well-established families who were able to limit competition, so that economic expansion was slow and fairly well-regulated.

Residential Changes since 1948

Taking 1948 as a base line, we can now assess the significance for Guatemala City's spatial organization of the changes that have occurred since that time. As compared with the years up to 1948, the subsequent population increase has been rapid. In the twenty-nine years from 1921 to 1950, the population of the city appears to have doubled; but in the fourteen years from 1950 to 1964 it doubled its size once again. In the last chapter we noted that the increase in migration to the city and the increase in the urban growth rate accelerated from the late forties to the present. Spatially, also, the city has dramatically increased. Guatemala City, as Caplow described it in 1948, was still mainly confined to the central zones, Zones 1 and 3. He noted the increasing importance of residential developments to the south of these zones and to the north and east. These developments, however, appear still to be in an early stage.

By contrast, the city in 1968 had extended beyond and even within the ravines mentioned by Caplow as barriers to expansion to include new planned and unplanned communities that lie as far as ten miles from the center of the city. Whereas in 1948 it would still have been possible to walk to the periphery of the major area of the city, by 1968 it required a thirty-minute bus ride to get to Planificada, located at the city's southern edge in what was farming country in 1948. The southern and western suburbs have extended and become specialized as homes for the middle- and upper-income groups; whereas to the north, west, and southwest large areas of lower-income housing have emerged. Zones that in 1948 were at the margin of urban development—such as Zones 2, 5, and 6—are now considered central zones and are fully urbanized. It is also apparent that the recent expansion of the city has outrun the capacity of the municipal authorities to plan for the absorption of the increase in population, which Caplow claims that they had been relatively successful in doing until 1948. Thus, not only does an estimated fifteen percent of the urban population live in shantytowns of the San Lorenzo type, but many of the legal neighborhoods lack adequate sewage disposal, electricity, and water supply.

The extent of change should not, however, be over-emphasized. As compared with the industrial cities of Britain or the United States, Guatemala is still relatively undifferentiated residentially. Despite the considerable growth of middle- and upper-income suburbs. many people from these categories continue to reside in the center of the city. The pace of urban renewal in the center has been slow, and Caplow's description quoted above could still serve as a description of many central city areas.

There is a slow replacement of relatively unspecialized economic and residential uses by modern multistorey buildings devoted to offices and specialized retail and whosesale outlets. Likewise residential streets are becoming more homogeneous as buildings are torn down or converted to suit the predominant residential pattern. In 1968, Guatemala City was thus in the midst of the slow transition of the type described for other cities in developing countries, but gradually a pattern of dominant use is beginning to emerge in the different subareas of the city. The argument to follow has many similarities with that developed on a more statistical level by Abu-Lughod with respect to Cairo. One of the most important comparative differences is the lesser importance of the migrant status/ ethnicity variables as factors in differentiating residence in Guatemala City.[7]

As more and more people have come to Guatemala City, so the competition for existing housing has increased. The pressure of this demand for housing has been met partly by increasing urban densities and partly by the spatial extension of the city. Both processes, however, can be expected to have similar consequences for the residential mobility of low-income families. As densities increase and the city extends, so it is more likely that those who sell property or rent it begin to specialize in their clientele. In the densely settled central urban zones, landlords attempt to sell the smallest amount of space for the most money and the least trouble, so that families with a large number of children cannot afford the space they need and are not welcomed by landlords. In contrast, in more peripheral zones of the city, or in shantytowns, families are catered for at lower cost but at the expense of a long journey to work or of unsanitary conditions.

This is basically what the process of differentiation means to families seeking suitable accommodation. This process is not completely homogeneous, and it is still possible, though less

[7] Janet Abu-Lughod, "Testing the Theory of Social Area Analysis: The Ecology of Cairo, Egypt," *American Sociological Review* 34, no. 2 (April 1969): 198-212. A similar analysis is conducted by Brian Berry and P. H. Rees, "The Factorial Ecology of Calcutta," *American Journal of Sociology* 74, no. 5 (March 1969): 445-491.

common than before, for people of different income levels or at different stages of the family cycle to locate near each other. As a son grows up and sets up house, he finds it too expensive or too inconvenient to locate near his parents. Thus, they may be living far outside the center where they obtain more space and the son may prefer to rent a room in the center and have easy access to his work and city amusements. A similar process separates other long-established relationships, and residential neighborhoods increasingly cease to be communities in which kinsfolk, workmates, and lifelong friends reside together.

Residential Careers

Understanding the changing significance of the two neighborhoods as residences for certain categories of the poor enables us to assess the biases that may affect the subsequent analysis of their occupational and residential careers. The discussion of residential careers is thus in part a device aimed at clarifying the factors intervening to affect the characteristics and behavior of this sample. It underlines a methodological problem with my attempt to describe the processes of change in city life by using cohorts to look at the characteristics and experiences of city residents at different points in time. Such a reconstruction is unsafe because coming to or moving from a neighborhood is influenced by differences in household characteristics and careers. Since my sample only contains survivors of previous cohorts, their survival may indicate that they have special characteristics.

Despite these warnings, I proceed with the description of changes over time and hope that my difficulties will help others to anticipate more successfully the range of data and samples they need to accurately describe changes in urban careers. I also feel that the results I report are not simply produced by selective factors in the survival of these residents. The results form a trend that is both coherent and plausible. Furthermore, before stressing the importance of particular changes, I have tried as far as possible to check them against my observations and against the accounts of residents.

The process of residential differentiation has proceeded apace since 1948, and families in both neighborhoods have experienced it during their urban careers. To judge its impact we begin by comparing migrants and those born in the city who, in the traditional organization of the city, are likely to be residentially, as they are occupationally, segregated. As Caplow describes the situation in 1948, migrants to the city were likely to settle in the zones peripheral to the central zones. City born were thought to be located in such zones as 1 or 3 and to be relatively stable from generation to generation. Thus, in 1948, Caplow thought that migrant status was probably the most important variable determining where people lived; but it is doubtful whether this assessment was a completely accurate one even then. Certainly, the presence of cheap rented accommodations in most urban zones at the time makes it likely that migrants could find their way into most areas. To explore these possibilities, the 1948 residences of those born in the city and of migrants are compared with the note of caution that we are looking at a sample that, either socially or spatially, is peripheral to contemporary urban life, and so their residential origins may also have been peripheral.

Table 12. Zones of Residence of Migrants and City Born in 1948 (Male Heads of Household) in Percentages

	One	Three	Five	Four and Eight	Others	Total
Migrants[a] N = 62	26	11	19	11	33	100
City born N = 48	17	23	23	12	25	100

[a]The reduced number of migrants is because only a minority arrived in the city by 1948.

In 1948 there were some differences in the zones of residence of those born in the city and of migrants, but these differences were not considerable. Thus, 25 percent of the city born were residing outside the central nucleus of the city that included Zones 5, 8, and 4 as well as Zones 1 and 3, in comparison with 33 percent of the migrants (Table 12).

Almost all those in the city in 1948 were concentrated in the various central zones, and it appears that sections, at least, of all those zones served migrants as well as the city born. The data also indicate that the expansion of the city has indeed involved the physical mobility of families and that the large majority are now living in very different zones to those in which they lived in 1948. These data do not at first sight accord with those on the first zone of residence of migrants and city born which show a greater discrimination. Whereas 60 percent of the city born first lived in the two central zones, Zones 1 and 3, 32 percent of migrants took up their first urban residence in such zones; but this comparison is affected by the comparatively late arrival of migrants in the city. Thus, while all those born in the city were necessarily resident before 1948, the majority of migrants arrived later, so that in effect we are comparing the zones in which those born in the city lived in the 1930s and 1940s with those in which migrants lived in the 1950s and 1960s. The last but one zone of the sample (i.e., the zone of residence before movement to their present neighborhood) is less affected by differences in time of arrival and shows that, while 28 percent of the city born were resident in Zones 1 and 3, 18 percent of migrants were so resident. If we now juxtapose the residential data in their true time order, we find that the gradual process of movement away from the central zones clearly emerges, and that migrants and city born become less segregated as the city born cease to reside centrally (Table 13).

Those born in the city have been somewhat less residentially mobile than migrants, and the pattern of their mobility has in many cases been to move from their zones of origin to their present neighborhoods in a single move. By comparison, migrants have been more mobile, partly, I would suggest, because as in the case of jobs, they have to spend more time seeking out suitable locations.

The population growth in the city is accompanied by a displacement of those "living centrally" to more peripheral zones. In this respect the process is similar to that described in the

Table 13. Percentage of Migrants and City Born Resident in Zones One and Three
Ordered by Time Sequence (Male Heads of Household)

	Earliest Time (1948 for Migrants, First Zone for City Born)	Intermediate (1948 for City Born, First Zone for *All* Migrants)	Latest (Last but One Zone)
City Born	60	40	28
Number	(50)	(48)	(50)
Migrants	37	32	18
Number	(62)	(151)	(151)

growth of cities in the United States in the early part of this century.[8] In contrast, however, since migrants and city born are competing on relatively equal terms in Guatemala and are not distinguished by pronounced cultural differences, the movement that occurs is not characterized by differences in the migrant status of those that move, with each cohort of migrants displacing the earlier one to a more distant zone. Instead, as migrants become residentially mobile, so their dispersion is accelerated as those recently arriving join relatives and friends throughout the city.

To extend this analysis to include variables that do influence residential mobility within the city, we now consider the peculiar position of the two neighborhoods and examine the types of urban career that have led families to these residential destinations.

The peripheral legal neighborhood Planificada is a recent phenomenon, and its final incorporation within the city's boundaries came only in the period of the study. It is thus a concrete expression of the city's rapid expansion. The shantytown also represents important aspects of the city's develop-

[8] See Amos Hawley's account in *Human Ecology*, pp. 371-404, which summarizes the literature on the forms of urban expansion and the role of population succession in this. Even in the case of these American cities it has never been entirely clear to what extent the various migrant and other social groups moved homogeneously, displacing other populations. See Paul Hatt, "The Concept of Natural Area," *American Sociological Review* 11(August 1946): 423-427.

ment. The burgeoning shantytown settlements of the city are the result of a rapid growth unaccompanied by an equivalent expansion of urban housing. Since these neighborhoods bear a special spatial and social relationship to the rest of the city, the increasing spatial differentiation of the city means that families who come to them should have special characteristics.

This investigation also has broader implications; for, although we are confined to two low-income neighborhoods, they are neighborhoods that differ on an important dimension in the current rapid urban growth of developing countries—the legality of settlement. The shantytown San Lorenzo is an illegal settlement, and communities of its type are thought to epitomize residential marginality. Many accounts stress that shantytowns in Latin America are the locus of social disorganization and the first home of the disorientated—whether they be recent migrants or social misfits.[9]

San Lorenzo was founded in 1959, when almost all of its present shacks were erected. Planificada was laid out in its present form during the 1950s, and it attracted large-scale settlement toward the end of that decade. Comparing the first settlers (those families who came to the neighborhoods in 1960 or before) indicates the social forces present in actual and concurrent examples of the city's expansion.

In comparison with the legal neighborhood, a higher percentage of family heads entering the shantytown were females who were either widows or separated from their husbands (34 percent in the shantytown as against 9 percent in the legal neighborhood). Of the male heads of household, 52 percent of those who came to the shantytown around 1960 were at that time self-employed workers or employees in trade or service; 39 percent of those coming to the legal neighborhood were so employed. These are the jobs in the city that are most subject to fluctuation and to the possibility of having periods of low or no earnings. Family heads moving to the legal neighborhood in

[9] Carolina Mariá de Jesús, *Child of the Dark: The Diary of Carolina Mariá de Jesús.*

this period were more likely to be employed in fairly large-scale urban enterprises. Further, settlers of Planificada were more literate than those of San Lorenzo, but the difference is small (48 percent compared to 43 percent) and the age distribution was approximately the same. These differences in the characteristics of the early settlers are relatively consistent with the view of the shantytown as socially more marginal. But there is an exception, to which we will return later, in that heads of families are less likely to be born or reared in the city from age eleven or before in Planificada than in the shantytown (45 percent city born or reared in Planificada and 52 percent in the shantytown). At this period there is no difference between the two neighborhoods in the number of children in the entering families who average 2.7 children.

It also appears that those who founded the shantytown often had other characteristics—not revealed in the survey indices—that relate to an insecure urban position. In the accounts of the founding of the shantytown, it is often the wife that takes the initiative in securing a space in the emergent neighborhood. In three of the ten life histories, it is the woman who negotiated for space in the absence of the husband. During his absence from the city, Pablo's wife heard from gossip at the market that the shantytown was being erected and wrote to him to come back and help her erect a shack. In this case, as in others, the husband's job involved travel outside the city and long absences. Consequently, the wife was often alone in the city with the children and, living in rented accommodations, was liable to be out on the street if the husband delayed in sending money for rent. Many of the founding families were in broadly similar positions; they include, for example, single men and families of traders who were constantly traveling about the city or about the countryside. For them, rented accommodations proved too insecure a base since, in their absence, their accommodations could be rented out to others and their belongings would disappear. It also appears that coming to the shantytown is not only associated with a marginal job position, but often with changes emphasizing the insecurity of the job. In the life histories several of the accounts tell of the failure of a job or of a dramatic change that preceded the movement to the shantytown. For Fausto it was the failure of a small bread business he and his brother had set up in the city and his transition to street peddling. For Isabella it was the arrest of her son and consequent loss of an important income that is cited as a contributing reason for the move. José settled there on his final return to the city after his unsuccessful attempts to make a living in agriculture. For Pepe it was the end of his barber business and his taking up a job on the buses.

For others, moving to the shantytown means saving rent and its possible investment in business or family expenditures. For some small businessmen in the shantytown, their move came at a time when they needed to make important, if marginal, savings to build up their enterprises. Thus Angel moved at a time when he was paying for his barber's equipment because the savings on rent would ease his debts. Coming to the shantytown thus represents an attempt by relatively experienced urban dwellers to cope with changes in their urban position, and there is evidence that the settlement represents a more conscious and coordinated movement of people than is usual in the pattern of urban development. It has been reported from other areas of Latin America that the invasion of land to build a shantytown is an organized event with considerable preparation before the day of the invasion. Shantytowns have in fact been seen as a possible solution both to the problems of housing in Latin America and to the problems of community organization.[10] In Peru, especially, there is considerable evidence that squatter invasions are highly organized events. It appears that the invasion of San Lorenzo was also in many respects an organized response to the problems of housing.

[10] William P. Mangin, "Latin American Squatter Settlements: A Problem and a Solution," *Latin American Research Review* 2, no. 3(Summer 1967): 65-98; idem, "Poverty and Politics in the Cities of Latin America," in A. Bloomberg, Jr., and H. J. Schmandt, eds., *Power, Poverty and Urban Policy*, pp. 397-432.

From the accounts of those who took a leading part in the invasion, it is apparent that the possibility of invading had been a topic of discussion among men in the contiguous legal neighborhood and informal meetings had been held to consider the possibility. They already had an example of the possibility of invading land in that the land farther down the ravine had already been occupied by squatters. From the first days of the invasion, a committee of invaders was set up—called the pro-invasion committee—which was active in regulating the distribution of space and in making contacts with the press and political figures. These aspects of the founding of the shanty-town will be discussed later, but at this juncture it is important to note that the shantytown did not represent a desperate last resort of those unable to find urban accommodation, but was the achievement of people who, while they had pressing needs, also had the urban skill to plan what they were doing. Indeed, after the first weeks of the invasion it appears from the accounts that settling in the shantytown had become a formal procedure involving obtaining permission from a squatter's committee and showing adequate building materials.

The burgeoning of shantytowns, according to this argument, is thus not the response to the accommodation needs of recent migrants. Rather it is the response to the needs of those who in various ways have been "displaced" by the growth and differentiation of the city, whether people born in city or long established migrants. It is to people who find it increasingly difficult to find accommodations to suit their needs or who are placed in an increasingly insecure job position that shantytowns have most appeal: they require little capital outlay from a squatter but instead the ability to mobilize contacts and resources, especially building materials.

In contrast, moving to Planificada at this period did involve financial outlay, but was attended by greater physical comfort and legal security. Those who moved to Planficada to buy lots were able to purchase them relatively cheaply, and the prices were not beyond migrants with money from the sale of small rural landholdings. This is one reason for the greater proportion of provincial migrants in Planificada than in the shantytown. It provided them with a secure base from which to seek urban work. It also provided space and pleasant conditions for urban workers in the better paying and more stable enterprises; they could purchase a lot over time, and their job security made this feasible.

In addition to these categories were the early renters who often rented from the original buyer and set up a shack on an empty lot. Other families built more than one shack and rented out the ones they did not use. These different procedures brought different social groups to the neighborhood and a consequent diversity of housing types. Evidence of this diversity is still apparent as one walks down any of the streets and passes shacks of the type found in San Lorenzo followed by a well-designed and spacious house occupying the whole lot and then by an empty lot or by an adobe house whose front is given over to a store. However, at this period, renters and owners of lots showed similar jobs age, and family characteristics. Planificada was still sparsely inhabited and had few urban services and thus, though a pleasant dormitory for urban workers, it had few attractions to create employment within the neighborhood.

After the establishment of the shantytown, there has been a constant turnover of population—approximately 7 percent a year. The leaving population has been replaced, but those who came after the settlement came to very different conditions than did the founders. Though still illegal, the shantytown had gained a relatively stable existence, and the incursions of police and military had long ceased. Furthermore, rudimentary services such as public latrines, electricity, and public water had been installed. A similar process of stabilization has also occurred in Planificada, which has filled with people, and few empty lots exist. Urban services have been increasingly provided. In all, Planificada has become increasingly self-sufficient and less a dormitory appendage of the city. There is now a considerable local market and enough purchasers to justify an increasingly extensive infrastructure of craftsmen, merchants, and service workers. City neighborhoods thus have a development sequence of their own, and this sequence is an independent factor in attracting residents, as is seen by contrasting San Lorenzo and Planificada in the years after 1960.

When we compare the characteristics of people in the two neighborhoods who came after the period of first settlement— those families who came in the years after 1961—some striking differences to the account of the earlier settlement emerge. The proportion of single females who come with their children to set up house in the shantytown has diminished from the earlier 34 percent to 18 percent. In Planificada it remains much the same, at about 8 percent. Among the males who come in this later period, the first notable change is that the proportions of people in what we earlier characterized as unstable occupations (self-employment trade, and services) become reversed with respect to the two neighborhoods, increasing in Planificada and decreasing in San Lorenzo. In the period after 1960, it is in Planificada that people in such occupations predominate, with 54 percent of entering males being so employed compared to 43 percent in San Lorenzo. The second notable change is that the number of children of entering families increases in both neighborhoods, but this increase is most marked in San Lorenzo (the average number of children of entering families increases from 2.7 to 3.4 in San Lorenzo and from 2.7 to 3 in Planificada). What appears to be happening is that, after its initial settlement, the shantytown of San Lorenzo has come increasingly to serve as a place for families whose housing problems are related more to family size than to employment. In line with this argument is the increase in the proportion of migrants who came to San Lorenzo after 1960 (63 percent who were not born or reared in the city). With its increasing incorporation into the city, the shantytown has become a regular part of a migrant's search for accommodations and less the resort of those displaced by incoming migrants. In the period since 1960, several families of recently arrived migrants have come straight to relatives in San Lorenzo or through contacts have made inquiries about vacant lots.

In Planificada what lies behind the increasing entry of workers in trade, services, or self-employment in the period after 1960 is that the neighborhood is more densely populated and is more suited to trading and service activities. The center of the city, including San Lorenzo, is so overcrowded and competition so fierce among the self-employed that they have become hostile environments for those whose work is not stable. We will see later in this chapter that the self-employed in San Lorenzo have become increasingly dependent on central shops and agencies for their work. Also, the amount of space in the shantytown is not sufficient to conduct one's own business whether it be that of an independent craftsman or a trader who must store his goods.

In contrast, Planificada not only provides sufficient space but also sufficient population for the self-employed, for traders and service workers to find local work and local clients. Also, those coming after 1960 have increasingly been migrants (65 percent of those arriving) and especially migrants from the contiguous rural areas. The links established with these areas are of a kind to favor trading activities. Thus, several families in the sample trade in agricultural products through their contacts in their home region.

Accompanying these trends has been the increasing differentiation of renters and owners. The renters who have come since 1960 are increasingly young married couples or single males, while the owners are heads of families at the end of their family cycle. In these ways, Planificada provides a beginning and a terminal point in an urban residential career. Young families come to Planificada to rent and pursue their occupation. As their family grows it becomes more difficult to make do with the confined quarters available in the neighborhood, and they move out in search of better accommodations. Their next move may well be to one of the shantytowns emerging at the city's periphery. They will have established the contacts to obtain information about them and the freedom from rent and interference may suit their budget. Ultimately, if the family builds up its resources through the husband improving his job or through the children getting jobs and contributing money, they may return to a neighborhood like Planificada, this time to purchase.

This is a simplified and artificial scheme of urban residential movement, but it does seem that the two neighborhoods cater not only to people with somewhat different socioeconomic characteristics but also to people at different stages of the life cycle. Indeed, several San Lorenzo families in the survey sample had originally rented in Planificada before moving to the shantytown, while I recorded two cases of San Lorenzo families, both with some adult children and the father in a well-paying, stable job, who moved out during the three-year period of this study to a legal neighborhood adjoining Planificada where the government was selling cheap housing.

Unfortunately, I was unable to obtain complete information on the destinations of the families that left the shantytown during my stay there. The information that was obtained does fit the picture that is being developed. Some of the families—those with stable jobs, with their children growing up and beginning to earn—left the neighborhood for the new government housing projects emerging on the city's periphery. Other families, mostly successful small entrepreneurs, left San Lorenzo for nearby and centrally located neighborhoods where they purchased fairly spacious housing lots and continued their established business. Some heads of household who had been living with their wives in San Lorenzo and leaving their children with the grandparents in the city returned to rent in the city as a result of obtaining a better-paying job and the opportunity to get a larger house. There were also some families who left for other parts of Guatemala, to work either on plantations or in some of the developing provincial towns.

San Lorenzo is a neighborhood that over time has become a regular feature of urban residential organization attracting families in a certain phase of their family cycle rather than, as initially, families with insecure urban positions. The shantytown has thus become a stage in an urban residential career. Many families will never leave it, but it is significant that since its founding half its original population has been replaced. Also, almost all those who have remained assert that they intend to leave it and could cite concrete plans for doing so. Only a very few families constantly asserted that they regarded the shantytown as a permanent home. The lessening of commitment has grown with the development of the neighborhood. The more the neighborhood has approximated other low-income neighborhoods in its housing, services, and the people it attracts, the less it has become regarded as a permanent home community by its residents.

The position of Planificada is somewhat different. While it is a transitional phase in the residential careers of those renting, it has become a permanent home for those who own the housing lots. As the neighborhood has developed in population and services, so it has become a more viable community for the home owners. The contrast with San Lorenzo is that Planificada has increased the commitment of its home owners with time, while in the shantytown development has reduced the special characteristics of the neighborhood and has led it to be increasingly regarded as transitional.

This analysis of the characteristics of those coming to the two neighborhoods at the approximate period of their foundation and of those arriving subsequently indicates the direction of the city's own spatial differentiation. Unlike large industrial cities, Guatemala City has not developed large-scale industrial and service activities with fixed urban locations. There is also the development of small peripheral services and industries. Under these conditions, the central urban zones have increasingly differentiated to provide accommodation for people in lower socioeconomic categories and in various stages of the family cycle. At the periphery of the city are emerging what are almost satellite cities with their own economic base. These provide differentiated rental accommodations for low-income urban workers, many of whom will work locally and also provide the more successful and those ending their family cycle with permanent homes. Regardless of the legality of the settlement, a neighborhood becomes absorbed into this spatial organization, attracting people whose needs are locational as well as social. For example, whatever the dynamics of change that results from a shantytown's internal social organization, a powerful constraint on behavior is the position of such a neighborhood within the spatial and social differentiation of the whole city.

Placing residential mobility within the context of the general processes of urban development should not obscure the importance of the particular relationships of families to their mobility. Thus, the arrival of families in San Lorenzo has to be explained in terms of the personal networks in which they have been involved. Everyone from whom an account of the invasion was obtained stresses the part played by friends or kin. In some cases they were told by friends of the possibility of getting a housing space in the invaded land. In other cases, kin journeyed across the city to tell them of this possible solution to their problems. Indeed, one apparent characteristic of those who invaded is the existence among them of sets of relationships that had directly or indirectly existed prior to their invasion.

The importance of personal relationships in recruitment indicates another feature of the families who invaded San Lorenzo. The majority were already resident in the zone in which the shantytown is located. In that respect, the invasion was a local phenomenon undertaken by people with considerable local experience and many local contacts. As we shall see later, this circumstance is important in understanding both the early organization of the shantytown and its subsequent history. Families who were not residents of that zone were recruited by friendship and kinship networks that included people living there. Pepe, who was living in Zone 7, heard of the possibility of coming to the shantytown from his friend who lived in the neighborhood just above the present location of the shantytown.

The extent to which recruitment to this neighborhood has been based on propinquity illustrates a more general characteristic of urban residential mobility. Movement from one residence to another is most likely along lines of familiarity; people search out accommodations within a city in areas with which they are familiar and where they have contacts. Though friends and kin become distributed over the city, this distribution is not likely to be random but to be disproportionately concentrated in contiguous neighborhoods, so that when most people move residence it will be to areas fairly close by that meet their new requirements. This can be seen by comparing the prior residences of those who came to San Lorenzo and those who came to Planificada. In both cases the last zone of residence of most families is in a zone that lies in the same geographical area as their present residence. Indeed, the distribution is quite dichotomous. In San Lorenzo only 15 percent of the inhabitants last resided in the zones that provide the majority of inhabitants for Planificada, and in Planificada 30 percent last resided in the zones (including the central Zones 1 and 3) that provide the vast majority of inhabitants for the shantytown.

Indeed, even as far back as first zone of residence in the city, there is still evidence of a geographical distinction between San Lorenzo dwellers and those in Planificada. Over half of the shantytown dwellers originate in the central zones, and a further 29 percent originate in other zones contiguous to the shantytown. By contrast, 34 percent of the families in Planificada originate in the central zones, and 40 percent originate in the zones peripheral to the city that are in the same area as the legal neighborhood.

Whatever the reasons for people's residential moves, they describe a path in which origins do affect outcomes—the places and personal relationships with which an urban career is begun influence subsequent moves—even when the move is to the illegal settlement of a shantytown. Consequently, no urban sector can reasonably be characterized as completely marginal since it is linked to other areas and social groups within the city.

The Process of Economic Change

The increase in city size has come to a large extent through the addition of migrants whose characteristics make them highly competitive with the city born. Since Guatemala's growth has been an unplanned urban growth, competition for the scarce resources of the city is thus likely to be one variable determining change, and the significance of this competition needs first to be considered.[11]

Consider the procedures adopted by employers for selecting employees in face of increasing competition for jobs among people who have migrated to the city. The employer is unlikely to have personal knowledge of the applicants or of their family and employment background. He is thus likely to use some general measure of their fitness for work such as, for example, their level of education or their physical fitness. As more people are recruited on this basis, such general selection criteria influence employment of the city born also. Thus, although contacts with an employer or his established workers and the reputation of a previous employer continue to influence recruitment, this occurs within a framework set by general standards of recruitment. This is similar to the process described in the previous section as occurring with respect to residential accommodations.

Whatever the rate of economic expansion and planned change, it is to be expected that an increasing population entails an increase in the number of enterprises providing services and consumer goods and an increase in rudimentary as well as more formal accommodations. These increases further differentiate

[11] The emphasis on competition as an underlying dynamic of urban organization is similar to Robert Park's treatment of competition as one force differentiating the ecological organization of the city. See Robert Park, "The City: Suggestions for the Investigation of Human Behavior in the Urban Environment," in E. M. Burgess and R. E. Park, eds., *The City*, pp 1-46.

the housing and job market, and its resulting complexity makes it less likely that either employer or landlord will rely on reputational characteristics in evaluating applicants. For example, an owner of a workshop is not likely to know much about the myriad of other workshops in which an applicant has gained his experiences and must rely upon general guides such as literacy or physical appearance.

According to the model of change set out above, the years since 1945 should be years in which city dwellers find themselves less able to find work through friends and kin and are increasingly forced to depend on their own initiative to get employment. In discussing the occupational careers of poor people, we will be talking about the poorer and less well-educated sectors of a city that is itself economically under-developed. The analysis is thus an exploration of the social consequences of an urban growth unaccompanied by adequate industrialization.

There is a great contrast between the description I give of occupational mobility and that reported for the more economically dynamic city of Monterrey, Mexico. The authors of the Monterrey mobility study are able to show considerable amounts of upward occupational mobility, both within and across the manual and nonmanual occupational categories.[12] Furthermore, they are able to use the term "occupational career" in its precise sense of an orderly and predictable occupational advancement within a work setting and to show a considerable proportion of their sample experiencing such a career.[13] Undoubtedly there are white-collar workers and skilled workers in Guatemala City who have career moves in this sense, but the inconsistent patterns of job mobility that I describe are not simply a reflection of sampling bias. They also reflect the real differences in economic opportunity between an expanding industrial economy, such as that of Monterrey, and the more informal and uncertain economy of Guatemala City.

[12] Jorge Balán et al, "The Lives of Men," chapter 8.
[13] Ibid., chapter 8, p. 23.

The contrast between the two cities brings out the fact that social and economic development is not an undifferentiated process, but one whose possibilities and disadvantages depend on the particular political and economic context, both local and foreign. The discontinuities in job experience in Guatemala serve, however, as interesting variables in the exploration in subsequent chapters of the conditions of collective organization.

The Changing Basis of Occupational Recruitment

An employer or landlord is faced not only by increased competition for jobs or housing but also by increased competition among particular groups of people. The characteristics that are used in selecting among those competing are thus dependent on the characteristics of the people competing. It is at this point that the process of differentiation in Guatemala diverges from that of other countries and cities whose growing population evidences characteristics, such as ethnicity or education, that are different from those of the people making up Guatemala City's growth.

In Guatemala City there are few evident and stable social or economic characteristics that can serve as a basis for differentiating the population. In the last chapter we saw that ethnicity, migrant status, or even level of education are not readily adaptable to this purpose. The number of years completed in school has different significance in different parts of the country, and certificates of educational competence are not given except for completing a definite stage of the process, which few do. Likewise, among manual workers there are no formal certificates of work skills. Apprenticeship in both traditional and industrial crafts is a highly informal process that is rarely supervised by government or a labor union. The most a worker has to show for his skill is usually a handwritten note from a craftsman certifying that he has been an apprentice and is now competent at the job. Under these conditions, the readily available characteristics for distinguishing among job applicants are their age and literacy. Neither of these characteristics allows fine or particularly stable discriminations to be made among the population. Before pursuing the implications of this change, we need now to see if the available data support the preceding argument.

The argument so far is that since 1945 employment in Guatemala has become increasingly less based on an employer's knowledge of the background of his employees and based more on individual characteristics, especially age and literacy of workers. To indicate the importance of ascriptive relationships in obtaining a job, we can use the distinction between migrants and city born. The male heads of household in the two neighborhoods are over twenty and the large majority of those born in the city were born there and grew up in the years prior to or around 1945, when the city was experiencing a slow rate of growth. In this period we would expect the city born to have lived in neighborhoods and to have developed relationships that enabled them to obtain jobs in long established city enterprises. Thus, if an employer's knowledge of a family's reputation, of a neighborhood, or of a previous employer was the most important criterion by which he selected and employed his workers, then the early careers of city-born workers should be distinct to those of migrants. On the other hand, migrants lacking relationships with established urban employers should find jobs in unstable or newly established enterprises or become self-employed.

This model will not be completely congruent with the city's employment structure, especially as increasing numbers of migrants enter into relationships that give them access to long established firms. Also in this particular sample, the city born probably include a higher-than-average proportion of people who are "drop-outs," for one reason or another, from a stable occupational career; the very fact of being in the neighborhoods argues for that. Yet, despite these qualifications, the continuance of a traditionally organized employment system should still be reflected in certain qualitative differences in the employment of migrants and city born. City born should be more concentrated in traditional craft and industrial enterprises and less concentrated in trade, services, and construction work.

We can use the sample to explore the relation of migrant status to employment in 1946, a year in which a traditionally organized employment system should still be evident, by isolating a cohort employed in the city in this year and which in terms of age range was then in its occupational prime.

This cohort analysis is subject to the same objections that I outlined with reference to residential careers. It is possible that the selective recruitment or survival of residents with particular combinations of educational and migrant status characteristics influences the difference I report. I have, however, considered the various types of selectivity required to provide an alternative explanation to the one offered here, and I still consider the present explanation not only more theoretically plausible but also more economical. Also, using comparisons within cohorts on literacy and on migrant status means that the differences reported are not produced by a change in the distribution of these characteristics over time.

Taking males born between 1905 and 1926—aged between twenty and forty-one in 1946—and classifying their occupations according to their migrant status show that being a migrant or being reared in the city (born in the city or arriving before the age of twelve) is clearly related to the types of jobs they enter. The city reared are more likely to be found in established economic enterprises. Literacy is defined by making the arbitrary distinction between those with three or more years of formal schooling and those with two or less years (illiterates). I found that respondents used these two response categories in the questionnaire as proxies for their degree of literacy. "Established economic enterprises" is the term I will use to cover employment in craft industries, workshops, and factories, and it will also include office work and employment in transport. The reason for including transport is that this constitutes one of the best and most stable jobs in the city, whether as a bus driver or as a conductor. In contrast, self-employment, trade, services, and construction are much more subject to seasonal fluctuations and are the type of work that can most easily be expanded to include new workers. For example, there are certain limits to the number of workers that a factory or workshop can employ, but it is always possible to have another peddler, barber, or unskilled laborer. The distinction is intended to relate to ease of access to jobs. For that reason the category of city reared is used rather than city born. This not only increases the number for statistical purposes but also relates to the possibility of an individual developing contacts with employers and within the older established urban neighborhoods.

In the same year, literacy also influenced employment, but its effect is strongest among the city reared (Table 14). The conclusion then is that in 1946 migrant status strongly influenced a person's chances of being employed in established enterprises, but that being literate was a further requirement for such jobs.

In contrast, we take a male cohort born between 1927 and 1948 and look at their occupations in 1968, the year in which this cohort has the same age range as that born 1905-1926

Table 14. Occupations in Guatemala City. Males Born Between 1905 and 1926 in 1946. (Percentages)

	Born or Reared in City		Migrant		Total (Migrant Status)		Total (Literacy)	
	Literate	Illiterate[a]	Literate	Illiterate	City Born	Migrant	Literate	Illiterate
Established enterprises (factories, workshops, offices, transport)	75	40	27	37	67	33	56	37
Self-employment, trade, services, construction	25	60	73	63	33	67	44	63
Total	100	100	100	100	100	100	100	100
Number	(16)	(5)	(11)	(16)	(21)	(27)	(27)	(21)

Source: Male heads of household from survey.
[a]Two or less years of formal schooling.

Table 15. Occupations in Guatemala City. Males Born
Between 1927 and 1946 in 1968. (Percentages)

	Born or Reared in City		Migrant		Total (Migrant Status)		Total (Literacy)	
	Lit-erate	Illit-erate[a]	Lit-erate	Illit-erate	City Born	Mi-grant	Lit-erate	Illit-erate
Established enterprises	56	17	46	33	43	41	52	25
Self-employed, trade, services, construction	44	83	54	67	57	59	48	75
Total	100	100	100	100	100	100	100	100
Number	(36)	(18)	(26)	(21)	(54)	(47)	(62)	(39)

Source: Male heads of household from survey.
[a]Two or less years of formal schooling.

(Table 15). The relation of migrant status and literacy to type of occupation is almost the reverse of that in 1946. In 1968, it is literacy that is the most important in discriminating between migrants and city reared, while migrant status does not appear significant.

Between 1946 and 1968 migrant status ceases to be significant as a criterion for a job in established urban enterprises. To discover more exactly when this shift occurs we can reorganize the survey data to take three cohorts—those born between 1911 and 1921, those born between 1922 and 1932, and those born between 1933 and 1943. By taking the occupations of these cohorts in 1946, 1957, and 1968 respectively, each cohort is of the same age range—from twenty-five to thirty-five years old—and in its occupational prime.

Those reared in the city are most likely to be employed in established enterprises in 1946 (Table 16). With each succeeding cohort, however, those reared in the city become increasingly employed in services, trade, construction, or are self-employed. In contrast, migrants, despite the overall increases in the proportions of urban workers in these activities, show little change in type of employment between the three time periods.

As a consequence, migrant status only makes an important difference to type of employment in 1946; subsequently the
differences in the participation of migrants and city reared are
not significant.

If we look at the bottom section of the table, this trend also
appears among the first occupations that members of these
cohorts enter after age twenty, so that the type of employment
of migrants and city reared converges with time. Comparing
these first occupations with the subsequent occupations, a
contrast appears between the first cohort, who "improved"
their position by increasing their employment in established
enterprises and the last cohort, who became less likely to be so
employed; this occurs earlier for the city reared than for the
migrants. This means for the most recent group that their career
prospects of getting stable employment with time have diminished and is evidence for the change in the significance of age to
which we return later. A similar trend occurs among the cohorts
used in Tables 14 and 15—those of 1905-1926 and
1927-1946—though the data are not presented.[14]

Workers' responses to a question asking how they obtained
their first city jobs give some direct corroboration to the argument that the change described above is related to the declining
significance of locally based relationships for job recruitment.
In this system, a worker gets his first job by a friend or a
relative "speaking for" him to an employer, and it is the reputation of these sponsors that gets him the job. This applied as
much to migrants as to the city reared; the only difference is
that under this system young migrants are recruited to the more
marginal occupations where they are likely to have contacts.
Unfortunately, this question was not asked of those born in the

[14] These cohorts are created from the same sample of respondents. The respondents used in the cohorts of Tables 12 and 13 are thus in almost all cases the same as
those used in the cohorts of Table 14. There is, of course, no coincidence between
respondents used to make up the 1905-1926 and the 1927-1946 cohorts, or between
the members of the cohorts in Table 14. Total numbers in these tables will not
include the entire male survey sample, since some respondents would not have arrived
in the city at the appropriate dates.

Table 16. Percentage of Males Employed in Factories, Workshops, Offices, or Transport at Different Time Periods

	Cohorts		
	Born 1911-1921	Born 1922-1932	Born 1933-1943
	Job in 1946	Job in 1957	Job in 1968
City born or reared	70	44	42
Number	(10)	(23)	(29)
Migrants	34	45	38
Number	(18)	(22)	(29)
	First Job		
City born or reared	60	53	52
Number	(10)	(23)	(29)
Migrants	23	32	55
Number	(18)	(22)	(29)

Source: Male heads of household from survey.

city, but it is confined to migrants (including the city reared ones). It is clear, however, that from 1955 onward people are less likely than previously to say that they had obtained their jobs through the aid of friends and relatives (Table 17). Friends and relatives received equal weight throughout the period as means of obtaining jobs and are thus not distinguished. After 1955, the majority of those getting their first job claim to have done so through their own initiative. This period is significant because it is just the period when migrant status ceases to influence type of occupation (Table 16). At the time that migrant status is completely replaced by literacy as the apparent credential discriminating the occupations that people have, so too being personally sponsored becomes less important in occupational recruitment. Though the time periods used here are not congruent with those used in Chapter 2, it also appears that the decline in the importance of sponsorship coincides with what I claim to be the period of most rapid immigration to the city. The uncertainties and extent of growth of that period may have served as a catalyst in the decline of reputational factors in job recruitment.

Table 17. First Job by Year of Entering City Labor Force:
Male Migrants (Percentages)

How Job was Obtained	Pre- 1939	1940- 1944	1945- 1949	1950- 1954	1955- 1959	1960- 1964	Post- 1965
Through own initiative	34	43	38	33	71	58	83
Through friends or relatives	53	43	54	59	21	32	17
Other (e.g., came as soldier)	13	14	8	8	8	10	
Total	100	100	100	100	100	100	100
Number	(38)	(21)	(13)	(27)	(24)	(19)	(6)

Source: Male heads of household from survey.

These data should not be taken to mean that personal relationships are no longer useful in obtaining jobs. Through my
own observations and through conversations, it was clear that
such contacts continue to be important, but respondents
interpreted the above question quite literally to mean the actual
securing of a job. Though friends and relatives were usually the
source of information about jobs, they would not be seen as
getting the job for the individual unless they actually arranged it
or made the introduction. Responses to this question thus inevitably underestimate the continuing importance of friends
and relatives in job recruitment.

It is evident from the data already presented that age does
affect a person's occupation. As workers grow older they are
increasingly likely to become self-employed and less likely to
retain jobs in large-scale enterprises. We can see the effect of
this process on the present distribution of occupations in the
sample; classifying the sample by age and their occupational
position shows that older people are more likely to be self-
employed and less likely to be employed in large or medium-
sized enterprises. (Table 18).

The clear trend in this table is partly produced, however, by

Table 18. Age and Occupational Position of Heads of Household (Percentages)

Position	Age			
	20-32	33-44	45-56	57 and Over
Self-employed	37	44	56	77
Sole employee (i.e., watchman)	18	12	17	7
Employed in small enterprises (under 10 people)	22	13	7	6
Employed in large enterprises (10 people and over)	23	31	20	10
Total	100	100	100	100
Number[a]	(65)	(75)	(70)	(38)

[a]Includes both male and female heads of household; four did not answer.

the greater likelihood that self-employed people have of remaining in the two neighborhoods. The presence of substantial numbers of older, self-employed workers does create a climate in which younger workers often assume that self-employment is an inevitable career destination.

It is difficult, however, to demonstrate that age has had an increasing significance for occupation over time, to become like literacy a major means of differentiating the working population. The difficulty is mainly a methodological one since, even using life-history material, it is not easy to compare older workers at different periods. To isolate a cohort of workers aged forty to sixty in 1946 would require a substantial segment of the sample presently aged from sixty-two to eighty-two, and few people live that long in Guatemala. Thus, we must base the claim that age has become increasingly important for taking on or staying in established enterprises on such evidence as the increasing tendency for more recent cohorts to move away from employment in established enterprises from first to actual job.[15]

[15]Compare the findings from Monterrey, where age is clearly not related to becoming self-employed (Balán et al., "The Lives of Men," chapter 8, p. 40). This underlines the difference in the meaning of self-employment within the more industrialized economy of Monterrey.

The Significance of Occupational Change

The declining significance of reputational factors in job recruitment means an increase in job mobility and a greater discontinuity in the occupational careers of these workers. This occurs partly because age and literacy are not qualifications that commit an individual to any particular type of job. Consequently, a worker can seek out better job opportunities, but lack of personal commitments also means that he is more easily replaceable. Also, with the proliferation of small enterprises the work situation itself becomes more unstable and sensitive to changes in the economic climate of Guatemala. Newly established enterprises do not have stable relationships with a clientele in city or countryside. In time of prosperity, the number of enterprises increases and established ones take on additional workers to meet the demand, but during economic depressions or those fluctuations occasioned by political events, enterprises fail and lay off workers.

Under these conditions, a successful occupational career is one in which a worker seeks out stable and well-paid employment moving from one job to another as circumstances change. Those who are old and illiterate and cannot easily compete are thus likely to remain in, or soon enter, a marginal occupation where the income fluctuates with economic change or is so low as to make no difference. In contrast to those situations where the change occurs because large enterprises demand higher qualifications of their workers, individual characteristics become important to job recruitment in Guatemala City as a worker shifts from one small, ill-equipped workshop to another, as he sets up his own workshop with no more equipment than a sewing machine or a few rudimentary tools or helps others to peddle merchandise around the city.[16] This movement does

---

[16] In the contrasting case of Monterrey, Mexico, the increasing importance of qualifications appears to occur through large-scale industrial enterprises raising their recruitment standards. See Jorge Balán, "Migrant-Native Socioeconomic Differences in Latin American Cities: A Structural Analysis," *Latin American Research Review* 4, no. 1 (February 1969):3-29.

include larger and more formally organized enterprises where literacy is more closely tied to job position; but, in general, the emerging significance of literacy and age occurs as workers move from job to job, seeking better employment or trying to avoid entering low-paid marginal employment.

To convey a sense of the type of mobility that is being discussed, two cases of job mobility are presented; one of these is city born and the other is a migrant. Both cases emphasize the diversity of the mobility and its sensitivity to economic and political events.

Luis: a migrant, literate, in his late thirties

Luis came to the city at age fourteen from a departmental capital located some 150 miles from the city. His elder brothers had preceded him and were working as tailors in the city. He came to live with them, and they got him an apprenticeship in the small clothes factory where they were working. There were about forty-eight workers in the factory supervised by three specialist tailors. The factory was local. Luis describes his ten working years in the factory, emphasizing the prosperous economic conditions of the early revolutionary years: "Peasants would come to the city to buy shoes, clothes, food, and would not even bargain." Working conditions were being improved by industrial legislation that protected the worker, guaranteeing a six-day week, overtime, and a minimum wage. A union was formed in Luis's factory, and, in the last years of his stay that coincided with the regime of left-wing President Jacobo Arbenz, Luis was active in labor disputes. He had married and describes this 1952-1954 period as one when he was working hard to maintain his wife and yet active against exploitation by the factory owner. Luis was still living close to his brothers. With the fall of Arbenz, Luis describes the worsening conditions in the factory due partly to the owner's taking advantage of the conservative regime to reduce workers' benefits and partly to an economic recession. Luis quotes the figures for the reduced output of the factory in this time. In 1956 he lost his job shortly before the factory closed due to the backruptcy of the owner. He set up independently as a tailor in the zone. At first, he claimed to do reasonably well and soon bought sewing machines and hired assistants to help with the work. Then, his business failed and Luis began to work in small tailor shops. He describes his work in this period from 1956 onward as moving from shop to shop in search of adequate work. He claims that, due to competition from Salvadoran products, it was becoming increasingly difficult to get enough work to make ends meet. Where before he was given five pairs of trousers to work on in a day, he was now given five pairs to work on in a week. Finding his rented accommodations too expensive and having married again and had children, he invaded the shantytown. In subsequent years, while still seeking work from tailor shops, he sought other forms of remuneration, often, as we shall see, political. He also occasionally travels to the provinces, especially the remoter parts, taking his sewing machine with him and hiring a mule to carry his equipment. He sets up in village fairs and does on-the-spot tailoring. He claims that his income in 1968 from tailoring was about a third of what it was in 1954.

José: city born, literate, in his early forties

José's father apprenticed him in his early teens to a local butcher's trade, but he did not like the conditions of work and a few years later he joined his uncle in his small business of making such leather goods as saddles, bags, and the like. He served out his apprenticeship and began to work, but, after getting into trouble in the city, he took to the provinces and moved around small towns working for months at a time as a leather worker. He returned to the city just before the revolution of 1944 and became an active participant. For his efforts, he became a member of a city police force set up to keep order in the period following the revolution. He returned to work with his uncle and continued working there until 1954, in the meantime moving his zone of residence several times. In the disturbances following the counterrevolution of Castillo Armas, he left the city and took a job as a docker in the port of San José. This job he got through a contact there. In the same period he applied for and got a small parcel of land where he located his family and started a small farm. He got into trouble on the docks, being prominent in labor disputes, and lost his job, then dedicated himself full-time to the farm. This work went well, but again personal and political disputes surrounded his rights to the piece of land, and influential people desiring his land had him removed from it. He tried again with a poorer piece, but eventually in 1962 he returned to the city, went straight to the shantytown to get a lot, and started to work in his old trades of leather work and pork butchery. He finds that leather working is no longer remunerative because of the decline in demand for saddles and competition from imported material. Increasingly he set himself up in independent work, buying pigs and cattle, slaughtering them, and selling the meat to whole-salers and retailers. He continued in this work full-time until 1968, when his work in political organization got him an office job with one of the political parties.

We can now look at the evidence for the increase in job mobility over time, especially among those categories of workers who are able to take advantage of available opportuni-ties and who need to better their position. First, taking the whole sample, but excluding females, job mobility is classified by age, literacy, and migrant status to see if these different characteristics affect mobility.

The mobility being described is one between different types of jobs, that is, between tailoring, carpentry, street peddling, etc., though often these jobs are within the same general job classification. Shifts of location involving the same job are not included because they were not recorded satisfactorily. For example, the case of Luis reported on the previous page would be coded as having little mobility, since he has remained a tailor despite his shifts in work position. The figures reported con-sequently underestimate the true mobility of the sample, but doing so has the advantage that differences in the age or intel-

Table 19. Average Number of Years to Change Job since Age 20, by Age, Literacy, and Migrant Status (Male Heads of Household)

	Migrant Status			
	City Reared		Migrants	
	Literate	Illiterate[b]	Literate	Illiterate
Years to change (age 40 & under)[a]	10.8	11.1	4.4	6.2
Years to change (age 41 & over)	11.7	23.6	14.5	22.7
Number	(56)	(26)	(48)	(65)

[a]This refers to movement between different jobs, though possibly within the same category (e.g., shoemaker to tailor, though both craftsmen).
[b]Illiterate is here defined as those with two or less years of schooling.

ligence of a worker are less likely to affect his memory since he is recalling important career shifts.

One striking difference is that between older and younger workers. (Table 19). Older workers are the less mobile over their whole careers, which means that in terms of the number of years they have spent in the city they have made proportionately fewer moves than the younger men. Literate workers are more mobile than illiterate workers, thus indicating that better qualifications lead to mobility as workers seek out the better jobs and are not tied to marginal employment. It is in similar terms that the greater mobility of migrants is to be interpreted. Since they are likely to first come to the city in their occupational prime (and the data reported here are of job mobility since age twenty), they spend more time seeking out jobs than the city reared who will, by this stage, have sought out their preferred niche and who will be relatively stabilized until age or economic fluctuation forces them to move.

We can more directly examine these statements by comparing the job mobility of two male cohorts that have the same age range—one born between 1910 and 1930 and one born between 1928 and 1948. The cohorts overlap slightly, and the particular choice of years was dictated by the expediency of securing a sufficiently large range of working years before year points—

1950 and 1968—that are meaningful for our argument. The occupational moves recorded are those occurring since the age of twenty, an age when workers should be relatively stable in their occupations and more likely to remember the moves they have made. Indeed, memory presents a greater difficulty to the analysis of cohort differences, since there is a danger that people will remember more exactly what has happened recently and thus that the more recent cohort will report more moves just because they are recalling more recent events. To minimize this danger, the table reports only change in job category, that is change from being a craftsman to being a trader or factory operative. Since such changes involve quite different skills and relationships, they are more likely to be remembered.

The more recent cohort has moved more frequently during the age period twenty to forty than the earlier cohort; this remains true when calculated according to the average number of years spent in the city (Table 20). Thus job mobility, even when calculated by move between very different types of jobs,

Table 20. Mobility between Job Categories of Two Cohorts Born 1910-1930 and 1928-1948, by Migrant Status (Male Heads of Household) in Percentages

	Cohort 1910-1930, from Age 20 to 1950			Cohort 1928-1948, from Age 20 to 1968		
	Migrants	Both	City Reared	Migrants	Both	City Reared
Changed job category	46	37	29	62	48	36
Did not change	54	63	71	38	52	64
Total	100		100	100		100
Number	(26)		(28)	(45)		(52)
Average number of years to change[a]	13.1	14.7	17.1	6.9	10.7	21.2

[a]This calculated according to the number of years, from age 20 to either 1950 or 1968 depending on the cohort, the individual has spent in the city.

has increased over time. It is also clear from the data that migrant status is significant for mobility at both time periods. We know that migrants have become increasingly similar to the city reared in terms of the proportion in established enterprises, so their greater job mobility relates to the process of stabilization mentioned earlier. Arriving in the city labor market relatively later, migrants are likely to spend more time seeking out good job possibilities and thus be more mobile than those reared in the city. This argument can be further checked by looking at the job mobility of the city reared up to the age of twenty. In that period, the city reared were almost as mobile as migrants are subsequent to it. Thus, 48 percent of the city reared in the 1910 to 1930 cohort changed their job category before twenty, and in the 1928 to 1948 cohort 58 percent made this change. Interestingly, these figures also show an increasing mobility over time, even for the early years in the labor market.

The changes being described are not just of academic interest; they involve considerable discontinuities in the occupational careers of our sample. One prevalent career movement, to which we have constantly referred, is the increasing likelihood that workers shift to self-employment or low-paid work in construction or services as they grow older. This shift is often a painful experience, as those who enter the labor force as industrial or craft apprentices spend considerable efforts to continue in such work and ultimately have to eke out a living in seasonal employment or low-paid unskilled work. One illiterate city-born worker in the shantytown began his occupational career as an apprentice tailor. He worked a little in the city with this trade and also moved around the provinces. When he returned to the city in 1956, the only job he could obtain was as an unskilled laborer in a small sawmill. He aspires to get a permanent job as a construction laborer with the municipality or to take the trade of tailor again, but in the three years of my acquaintance was unsuccessful and was one of the poorest paid of all the shantytown workers. Another city-born shantytown dweller who finished primary school was apprenticed as a mechanic. In his early occupational career in the years following the revolution, he was employed in large-scale industrial enterprises. By the 1950s he was employed by small workshops, and at the time of the study he earned an occasional dollar breaking down old cars at a neighborhood junk heap.

These examples merely dramatize something that results from the structure of job recruitment under the conditions of the rapid growth of Guatemala City. These discontinuities are also true for those who remain within their occupation. Thus, the rapid increase in the labor force also means that within an occupation there is increasing competition for the good jobs and the good profits or wages. Workers, as in the case of Luis described earlier, who began their careers in the city in the years up to the late 1940s speak with nostalgia of the stable working conditions of jobs in these years. Traders, for example, emphasize that they could sell for higher profits and turn over more merchandise than they can now. Craftsmen such as tailors and shoemakers, who face increasing competition from factory-made products often originating outside Guatemala, cite the much higher incomes they earned in the early years of the revolution. However accurate these complaints, the important thing is that workers in most occupations believe that their material condition has not substantially improved, and the reference points they use in interpreting present possibilities often are their early career experiences.

Apart from these general discontinuities, there are those discontinuities that arise because the careers of the workers straddle the changes that have taken place. Basically, we have been describing a change in the way different generations of workers enter the labor market. During a worker's occupational prime, what matters for his subsequent mobility is the job category in which he starts, and there is little evidence that, during their prime, workers move between jobs in established enterprises and those in trade, services, or construction, or between being employed and being self-employed. Looking again at the data on the three cohorts born in 1911-1921, 1922-1932, and 1943-1953 (Table 16), there is little difference between the first and subsequent jobs of each cohort as to whether they are in established enterprises or not. Indeed, comparing the very first urban jobs of the whole sample with their occupations in 1968 also indicates considerable continuity as far as these broad distinctions are concerned. Of those who started in self-employment, 78 percent continued in it in 1968, and, of those who began in trade, construction, or the services, 70 percent were still in those categories in 1968.

One major way in which the change in the basis of job recruitment has affected workers in the neighborhoods is to differentiate the job careers of the different generations.[17] Younger workers, for example, are less likely to have experience in workshops or factories than older workers who, in turn, may be less familiar with the emerging trading or service activities. This means that fathers and sons are less likely to have jobs in common and to be of use to each other on the job. Less than half the eldest sons of workers in the sample have followed in the same general job category as their fathers, let alone in the same job or enterprise; it was noticeable during field work that many parents made a point of advising sons not to follow in their occupations. Thus, craftsmen such as tailors, shoemakers, or carpenters, when commenting to me on the difficulties they encountered in making their living, would often turn and point to a son and say that he was in, or was going to enter, a different type of occupation.

This generational discontinuity is also associated with a discontinuity in individual careers. Changing the basis of job recruitment has meant that some workers entered the job market with characteristics that later enabled them to secure a different type of job or that later proved a handicap for continuing in the job they have. Movement to the services, trade, construction, or self-employment is more pronounced among those

[17] The Monterrey mobility study reaches a similar conclusion (Balán et al., "The Lives of Men," chapters 8 and 9).

who were "wrongly placed" according to the present job requirements. Thus it is the city reared who show the greatest mobility to those more marginal occupations, and among them it is the illiterate city born who are most mobile. They had secured work in established enterprises at a time when this was based on reputational characteristics and thus became the category most likely to lose it when they grew older and when the basis of recruitment changed.

In the account of an occupational career that follows, the personal discontinuities involved in the changes in occupational recruitment are directly related to the emergent effects of age, educational qualifications, and migrant status that have been so far described.

Pepe: literate, migrant, in his fifties

Pepe was born in the small town of Momostenango in 1914 and spent his youth and early adulthood in the nearby city of Quetzaltenango. He reached the sixth grade of primary school. In Quetzaltenango he learned the trade of barber and also became an active member of a marimba band. His move to the city in 1940 was occasioned by a message from a close friend he had made in the marimba band who had preceeded him to the capital. This friend had many relatives and friends in the capital and was relatively highly educated, having completed his accountancy qualification (equivalent to competing secondary school). Pepe was given free room and board by the friend, and they both sought work as barbers. Pepe went from barber shop to barber shop and eventually was taken on as an assistant. Shortly afterward, his Quetzaltenango friend got together enough money from his contacts to purchase his own barber shop, and he invited Pepe to become his partner. The business did relatively well, and the friend rented a second barber shop but left barbering when he got married. He sold one shop and left the other business with Pepe. Pepe continued in this business, making a wide circle of acquaintances through the shop. One of these was a qualified male nurse who, after the revolution of 1944, obtained employment as a hospital nurse in one of the large city military bases. He spoke at the base for Pepe, who got a job as one of the base's barbers. Pepe continued with his private barber business in his spare time. He also learned a little of the business of a medical attendant by assisting his friend with his work in the base hospital. After a year or so of this work, Pepe returned to his own barber business, which he now supplements with a little work as an unqualified nurse, giving injections for a small sum. By this time, Pepe has made several residential moves; starting in the center of the city, he moved out to the peripheral zones, first to Zone 12 and finally to Zone 7.

It is in Zone 7 that he conducted his barber business. He continued working as a barber until 1959, when his first friend from Quetzaltenango secured him a job as a bus inspector with a large bus company. The same year he moved to the shantytown after being told of the possibilities there by another friend who had lodged with him when he was a barber in Zone 12. The first friend had, by this time, himself secured work in line with his original accountancy qualification and is an accountant in the head office of the bus company. Pepe stayed in his job as bus inspector until 1967, when he voluntarily resigned to set up shop in the local market of the shantytown. He obtained this shop through a political contact he made as president of the Betterment Association. Even while he was a bus inspector, he maintained a small shop in the shantytown, which his wife ran, and he also did a little barbering and giving injections in his spare time. The reasons he gave me for his move to the shop in the market were his health and inability to keep the long and tiring timetables required for inspecting city buses. He also said that he wished to build up a little business and capital to keep himself and his wife in their old age.

We can now construct a general description of the types of occupational career experienced by low-income workers. At the beginning of a worker's urban occupational career, he has neither the experience nor the contacts to find good employment and, especially, good employment in established enterprises. Also, the decline in the proportion of apprenticeships means that both migrants and city born are likely to take whatever job is available. As they accumulate experience and contacts, they move relatively frequently before stabilizing their occupations around age twenty if they are city reared and later if migrants. If they are literate they are usually successful in finding some relatively well-paid job in established enterprises; but if they are illiterate they are more likely to begin in low-paid employment and to remain in such employment despite changes of jobs.

As they grow older, workers shift to self-employment or low-paid marginal occupations; illiterate workers are especially likely to do so. Yet for all these workers, it seems that sooner or later age makes them marginal to being employed in established enterprises and one of the most frequent topics of conversation with workers in such enterprises is the prospect of their becoming self-employed or taking on some service or trading job. This means that workers, as they grow older, must take into account not only the social relationships relevant to their present occupation but also those that will aid them in a future and often quite distinct type of occupation. In this way, the life cycle has a dynamic of its own with respect of the job behavior and social relationships that an individual considers relevant to his interests. Much of the movement described is not forced through losing a job, but brought about by an individual's assessment of his present position and prospects. This is even true, as we saw in Pepe's case, of many moves to self-employment and to other unstable occupations. As workers grow older they may prefer less arduous work and a more flexible timetable.

Separation of Work and Residence

The profileration of small enterprises and the occupational mobility that has been described are associated with an increasing separation of the place of work and the place of residence of these workers. Another expression of the decline of reputational factors in job recruitment is that workers cease to be primarily recruited locally. Before 1945 there were some workers who made the journey to work, but by 1968 it was only a minority of workers who were employed even in such a large local area as the administrative zone in which they live. The major reason for this transition lies in the increasing differentiation of residential and industrial areas discussed earlier in the chapter. As the city has increased its population, residential areas have been developed on the periphery of the old city, while industrial activities have become increasingly concentrated in the center.

Unfortunately, data were not collected on the place of work of the sample at different stages in their careers, and consequently a statistical indication of the trend described above cannot be given. In Planificada, the majority of workers are currently working in the center of the city or in the developing industrial zones and spend on average forty minutes on their journey to work, but the location of this neighborhood at the periphery of the city makes it a somewhat extreme case. However, the shantytown is located centrally and belongs to a zone with a considerable concentration of established industry and commerce. Shantytown workers work in fifteen of the city's nineteen zones, and 70 percent work outside their own zone.

Conversations with workers and the evidence of the ten life histories suggest that this separation of work and neighborhood has been part of the life experience of workers. In the life histories, those working in the years before 1944 were without exception working in the zone in which they lived. By the late 1950s and early 1960s, the majority were working in zones other than where they lived, and they explicitly linked this transition to either the difficulty of finding housing where they were working or of finding work where they were living.

The increasing separation of place of work and place of residence further weakens the significance of reputational factors in job recruitment and makes it less likely that workers are committed to their jobs by residential as well as job-based social relationships. The process is, in fact, a cumulative one. As more people are recruited to jobs where fellow workers and clients are not confined to the local neighborhood, the more likely it is that they recommend nonlocal job seekers and inform such applicants of the possibility of work.

The significance of the separation of work and residence is a broad one, for it means that both a person's workplace and his job lie outside his immediate environment and become dependent on forces that are neither visible nor predictable. To the extent that a person's work was located in his neighborhood and depended on a stable local clientele, fluctuation and change were visible and understandable as part of a process affecting everyone around. With the rapid expansion of the city, even such urban workers as craftsmen who traditionally catered to a local clientele have become increasingly dependent on outside work. At the time that occupational careers become more discontinuous, so too the risks and uncertainties in an individual's working environment have increased.

The control of economic activities in the city has become increasingly centralized, but this process has not brought with it a concentration of economic activities. In this context, centralization means the increasing dependence of craftsmen, artisans, and laborers on centrally located businesses for their livelihood. The increasing competition for employment and the proliferation of small businesses have made the day-to-day operation of many enterprises hazardous and dependent on credit or some guarantee of stable work. This process is especially clear among the numerous craftsmen and petty traders in the two neighborhoods. Many of those began their urban careers attached to workshops or as fully independent workers, buying their raw materials and selling the finished products. Over the years, increasing competition has made the business of the independent craftsmen a much more hazardous undertaking. Whether he is a tailor, a shoemaker, or a carpenter, he must sell his products not only in competition with the increasing numbers of other craftsmen migrating from the provinces or newly entering the job, but also in competition with cheap factory-made products produced at home or abroad. The craftsman no longer has the advantage of servicing a local clientele since intraurban mobility means that even low-income families shop beyond their neighborhood boundaries. Also, increasing residential differentiation means that craftsmen are disproportionately concentrated in certain residential areas. For example, in the shantytown there are approximately 40 shoemakers among some 380 families.

In face of these difficulties, craftsmen have entered relationships with the larger urban workshops and commercial establishments. In the shantytown, most of the shoemakers who work in their own homes are working for a centrally located shoe retailing establishment. They receive raw materials from the shop and undertake to produce a certain quantity of shoes a week and receive a fixed price for these products. A similar relationship exists between many tailors and larger tailoring establishments, in which the neighborhood tailor goes from one city shop to another in search of work that is to be put out. Small traders not only depend for credit on large commercial establishments but often trade in the streets on commission using goods given them by a city businessman. It is this type of relationship that many workers are referring to when they call themselves independent in conversation or interview. Those workers who wish to remain truly independent must often go to considerable lengths to ensure themselves a clientele. In the shantytown a shoemaker, Lisandro, uses his wife to retail his shoes door to door in the city and hires a woman neighbor on commission to travel to the provinces to sell them at the markets.

The process that is being described is a consequence of the rapid growth of the city unaccompanied by substantial and evenly distributed economic development. The purchasing power of the mass of the urban population has remained low and thus there is not the extensive market available for the stable growth of a large number of urban industries catering to the population. Instead, there are a number of establishments catering to an international, national, and local middle and upper class clientele that accumulate sufficient funds to enable them to directly or indirectly finance a chain of smaller enterprises. A shoe factory, for example, may have a retail outlet in the center of the city and also "put out" work to a large number of small craftsmen.

The significance of increasing centralization is that it is a career experience of many workers in the two neighborhoods that they must take into account as they consider their next occupational move. For some workers, it means the increasing relevance of social relationships with social and economic superiors who have the social and geographical span needed to influence the allocation of jobs or credit. Many workers have experienced a shift from a work situation where they depend on local businesses or a local clientele—where they reside close to those with whom they did business or by whom they were employed—to a situation where their working relationships are divorced from their residence and often depend on socially and spatially remote people. This description is in many respects similar to that of the social consequences of the urbanization and industrialization of countries such as Britain and the United States. Yet there are important differences, because the process in Guatemala City entails the coexistence of many "pre-industrial" economic forms with industrial ones. Workers in the two neighborhoods have neither come to work in large-scale enterprises nor have they remained working locally and for a local clientele. These workers have neither social relationships binding their work and their residence, nor do they have the opportunity to form relationships with workers in the same category through common employment in large-scale enterprises.

Occupational and Residential Paths

The change in the basis of occupational recruitment is thus part of a transition in which individual workers must construct their own occupational careers with the aid of whatever contacts and qualifications they have at hand. A person's job is thus increasingly divorced from a stable context of family and friendship relationships, and movement along an occupational career does not reinforce existing relationships by adding common work interests to kinship and common residence. Though kin and friends may provide the information or contacts needed to obtain a job, they rarely are acting to include the worker in their sphere nor are they determining his career. Instead, a worker's job mobility is influenced by economic fluctuations beyond his control, and the successful worker is one who uses whatever resources are at his disposal to manipulate the range of opportunities. In terms of his work, a worker thus develops an extensive rather than an intensive set of relationships and this has important consequences for his orientations to acting with others.

Under the conditions we have described, the working world of low-income workers is characterized by the emergence of distinct occupational paths. Thus, for workers in marginal occupations whose mobility is over, social contacts have a less immediate significance than for literate migrants expecting to be highly mobile. These latter maintain and develop contacts with those who can help them to better employment. Conversely, those facing the prospect of becoming self-employed must think in terms of a different set of relationships to assist them in the transition. The nature of the path that the low income worker is describing and his stage along it becomes an important determinant of his readiness to enter into social activity and gives him differing perspectives on how to order his environment. In this sense, neither neighborhood represents a community of workers who can be bound to an activity by some overriding common interest; for each location contains people describing different paths and differently interpreting the social meaning of interaction.

Under these conditions, neighborhoods are made up of people at different stages of their jobs and residential mobility who are not bound by long established ties of interest and interaction. Their mobility, and especially the type of occupational mobility they experience, makes it difficult for them to reinforce existing relationships by adding new strands of shared interests. Yet, neither the occupational nor the residential paths that people describe are formalized by the existence of set skills or qualifications prescribing when and where a move must be made. Instead, personal relationships remain important as a means of seeking out opportunities and countering difficult situations.

This indeed is one of the central dilemmas facing these families in their urban careers; for they must have a wide span of relationships to effectively cope with their environment, but their mobility makes it difficult to establish strong and stable relationships. Also, since the paths people follow are distinct, they have different demands to make on their relationships. It is the various attempts of differently placed people to cope with these dilemmas that give its peculiar character to the organization of low-income families; looking at these families at one moment of their lives should not obscure the fact that the dynamic of their activity comes from the convergence of many different and ongoing careers.

4. The Span of Social Relationships

Our analysis now shifts to the present situations of families in the two neighborhoods and, in particular, to the social relationships they develop to cope with urban life. These relationships are not divorced from the career experiences that have been described; job and residential mobility affect both the quantity and quality of personal and organizational relationships and condition the impact of present situations on these relationships. It is also the case that relationships entered into in the past remain important as continuing frames of reference and as possible resources and obligations.

These social relationships are central to an analysis of social action because they represent the manner in which an individual relates to his environment. Through his relationships he receives material assistance, advice, and opinion and is directly exposed to the expectations of others. In turn, it is through their relationships that individuals undertake most of their urban actions, giving assistance and advice or acting in concert to achieve some goal. In these ways, the number and nature of an individual's relationships is closely linked both to their ability and readiness to act and to their openness to influences in their environment: the sets of relationships developed by families or social groups become in this way independent factors in social action. In this section, the analysis parallels the emphasis given in certain African urban studies to the importance of social networks and the structure of social relationships as additional factors in explaining behavior. For example, Kapferer shows how it is the particular structure of relationships in a work situation that determines how values and norms are interpreted and independently influences the outcome of apparently normatively orientated disputes, such as that of rate busting.[1]

It is in the analysis of the social relationships of families in the two neighborhoods that we directly approach one of the central issues of this study: the capacity of low income families to organize their environment. First, the social relationships that individuals develop affect their capacity to be consistent in their actions. By this I mean that someone may be active in attempting to organize his environment, but his activities come to nothing if the pursuit of one hinders the pursuit of another, as happens, for example, when religious activities consume possible economic surpluses and prevent their reinvestment. Indeed the capacity of individuals or social groups to better their position is closely related to their ability to use a variety of activities to contribute to their purpose, whether these activities be economic, political, religious or social.[2] The consistency of individual or group activities is closely related to the number and nature of the social relationships present, and the more these relationships are dispersed and take in people with

[1] Bruce Kapferer, "Norms and the Manipulation of Relationships in a Work Context," in J. C. Mitchell, ed., *Social Networks in Urban Situations.*

[2] See, for example, Norman Long, *Social Change and the Individual: A Study of the Social and Religious Responses to Innovation in a Zambian Rural Community.*

differing expectations the more difficult it is to achieve consistency. This is also an often overlooked aspect of the Weberian emphasis on the relation between ideology and social change: thus one aspect of the relation between the Protestant ethic and the development of capitalism is that it facilitated the coordination of the various secular activities for economic enterprise.[3]

Social relationships have also more immediate significance, since it is through them that the risks and uncertainties of urban life are reduced. We have already seen that the nature of the city's growth creates conditions of mobility and insecurity. Faced with these conditions, urban families must secure what assistance they can get and identify reliable sources of help and advice. For low-income families this task is made especially difficult because they are the most mobile sector of the urban population. Poor families, and this is especially true of those in the shantytown, are less able to identify their fellows, and be themselves identified, by publicly accepted standards of reliability. Their physical appearance, their clothes, and their speech all contribute to identifying them as the very sector of the urban population that is not worthy of public trust. In the pragmatism with which Guatemalans, like others throughout the world, evaluate their fellows, "respectable" people are those who, because of their type of job, social position, or material possessions, are subject to significant costs if they violate public trust. By such criteria few if any of these families have the emblems that merit such trust.[4] For low-income families it is the personal relationships they develop that are the essential means of organizing their environment and of making it secure for their activities. Securing one's personal environment is not

[3] Max Weber, "The Protestant Sects and the Spirit of Capitalism," in H. H. Gerth and C. Wright Mills, eds., *From Max Weber: Essays in Sociology,* pp. 302-322.

[4] Gerald Suttles, *The Social Order of the Slum,* pp. 6-9. Following Suttles, this analysis also distinguishes the capacity of poor people to individually order their environment through extending personal relationships and their capacity to order it as a group through concerted action.

necessarily compatible with organizing with others for joint objectives, since the more effort a person puts into securing his personal environment, the less likely he is to coordinate his activities with others.

Variations between families in the extent and nature of their relationships thus directly relate to the capacity of these groups, whether neighborhood, occupational or religious, to consistently manage their environment and to change it through their actions. The first consideration of this chapter, then, is the impact of the changes described in the previous chapters on the dispersion and frequency of social relationships.

Segmentation

We have already noted that Guatemala City is a place where an individual's personal relationships are unusually important to his daily life. The absence of set procedures for providing urban administration, welfare services, or even jobs means that a personal contact is highly important in getting by in this world. These contacts provide information about the availability of jobs, recommend an individual to an employer, give loans and other assistance in times of shortage, and generally assist in negotiating the problems that people meet in their urban life. These services, in a sense, substitute for the formal procedures of other urban environments, intensifying the social relevance of personal relationships.

In some informal urban environments, the importance of personal relationships means that those that an individual has are used in a variety of urban situations. Kinsmen are also neighbors, workmates, members of a political party, or of a religious sect, and the urban situations through which people move are integrated by the same sets of people. Mitchell relates such a coincidence of contexts to the familiar problem of distinguishing the nature of the differences between small-scale societies and large-scale ones. Where people carry out a variety of activities in the company of the same set of people, there is, as Mitchell puts it, "a strain towards consistency in behavior."[5] An individual's relationships are thus intensified, are often locally based, and provide some security of action in a fluid and unpredictable environment. In contrast, the previous chapters have led us to suspect that the types of mobility present in Guatemala City segment an individual's relationships, so that he interacts with different people in his different urban activities. This is an apparent characteristic of life in the city as well as in the two neighborhoods, and with the exception of certain religious sects, intensively interacting groups are not evident. These impressions are substantiated by the data that indicate that the neighbors, friends, and workmates of our families are distinct from each other.

Both husbands and wives were asked to list on a simulated family tree their parents, grandparents, uncles, aunts, and cousins. The number of these entries was limited by requiring them to give specific information about the place of residence, occupation, and the number of visits they made. They listed some one thousand kin who were living in the city; but in the majority of cases these kin did not live in the same zone as the families, nor did they have similar occupations. Sixty-three percent of the husbands did not have a job in common with a single kinsman, and those that did have jobs in common were not necessarily working in the same enterprise. Even when wife's kin were also included, 58 percent of the husbands still had jobs that were different from their own or her kin. Some of the jobs held in common with kin, such as construction labor, have few specific skills or work traditions attached, and it is unlikely that shared work traditions are an important element in relationships between kin.

Kin are more likely to reside locally; approximately 35 percent of kin live in the respective zones of the two neighborhoods; but both these zones represent large populations total-

[5] J. C. Mitchell, "The Concept and Use of Social Networks," in *Social Networks in Urban Situations*, pp. 46-47.

ling some 75,000 people, and even on a purely random distribution of population we would expect some 14 percent of kin to be living in them. Since the city's population is not randomly distributed, the expected percentage would be much higher if we took into account only the low-income population likely to live in either zone.[6]

The available data on friendship is confined to males: one set of these are husbands' estimates in the informal interviews of whether the friends they see frequently are from the neighborhood or from elsewhere in the city. Friendship is not a precise category, and its meaning is explored in a later section of this chapter, but for our present purposes it refers to those others with whom people spend time and exchange favors.[7] Few admitted to having no friends and, of those who saw their friends frequently, in 59 percent of the cases these friends lived outside the neighborhoods. In response to the survey, fewer husbands said that they had friends, but the term used, *amigo de confianza* or close friend, was stronger than that used in the informal interviews. However, of those that cited having and visiting good friends, 51 percent said that these friends lived outside the zone. In these different interview contexts, the conclusion is the same: most friends do not live locally. Furthermore, in only two cases were these close friends kin and, in 53 percent of the cases, these close friends had jobs that were not even in the same category as those of the respondents. Such friends are thus often different not only from neighbors and kin, but also from workmates.

Common provincial origins are likewise not the basis for intensive interaction. Migrants are from diverse backgrounds, and the identifiable groupings of migrants from the same area in

[6] This relates to the earlier discussion of the ecological differentiation of the city. Zones such as the ones were are discussing attract only a certain segment of the population. Wealthier families, for example, would live in the outer suburbs or the more select areas of the inner city.

[7] These data were obtained through semi-structured interviews in which I had the chance to elaborate a little on the term "friend," defining it as someone with whom one enjoyed spending time and whom one would approach for small favors.

the two neighborhoods are mainly composed of recently arrived migrants who have come directly to either neighborhood to stay with longer established kin. Migrants who have been resident for some time in the city show little preference for associating with people from their home village or town. This is evidenced by the marriages of people in the sample. Only a minority of these marriages are between people from the same village or town, and even those born in the city are as likely to marry migrants as to marry others born in the city. The majority of marriages are mixed in the sense that they are between people originating in quite distinct sections of the countryside, and regional relationships do not form the basis for one of the most significant stages in an individual's urban career—his decision to take a wife and start a family.

It is true that one factor in these marriages is that the respective families have been neighbors or friends and that in some cases the husband met his wife through working with her father or one of her brothers. In most cases, however, the families of husband and wife know little of each other, have few experiences in common, and rarely interact. For example, during field work I observed three marriages in San Lorenzo that involved families that knew each other and that were living in the neighborhood. In two of these marriages, one set of parents disapproved of the other as not "respectable"; while in the third case—that of Pepe's daughter—both sets of parents were good friends but rarely met socially. The circumstance that the spouses' kin are usually either strangers or share few experiences in common is a further important factor in segregating the kinship interactions of the pair. This itself removes an important constraint on the cohesion and stability of marriages, since in many cases the separation of spouses affects no other relationships beyond those with the children and those with the parents of each spouse separately.

The differences reported earlier between the two neighborhoods also affect the segmentation of relationships. In San Lorenzo people are least likely to reside in the same zone as kin or have occupations in common with them and are most likely to have friends living outside the zone. As San Lorenzo has become a stage in urban careers, so its families—especially the younger families who have mostly arrived after its foundation—increasingly separate their neighborhood contacts from those of job and kin. In contrast, Planificada, in becoming more self-sufficient, caters to a wider range of families, which are able to maintain a greater proportion of their ties within the neighborhood. The location of Planificada also makes it more difficult to maintain ties outside the zone and thus encourages the concentration of active relationships. Of the *amigos de confianza*, 61 percent of males in Planificada have such relationships with people living in their neighborhood, in contrast with 31 percent of San Lorenzo males. The bases for these relationships are also likely to be less segmentary than is the case in San Lorenzo. In Planificada, 53 percent of the men cited other continuing relationships such as kinship, place of origin, or neighborhood as the original basis for the relationship; in San Lorenzo 24 percent cited such bases and the remainder cited work.

Table 21. Residence of Kin by Length of Residence in the City of Husbands and Wives (Percentages)

| | Migrants' Length of Residence in the City | | | | | | Age of Those Born or Reared in the City | | | |
| | 1-10 Years | | 11-20 Years | | 21 Years | | 20-39 Years | | 40 Years and Over | |
	H	W	H	W	H	W	H	W	H	W
Have one or more kin in same zone	64	65	62	54	36	44	73	65	38	40
Have kin in city but no kin in same zone	36	35	38	46	64	56	27	35	62	60
Total	100	100	100	100	100	100	100	100	100	100
Number[a]	(22)	(20)	(33)	(37)	(15)	(16)	(48)	(49)	(26)	(10)

[a]The sample size is affected by not including those people who have no kin in the city. In five cases, respondents did not provide enough data for them to be categorized.

Processes of Dispersal

This segmentation of relationships is occurring without the changes in economic and social organization with which it is normally associated. Occupations are not so specialized, the city not so complex, nor qualifications so different that individuals are likely to have interests that are different from those of relatives or neighbors. Instead, segmentation is linked to the length of a family's urban experience and to the consequent mobility to which both they and their social networks have been exposed. Taking the kinship networks of families, classifying migrants by their length of residence in the city and those born or reared in the city by their age, it is evident that in the case of both husband and wife, they reside farther from kin the longer they stay in the city (Table 21). Age, it should be noted, does not account for these trends, and classifying migrants by those under and over age forty still shows length of residence as having an effect.

When we look at the occupations of kin from a similar perspective, it becomes clear that dispersal of an individual's relationships is directly related to the decline in the significance of reputation and personal relationships for job recruitment. Thus, the older a person is the less likely he is to have jobs in common with his kin. This happens partly because there is more time for occupations to become differentiated; but old people are also more likely to be forced into marginal employment, and their kinship relationships do not prevent this mobility. Likewise, migrants who have arrived since the early 1950s have usually found work through their own initiative since, as we have seen, the changes in the economic organization of the city have made it difficult to place friends or relatives in jobs. These recent migrants are less likely than migrants with longer residence or than those born in the city to have jobs in common with their kin. It is only after some work experience that they are able to get into the better jobs that longer established migrants, including their own kin, already have.

The character of this process becomes sharper if we consider

Table 22. Similarity of Occupation of Kin, by Migrant Status and Literacy
of Respondents (Male Heads of Household), in Percentages

	Literate		Illiterate	
	Born or Reared in City	Migrants	Born or Reared in City	Migrants
Have no kin in similar occupation	62	80	42	69
Have some kin in similar occupation	38	20	58	31
Total	100	100	100	100
Number[a]	(52)	(35)	(24)	(35)

[a]This total is affected by not including respondents without kin in the city.

together the two factors that we saw to be crucial to the changing basis of job recruitment, literacy and being a migrant. Both factors are associated with higher job mobility, and their combined effect is to produce considerable differences in the extent that individuals have jobs in common with their kin. Thus, illiterates who are born in the city are the most likely to have jobs in common with their kin (Table 22). This occurs, I suggest, because they and their kin are likely to start within a locally based family occupational tradition, while their own lack of education makes job mobility a difficult and hazardous process. For both the literate and the migrants, however, kin are less occupationally relevant, and their mobility stochastically segments occupational and kinship relationships.

Length of residence in the city also appears to disperse friendship relationships. Thus, using the data from the semi-structured interviews which cover the entire sample, it is clear that the friends that heads of household interact with become increasingly based outside their locality the longer is their urban experience. (Table 23).

It is not only mobility that disperses friendship relationships, but also the quality of an individual's urban participation. Greater urban experience enables people to obtain work in different parts of the city and, through their jobs and other

Table 23. Length of Residence and Interaction with Friends of
Male and Female Heads of Household (Percentages)

Interaction[a]	1-10 Years	11-20 Years	21 Years or More	Born in City
With friends in neighborhood (weekly)	40	38	21	22
With friends in other parts of the city (weekly)	32	33	40	63
Interact infrequently	28	29	39	15
Total	100	100	100	100
Number[b]	(47)	(45)	(73)	(41)

[a]These data are taken from the semistructured interviews.
[b]The total is affected by nonresponse, which was particularly high among female heads of household.

encounters, to cultivate friends outside the locality. When we look at the survey data on close friends, it is those born or reared in the city and under forty whose friendships are most dispersed, and this dispersal is associated with working outside their zone. They cite work as the basis for their friendship and are usually still in the same job as their friend. In contrast, older people reared in the city and more experienced migrants are likely to have their friendships mostly outside their zone, but they are less likely to be in the same job as their friends, although this is cited as the original basis for the friendship. With increasing age, however, both migrants and those reared in the city become more local in their friendships, and the basis for these friendships is more likely to be one based on neighborhood. Thus a cycle exists in which experience creates extra-local friendships; these become increasingly divorced from work while remaining dispersed, but ultimately such friendships become locally concentrated.

The Level of Activity

This analysis suggests that those who are unable to maintain dispersed relationships are likely to have few active ones; even those who have attributes that lead them to concentrate their relationships are caught in the dilemma that kin and friends become dispersed, and many of their neighbors are involved in dispersed networks.

Old people in both neighborhoods say they interact less frequently with friends than do younger people, and with increasing age it becomes more difficult to maintain contact with kin dispersed throughout the city. Whereas 55 percent of husbands and 60 percent of wives between twenty and twenty-nine visit or are visited by five or more relatives in the city, for those couples over fifty only 11 percent of the men and 22 percent of the women have contact with five or more relatives, and about forty percent of both have no contact with relatives at all. This apparent isolation of the old should not be over-stressed. It is to some extent compensated by their having adult children who come to visit, and with increasing age the numbers of surviving close kin must necessarily become reduced. For many, however, it is a real isolation without close kin near at hand to call upon in necessity.

As people get older in Guatemala, they are most likely to need relationships to assist them in emergencies or to provide them with necessary contacts for getting irregular or independent work. Yet it is apparent that the ecology of the city makes it difficult for the older person to maintain a span of relationships. A person's contacts become spread out over the city as a person ages, but the time and distances involved in maintaining them become too expensive as an individual earns less, travels less on his work, and becomes physically incapacitated.

Equally constraining is the circumstance of being a female who is also the head of a household. Female heads of household, who are in almost all cases women separated from their husbands and with dependent children, are less likely than women living with their husbands to maintain relationships with kin either in the zone or outside it. Indeed, female heads of household maintain very few active kinship relationships at all, with 17 percent visiting five or more relatives and 46 percent visiting no relatives at all. In the case of these female heads of household it seems that the amount of work required to maintain themselves and their family without the help of the husband is such as to severely constrain the relationships they can actively maintain.

However, another factor appears to be operating. Female heads of household also appear to have less kin in the city than those living with their husbands. It is likely that females separated from their husbands are disproportionately drawn from those female migrants who have few urban relationships—they are likely to have come to the city as servants and to have developed few relationships outside their household. During the course of service they have taken up with a man, but the relationship is often an impermanent one. They contrast with those women who came to the city with their husbands or who came or were brought up as part of a family. In both situations, the choice of spouse is more likely to be made after some consideration and to be protected by a set of relationships. Single girls, especially servants, are in this respect less protected in the city.

Female heads of household are also less likely than males to say that they have close friends in the city (64 percent of such females have no close friends compared to 51 percent of males). Of those who report having close friends, two-thirds say that these friends are also neighbors. In contrast, women living with their husbands do keep up contact with their kin and to a somewhat greater extent than do their husbands with their kin. My observations suggest that apart from kin, wives maintain few extra-local friendships. Naturally they have people living close by with whom they spend time and can exchange services, but the mobility of friends and relatives and the likelihood that the female is tied to home duties circumscribe their active relationships.

Poverty has a similar effect, since it acts to limit resources and to make journeys too expensive; it is also true that poverty is associated with age and reinforces the likelihood of not maintaining contact with relatives. However, the significance of resources for maintaining contact with kin is clarified if we analyze the two neighborhoods separately. In Planificada, income has a consistent effect on maintaining contact with kin, and higher income means maintaining more contacts; but in San Lorenzo those earning the least—under thirty dollars a month—are more likely than any category other than those earning over seventy dollars to visit five or more relatives. When distance is less important (San Lorenzo is so centrally located that people can walk easily to the contiguous zones where many relatives are located) then the poor actively maintain relations with kin. A similar finding occurs with respect to friendship, with low income and distance acting together to reduce interaction. Economic resources are thus important in overcoming the limitation on interaction placed by spatial differentiation.

The number of social relationships a person maintains is also related to the quality of his urban participation; this is clear in the case of migrants to the city. Whereas their length of residence does not affect the frequency of their interaction with friends, it does affect the frequency of their interaction with kin. Recent migrants interact less frequently with city-based kin than do those with greater experience, and this relates to their continuing involvement in provincial relationships. Migrants with under ten years experience are much more likely than those with longer experience to visit relatives in the provinces, and over half of their visits to kin are to these relatives. In contrast, by the time migrants have been twenty years or more in the city, less than a quarter of their visits to kin are to kin in the provinces.

This relation between quality of participation and frequency of interaction is also true for occupation. Occupation determines the time people have available for participation in urban life and puts workers into contact with different types of people. Employed workers have regular hours and relatively stable wages and are also in constant contact with other workmates. It is not surprising that they should form a category likely to interact frequently with friends and have the facilities to keep up contact with kin on a regular basis. By contrast, the self-employed work alone, and their work is irregular and involves them in activity when others are socializing or relaxing. It is the self-employed who report the least frequent interactions with both kin and friends. This apparent isolation of the self-employed should not be overstressed, for although they interact less frequently than others, they were able in both survey and interview to cite as many sources of aid in times of necessity as any other type of worker. They prove themselves resourceful manipulators of urban relationships using latent ones as well as their presently active ones. The level of an individual's social activity is in these ways distinct from his capacity to cope with urban life.

However, the capacity to maintain a number of active social relationships does determine the style in which an individual copes; people who have few active relationships with kin or friends must focus on the neighborhood and on possible sources of patronage. In this way, since infrequency of interaction is associated with particular social attributes, these characteristics become associated with local commitment, conditioning the type and direction of local organization.

In concluding this analysis of the frequency of interaction it should be noted that the ecological position of the two neighborhoods does produce its expected effect. San Lorenzo inhabitants visit more kin (36 percent visit five or more kin compared with 26 percent in Planificada) and interact more frequently with friends (78 percent said in the semistructured interviews that they interacted with friends at least every week, compared with 65 percent in Planificada). However, in the case of the survey question on close friends, Planificada males were at least as likely to report having close friends (46 percent compared with 43 percent in San Lorenzo), suggesting that these locally based friendships substitute to some extent for the relative absence of kin living close by.

Differentiation

We must now consider the use to which these various relationships are put, remembering that families have unequal access to them and differ in the extent that their interactions are segmented among different sets of people. These considerations become more significant because the relationships we have been discussing also serve different purposes in coping with urban life. Those who do not maintain a range of relationships may have difficulty in coping with all their necessities, while the differentiation of relationships according to the tasks they perform is a further factor conditioning local cohesion and organization.

The argument that an individual's social relationships with kin, neighbors, friends, or workmates become specialized means of coping with their social environment has been mainly developed within the context of advanced, technologically based societies. In a recent exposition, data from the United States and Hungary were used to show how neighbors, kin, and friends are called upon for different services: kin being used for assistance in times of illness when long-term aid is needed, neighbors being used for short-term assistance or small services, and friends for specialized assistance and advice.[8] This pattern was clearer in the data from the United States than in that from Hungary, and those groups (such as bureaucrats) most subject to mobility showed the clearest differentiation in the use to which they put their various relationships. This differentiation occurs to cope with problems requiring different inputs of time and resources as technological change disperses kin, separates home from work and creates friendship groups united by their special interests. The efficacy of primary groups thus does not disappear with technological development, but the services they perform become more specialized to allow the flexibility needed for a mobile society.

The present data suggest than an equal differentiation occurs under the much less sophisticated technology of Guatemala. In so doing, they emphasize our earlier point that the emergence

---

[8] Eugene Litwak and Ivan Szelenyi, "Primary Group Structures and Their Functions: Kin, Neighbors and Friends," *American Sociological Review* 34, no. 4 (August 1969): 465-481.

of apparently "modern" forms of social organization is not necessarily tied to the level of the technology but also results from the instability created by rapid urban growth. Families in both neighborhoods are quite explicit in seeing their various personal relationships as having different functions. They frequently borrow small items from neighbors or call them in to assist with small repairs around the house. When it was a question of illness, however, they made a point of summoning kin, even though these were often living in distant parts of the city.

Several times I was asked to make a special trip to a distant zone of the city to ask close relatives to help out during a wife's illness. Women went to visit their own relatives, often even to the provinces, to help out in times of illness. In contrast, when it was a question of more specialized advice concerning a son's career or help to obtain work, families were adept in searching out a friend or superior who could give them advice.

This differentiation clearly emerges in the responses to the various interview and survey questions about the strategies families would use to meet different types of necessity. Two of these questions are drawn from the survey; one asking to whom families would turn if they needed a small loan and the other asking their resource in case of illness. Respondents were able to choose more than one of the alternatives: kin, fellow provincial, friend, workmate, neighbor, or that of having no recourse. The other two questions come from the earlier interviews with a partially different sample. These asked a respondent to cite his resource for advice and for obtaining a job. Since the survey did not include these latter questions, the interview data has to be used; but there is no reason to suppose that the responses are not comparable. Indeed, the range of answers to an interview question as to where a family would turn to obtain a small loan are almost identical with the answers given in the survey two years later.

Looking at the different uses to which the various relationships are put, it is family that is the most important in the case

Table 24. People to whom Families Turn in Emergencies (Percentages)

	Kin	Neighbor-hood Sources	Work (Workmates, Patrons)	Friends	Institu-tions (Welfare)	No Recourse
In case of illness	45	2	16	8	22	14
For loans	32	14	32	16	–	19
For advice	31	6	27	33	8	27
For help with a job	14	4	23	35	–	31

Note: Percentages do not add to 100 because of multiple choice.

of illness, but its importance declines as the service required becomes more specialized (Table 24). In turn, as the service becomes more specialized so the importance of friends increases. It is also in the case of the more specialized services that families find it harder to cite a possible recourse, and more of them admit to having no such recourse. Both neighborhood and work place are most important when it is a case of short-term and relatively unspecialized assistance; but it is clear that, in contrast to the situation reported in more developed countries, neighborhood relations appear to play a fairly small role in providing for the necessities of a family.

Using different types of relationships for different purposes is most likely to be the practice of those groups with a range of available relationships. Workers in the stable industrial enterprises show the clearest differentiation, using kin for illness and such emergencies, while relying on friends and workmates for loans and more specialized services. In contrast, those in more unstable occupations, where workmates are constantly being changed, use kin for the more specialized services as well as for illness.

Likewise, recent migrants have relationships that are more concentrated in their own zone and are less likely to differentiate those they call on for assistance, using kin or people from the same provincial area for the range of necessities. In this respect the position of older people is anomalous, for they live apart from their kin and are unable to maintain active relationships with them or with their workmates; thus older people use kin in illness and emergencies but are less likely than younger people to use them for loans or more specialized services; these latter cases are most likely to say that they have no recourse in such necessities.

The preceding analysis of the quantitative aspects of social interaction has important implications for the quality of social life among these families. These will be detailed in the sections that follow, but it is already apparent that neither neighborhood forms an interacting community. Although these families are not socially isolated, they do not possess that matrix of relationships that enforces a distinctive style of life and readily provides material and emotional security. Because such assistance is not assured by the conditions of their urban settlement, we can expect them to be unusually active in seeking out and using personal relationships.

The Content of Relationships

The fragmentation of personal relationships does not mean that the population is either socially isolated or inactive. We have already noted the frequency of interaction and the overall impression that emerges from field work is that of families who are highly active participants in urban life. Within both neighborhoods, especially in San Lorenzo, there is an impression of constant bustle, of people chatting to each other or going off to visit friends and relatives. Reserve, however, becomes apparent in the way they use their relationships; the quality of exchanges occurring between kin and between friends conveys its significance.

The net of kinship does not extend too far; the brother and sisters of one's parents are often treated as close kin, but relations with cousins are less imperative and often distant, unless these are the only urban kinsmen. Moreover, in large families individuals maintain close relationships with only some of their siblings and cite quarrels or differences in outlook to explain their distance from others. Indeed, one aspect of the mobility we have been discussing is the blurring of family relationships, since it entails the separation of spouses and their remarriage. Consequently, siblings may grow up in different homes or be children of different marriages.

In all the interactions between relatives I observed, there was an important element of reserve that was absent only when the relative, usually the mother, was living with the family. This reserve consisted in limiting the occasions on which close relatives were visited to obtain assistance. While relatives were used for advice and help in emergencies, families made a conscious effort not to ask relatives for small loans or other forms of minor assistance. On several occasions I observed men who had recently helped close relatives during illness or over an important family problem go out of their way to get a temporary loan from a neighbor or workmate rather than bother these relatives. Naturally, if relatives were the only available recourse, they would be used for small as well as large emergencies.

The reserve toward close relatives often resulted in interaction with them only in certain situations. Men hardly ever cited their relatives as possible recreation companions and would state that it was not suitable to be too informal with kin, especially when it was their wife's kin. This norm was often violated in practice, and husbands did go drinking with their own and their wives' relatives, but on these occasions they told me several times afterward that care had to be taken in order to maintain a certain degree of respect between relatives.

It was also a constant theme of conversation with families in the two neighborhoods that reciprocity had to be maintained in their relationships with kin. Families did not like to ask relatives for favors that they themselves could not reciprocate. Thus, in the few cases where families in these neighborhoods had relatives in significantly better occupational and economic situations than themselves, there was little evidence that these relatives were used more than other relatives. Indeed, some families accounted for their lack of interaction with such relatives as due to the fact that the superior status of their relatives made it impossible to maintain relationships with them. They talked of their professional or wealthy relatives as living in another world and said it was demeaning to themselves to continue to visit these relatives to ask for favors. Families in the shantytown often expressed to me a similar unease about visiting their relatives, because they felt they could not invite them back to their own homes.

Interaction with relatives of socially superior status is only a problem for a small number of families. Approximately 10 percent of the relatives of husband and wife are in white-collar occupations, and most of these are in minor clerical jobs. The sample we are discussing is not only itself a relatively homogeneous low-income group, but the relatives of these families are also concentrated in low-income occupations. In the few cases when families have a relative in a professional job, their interaction is specific and infrequent. One woman from San Lorenzo occasionally visits a sister who is married to a doctor and obtains a little help with her children's education. On the other hand, another woman with a sister married into a rich merchant family complains that she is not welcome at their house.

When we talk of these families operating with a norm of reciprocity, we are discussing the relationships among relatives whose occupational status, at least, is approximately the same. Both Pepe and José provide examples of the norm of reciprocity in action. Both of them have relatives whose position is somewhat better than their own in that these relatives own their own homes in "respectable" parts of the city and have stable occupations. Both see their relatives quite frequently and put greater trust in them than in any other urban contact. However, in the two years of my close acquaintance with them, both did as many favors for their relatives as they ever appeared to receive. José was constantly conducting business for his sister and helping her with the professional contacts she needed for her children's career. Pepe handled most of the negotiations concerning the rental and maintenance of a property that a sister owned and took no commission for doing so. Both received favors in return, usually in times of crisis or at times when help was important. The purchase of goods to start a small business, helping place a child in good employment, and assistance in times of prolonged illnesses are examples of the favors they received. Yet, the balance was maintained in the eyes of both parties. In the conversations I had with the two men, they always stressed the reciprocal nature of the services offered; their sisters expressed similar sentiments to me, even when talking privately.

The Conditions of Exchange

The significance of this emphasis on reciprocity becomes clearer if we now extend the discussion of the importance of trust in Chapter 1. The continuation of any relationship, even that between relatives, depends on exchange. These exchanges are not necessarily immediate, and relatives often exchange help in times of illness over the space of years. Neither are exchanges necessarily identical in content, and one member of an exchange may provide material services while the other or others may reciprocate through giving such nonmaterial returns as esteem and social approval.[9] Indeed, it is the nonmaterial returns that help exchange relationships to persist and develop. Whereas too rapid a material reciprocation terminates a relationship or confines it to specific activities, nonmaterial reciprocation provides a flexible basis for further and different types of exchange to develop.

Trust is an emergent property of such continuing exchanges and promotes stable social relations. But the social context is also crucial to the development of trust. This context determines the range of opportunities available outside a group and thus the relative significance for members of the services and social approval they receive within the group. As Blau points out, social approval has less pervasive significance as a restraining force in complex societies because the multiplicity

[9] Peter Blau, *Exchange and Power in Social Life*, pp. 97-106. My discussion is based on Blau, but readers should consult the original for the full range of the argument.

of groups and personal mobility enables deviants to escape the impact of community disapproval.[10] This is a severe limitation on exchanges when they occur outside of relatively enclosed social situations. When people are not tied by multiple ties and do not engage together in many activities, the range and certainty of exchanges are reduced. The value of esteem and the force of social approval are the greater when they are visible to others and when they occur in situations in which the members are to some degree constantly involved. Esteem or approval that is given or withheld apart from such social situations has only a personal significance and entails few costs or benefits.

In the environment of a city where relatives live apart and engage in transactions with a variety of people, families have no guarantee that kin will be at hand to provide them with the range of material services they will need, nor are they guaranteed that esteem or social approval constrain kin in any continuing personal or public commitment. For these reasons there is a stress on the norm of specific material reciprocity. Relatives are asked only for favors on important occasions, and these are of the kind such as help in illness, which relatives are those most likely to return.

To ask too many favors is to endanger the possibility of reciprocity and to make it possible that important favors will also be refused. This is a strong possibility, since urban mobility also makes it easier for relatives to escape unwanted responsibilities when they do not confront each other continuously and through the same sets of relationships. The lack of stable interactional contexts in the city makes it difficult to build transactions into the trust relationships that are basic to engaging in complex activity with others. Though kin are seen as basic urban relationships, they are not used to build a persisting base for urban participation. Such relationships, for example, are rarely the basis for economic or political action; they may recruit people for such action but they do not maintain it over time.

[10] Ibid., p. 114.

The above comments apply even more strongly to ritual kinship in the two neighborhoods. The institution of *compadrazgo* in Spanish America has often been cited as allowing individuals to form relationships with others who are socially or economically significant.[11] Basically, it is a relationship formed when a child is baptized and a godparent is required to stand as ritual parent. This godparent or *compadre* is thought to have responsibility for the child's moral welfare, and, in the event of the decease or neglect of the parent, the godparent is a possible guardian of the child. Families in both neighborhoods do seek godparents for their children, but their relationships with these appears quite distinct from that with godparents in rural areas.

I found little evidence that *compadrazgo* relationships served as a basis for continuing interaction of any kind within the urban milieu. People might interact with their children's godparents, but this was seen as part of the normal relationship between friends. Often families had ceased to see their *compadres* and, in some cases, could not remember their names. The category of *compadre* was hardly ever cited as a possible recourse in times of emergency or when in need of financial help. I analyzed the political and economic relationships in the shantytown to determine if *compadrazgo* played any part in the formation and maintenance of these relationships but could find no consistent evidence to suggest that such relationships played either an intended or an unintended part in the structuring of neighborhood organization.

In choosing godparents, families said that they tried to choose people whom they respected and who were not such close friends as to make them too familiar. This is the ideology of godparenthood, but it does not violate a common-sense interpretation of the actual choices of godparents. Despite the findings elsewhere in Latin America, there is no evidence from these neighborhoods that families made a practice of choosing

[11] Sidney W. Mintz and Eric R. Wolf, "An Analysis of Ritual Co-Parenthood (Compadrazgo)," in Jack M. Potter et al., eds., *Peasant Society*, pp. 174-200.

social superiors as godparents. Most of the godparents whose occupations I was able to note had occupations very similar to those of the father. The godparent relationships that Pepe has in the shantytown are with a meat salesman, a tailor, and a construction laborer. The godparents of his own children are tailors and barbers. Likewise, José chose godparents for his youngest child who were in the neighborhood and held relatively humble occupations; one of them subsequently became a political enemy. Since both José and Pepe have been active in politics and have entered into many relationships with middle-class professionals, it is the more interesting that they do not attempt to include one of these as a godparent of their children.

The weakness of godparenthood as a basis for enduring exchange relationships lies in the instability of urban life in Guatemala. Relationships made when a child is born are likely to be disrupted by changes of residence and occupation. Also, the instability of urban life makes it unlikely that a relationship made for one purpose will continue to be useful for a considerable period of time. For example, a godparent relationship established partly to cement an economic alliance becomes inappropriate as jobs are changed or as one partner moves to another area of Guatemala. Godparenthood is indeed basically seen by people in the two neighborhoods as too inflexible a relationship to be useful in their secular ambitions, although they are aware from rural experience that these relationships are used to make alliances and to gain access to wealthy or influential people. The exceptions are those women who work as servants in middle-class homes and who do invite their employers to become godparents to a child.

The Meaning of Friendship

Friendship has several meanings within the context of these neighborhoods, and in conversation or interview it is difficult to distinguish which meaning is foremost in a speaker's mind. There are a number of Spanish words that roughly translate the English term friend and friendship—*amigo, amistad, conocido*—and it is possible by adding intensifying adjectives to make the meaning more precise and to distinguish between acquaintances and good friends. But to these families, friendship refers not only to a relationship but also to a pattern of behavior.

This can be illustrated by citing one conversation that was necessary to elucidate what a speaker meant by saying that he had no friends. I observed, since I knew the respondent, that he was often in the company of others, exchanged loans with them, and seemed to treat them with a degree of familiarity. He agreed, but added that, to him, having friends meant trusting oneself to the company of others, drinking with them, being too open in one's confidences, and spending more time with them than with one's family.

To this respondent, friendship implied a pattern of behavior that in his eyes was to be deplored. To suggest that he had friends was to suggest that he wasted his time in useless activities and in dubious company. This contextual meaning of friendship is common among families in both neighborhoods and, as might be suspected, was most frequently cited by the women and those husbands who made most efforts to impress me with their "respectability." It derives its significance from two reinforcing circumstances. In villages and smaller towns it has been a traditional and public norm that individual families keep to their own business. Males who consort together in recreation and drinking are regarded as neglecting their families and jobs.

In the city this feeling is compounded by the conditions of instability that have been described. There is a great deal of alcoholism, and it is common for husbands to leave their wives and take up with other women. Also, families do not know their neighbors in the way that families in more stable environments build up such knowledge over time and often over generations. Consequently, to have friends is regarded by many as exposing the individual to the dangers and uncertainties of their urban environment. For these reasons, respondents were often ambiguous in answering questions about friends. Whatever

hesitations they had about citing their relationships were compounded by the difficulty they experienced in deciding
whether they should answer in terms of the ideology of relationships or in terms of their actual acquaintances.[12] This
illustration of the contextual meaning of friendship is particularly important to our analysis, since it also refers to a feature
of urban life that influenced respondents' behavior. Not only
was it the case that I was often confused by the use of the term
"friendship," but also it was evident that families were affected
by the ambiguity present in their perception of what the term
meant. To have friends is a valued attribute, since it means that
an individual has several recourses in an emergency, when he
needs loans or advice, or when he needs information and help to
get a job. Yet having friends is seen as making the individual
especially liable to the uncertainties and dangers present in the
urban environment, dangers that often occur when friends
betray trust and fail in their obligations.

In this situation, individuals' use and perception of friendship relationships appear to be of two kinds. They have
acquaintances with whom services are exchanged, with whom
they attend sports or movies, and with whom they engage in
political, religious, and even economic activities. These relationships are regarded as loose and are not seen as committing an
individual to do something contrary to his interests or to those
of his family. Relationships of this kind have little of the family
intimacy that in other conditions is often associated with
friendship. Friends of this type are rarely if ever invited into the
house and are often not even informed about important
domestic happenings such as the birth of a child or the
impending marriage of a daughter. In analyzing the pattern of
friendship of this type in San Lorenzo, it was apparent that
there was a constant turnover in membership of a friendship

[12] This ambiguity illustrates a general problem in the use of survey and observational techniques—they often fail to take adequate account of the social context to
which questions refer. It is wise to keep these caveats in mind when interpreting the
material presented on other forms of relationship.

group, and those at the end of my field work were often quite different from those at the beginning.

In contrast with this first type of friendship, there is also a friendship that is more permanent and unites families as well as individuals. These friendships are often formed between people born in the same town, village, or city neighborhood or with people who have shared significant common experiences in the past, such as army service or first employment. Such friendships are not usually with people living close by, and the joint activities in which such friends engage are usually recreational. It appeared to be a criterion for such friendships that they be not between people with common residential or occupational situations. This is understandable given the uncertainties and difficulties that attend such situations in Guatemala City. This characteristic of the relationship was more pronounced in the "disreputable" neighborhood—San Lorenzo—than in Planificada. The satisfactions derived from this type of friendship are intrinsic and mention is rarely made of any material transactions. Naturally such friends are possible recourses in times of emergency and occasionally spontaneously offer help, but this aspect of the relationship is subordinated in the minds of these families to the intrinsic satisfaction they derive. Such relationships do not involve transactions that expand in content and enable people to cooperate on a wide variety of fronts; they are specialized in that they allow people beset by uncertainties in their encounters to enjoy the company of others without suspicion of being exploited or betrayed. These relationships are maintained over time and are cited more frequently by the older, wealthier, and better educated in the two samples.

We can end this section by looking at the present social relationships of one member of San Lorenzo—Pepe. He plays a prominent part in the later discussion, and we have already seen glimpses of his career. He came to the city as a young, literate migrant, has been highly mobile occupationally and residentially, and now, aged fifty, he is setting up in a small shop in the market of the zone in which San Lorenzo is located. I came to know him well over the period of the study, and I closely observed the personal relationships that were a regular feature of his daily life during the six months in which he set up his store.

Pepe's relationships are dispersed throughout the city and in only a few cases, like those of kin and the people living in San Lorenzo, do the members of this network know each other. Even in these cases, however, it is Pepe who is the main link binding their acquaintance. Pepe's activities are also relatively compartmentalized, and the account below is intended to convey the extent to which a few of his activities overlap.

His main source of social visiting is his friend the shopkeeper in Zone 3, where Pepe and his wife are accustomed to go on a Sunday afternoon and stay for three or four hours taking a drink and watching television. His kin are his main sources of help in illness, coming to visit and help during a recent period that he was laid up in bed. Pepe visits them frequently, having meals with them and helping them with family problems and their financial affairs. His old-time friends also came to help with money when Pepe was ill; when he was let out of prison after an alleged attack on the local priest, these friends came from the various parts of the city to give their sympathy.

He relies on various neighbors for small loans and never to my knowledge bothered relatives or his older friends with such requests. However, he interacts socially very little with neighbors and claims that the only one he really trusts is Oscar, his son-in-law's father; but, apart from an occasional meal together and a visit to bingo, they rarely meet socially. Despite his lack of close friends in the neighborhood, Pepe is very active in neighborhood organization and spends much time in the company of other neighborhood organizers, but these relationships have not developed into more widely based exchanges. It is his longer-term friends that have provided the main sources of help in his business on a strict loan or credit and repayment basis. Some of these relationships—notably with his accountant friend from Quetzaltenango and with the owner of the super-market—have become more active as a consequence, despite several years of intermittent visiting.

The accountant, who has become an insurance salesman, heard from Pepe's brother, whom he saw in his taxi, of Pepe's new venture and came over to visit and to try to sell insurance. The other person who has helped extensively with the business is the local mayor, who is not a long-term friend of Pepe's but who has heavily committed Pepe to his political support. In religion, Pepe's relationships are also segmented from his others, and his daughter, who is constant in visiting and helping out, has become a member of a Protestant sect. Pepe is active in attending Catholic associations, but these are not locally based. Through these he has made contacts with priests with whom he corresponds and from whom he receives help in his community betterment work. He has also made a contact through these meetings with a prominent city lawyer who recently helped Pepe's friend, the tailor from Zone 7, by arranging a legal marriage for his daughter without charge.

During the period after the opening of his store, Pepe was visited by several old friends. One of these was the brother of a man who had got Pepe one of his first jobs and who had been engaged to Pepe's sister. The brother was now selling electrical goods and other hardware, and it was from him that Pepe purchased an ice-cream machine and a refrigerator on credit. At this time Pepe was finding sales low in his shop and was wondering whether he had made a good decision by setting up the business. However, on a visit to pay taxes at the municipal buildings he met an old friend, an army colonel who now holds a high municipal position. He had met the colonel when the latter was a sub-lieutenant and had played the marimba at his wedding. The colonel heard his troubles and persuaded him that the only solution was to open yet another store, obtaining for him the permit for a second stall in the market. Pepe decided to set his wife up in this, but the local mayor was furious, both because a charge of nepotism might be laid and hinder their political aims and because Pepe's credit was being stretched dangerously thin.

The above account of Pepe's recent friendship interactions illustrates several of the points that have so far been made. It is clear that he has made a series of friendships over time, but that some of these are latent. They provide Pepe with contacts with people in a wide range of economic and social positions, and their spread increases the likelihood of one of them being appropriate to a current problem. It is these long-term relationships, including those with kin, that have served him in the more important necessities, whereas neighborhood and more recent relationships are used for more immediate exchanges. Pepe characterizes his neighborhood relationships by saying that such people cannot really be trusted and, when pressed, admits that the problem is his lesser knowledge of them and of their relationships.

Maintaining continuing contact with long-term acquaintances, however, means that his stable relationships are the dispersed ones, and these are often intermittent in nature. One consequence is that he is easily pressured into inconsistent actions. Pepe maintains both an appearance and an ideology of respectability and hard work, and his friends respond by expecting such behavior. They provide help that is not easily combined to his present necessities and, for example, his relation with the colonel leads to inconsistent behavior in terms of the local mayor and his projects.

His relationships also are characterized by a restricted exchange of services. Pepe is careful not to use his close friend in the nearby neighborhood for loans or advice except in the severest emergencies. He expressed his attitude by saying that he does not want to bother them with small concerns and wants to keep their relationship a peaceful one, undisturbed by the problems he faces in his everyday life. It was clear to me that Pepe did see this relationship as an escape from the often worrying and depressing events in which he was involved, but he is also acting in a manner similar to that of other families by restricting his exchanges to those that can be reciprocated within his own conditions. He and his wife, for example, take small presents to their friends and naturally the social event has its own rewards for the participants.

We thus find a similar situation with respect to friendship as was noted with kinship. Enduring relationships are also limited in the content of their exchange—they are reserved for special needs and occasions for interaction. Other relationships—which are best labeled aquaintanceship relationships—are less enduring and orientated to the specific exchange of services and participation in common activity. The difference between these types of friendship relationships should not be overstressed. They merge into each other over time with respect to the content of exchange. They are differentiated, however, in the practice of people in the neighborhoods by the extent to which they involve the whole family and involve the exchange of life histories, attitudes, and aspirations. The enduring relationships appear to be fuller in all these respects; the partners to the exchange know more about each other and are more likely to involve the family in their meetings.

Patrons and Clients

The analysis of patron-client relationships is a further and special illustration of the limitations imposed on relationships by the instability of the urban environment. The existence of patron-client relationships has been noted in many parts of the world, especially in the rural areas of Latin America.[13]

Essentially the relationship is one between a social and economic superior who extends favors, often of a material kind, to a poorer person who gives service and esteem to the patron. The relationship endures and is often the basis on which

[13] Eric Wolf, "Kinship, Friendship and Patron-Client Relations in Complex Societies," in Michael Banton, ed., *Social Anthropology of Complex Societies*, pp. 1-22.

people mobilize political support and demonstrate their social importance.

There are elements of this relationship in the city and in the neighborhoods. Certainly, many people talk in terms of patrons and actively seek patrons in the urban environment. This is particularly true of those whose occupations are particularly uncertain and expose them to employment fluctuations. Construction laborers seek the patronage of engineers who appoint work gangs, and small traders seek the patronage of wealthy merchants or professionals who can extend them credit or trading privileges. Patronage relationships also extend over time and often originate in early experiences in the army, on government construction work, or in the home village.

In this context, it is important to remember that the working experience of most of this sample has included jobs in government service at one stage or another. Families, through such service, have had ample opportunity to make contact with influential members of their society, either in the close interactions of army life or in police or governmental construction work. These contacts are not forgotten by families in the neighborhood and are used when opportunity arises.

We have already seen examples of patronage relationships at work, such as when Prudencio used a contact with a colonel from his home village to obtain a police job or when Angel used a contact with another military officer to obtain other civilian employment. There is also the instance of an old construction laborer who about twice a year visits the colonel with whom he once served, performing small menial services for him.

We have already noted why such vertical relationships should be stressed in the Guatemalan context. There is such mobility and so few objective qualifications that individuals require assistance that can span social and geographical distance. To get a job in any part of the country or city it is useful to have a recommendation from an influential person—these recommendations stand instead of the reputational characteristics that have ceased to be relevant to job recruitment.

A similar argument applies to the administration of welfare payments and other urban services. The impossibility of knowing the circumstances of the many individuals who come for assistance and the lack of objective criteria to sort among applicants make personal recommendations a useful means of differentiating these applications.

There are, then, a series of reasons in the particular circumstances of Guatemala's environment for low-income families to actively seek patronage relationships. This search is complemented by the desire of many middle- and upper-status Guatemalans to obtain clients. This clientage is political in nature and must be distinguished from the inclusion of small traders or craftsmen in a marketing or production network.

In the political structure of the city, the ability to rapidly mobilize informal support is an important element in the strategies of middle- and upper-status people competing for influence and resources. Political party organization does not exist beyond the level of their central committees, and no permanent staff of professional party workers is maintained. Furthermore, party boundaries are fluid, and individuals move across them as suits their bargaining strategies. To some, an important element in their strategy is to launch their candidates for public office, particularly that of mayor of the city. As many as twenty candidates may be launched at any one time. To other individuals, the important thing is to demonstrate that they are able to mobilize support on behalf of another candidate or that they can influence part of the urban population to make or not make demands.

To achieve all these ends, these aspiring politicians require contacts among poorer sections of the population. Often these contacts are made by an immediate subordinate of the politician who then introduces them to the leader. Recruitment usually proceeds on the basis of existing social relationships. An employer approaches one of his workers. A priest approaches a parishioner and kinsmen as well as fellow provincials are used. The art of the patron is to build up a sufficient number of enduring relationships to form a basis for mobilization when it becomes needed. For this reason, patrons are ready and available to aspiring clients.

The process of patron-client formation is illustrated in the case of Pablo. Pablo has had varied urban and rural experiences that ultimately led him to become politically active in the neighborhood on behalf of radical political interests and also to take part in the local Catholic brotherhood. He has many kinsmen and is an influential figure in the neighborhood. His daughter won the neighborhood beauty queen contest in 1967, and the local parish priest contacted Pablo to introduce him to a prominent military officer, a kinsman of the president, and to get the officer interested in the welfare of the girl. The officer visited Pablo and secured employment for the girl in the government office of which he was head.

Pablo visited the officer at this office several times during the year, inquiring after the welfare of his daughter and relating to him events in the neighborhoods. Ultimately, the officer offered to have the girl sent with his sister to the United States where she would work as a house servant. Pablo agreed and throughout this period was in contact with the officer and getting small financial contributions from him to help in the activities of Pablo's Catholic group. When the officer began to think of his own political possibilities, Pablo was contacted through an intermediary to begin forming a group that would speak to others on the officer's behalf and start a local campaign for his election.

The above account can be reproduced with a different cast for many families in both neighborhoods. At election time, heads of families who have contacts with patrons are summoned to meetings, and they in turn work on their own relationships. These processes will in fact be analyzed in a more general and formal way in the subsequent chapters.

Families also think in terms of patron-client relationships. Their initial reaction to a well-dressed stranger is to gradually attempt to discover his potential as a patron. In discussing the

overall political climate of Guatemala, all except the ideolog-
ically sophisticated and the well-educated tended to depict
events in patron-client terms. Presidents of Guatemala are
frequently evaluated, in conversation, by whether they could be
considered good patrons or not.

The progress of a patron is occasionally a visible, and to the
outsider, ludicrous event in neighborhood life. One such patron
who held an important municipal position would occasionally
descend to the shantytown, with a foreign diplomat in train if
possible, and make progress down the mud streets, waving and
greeting people as he went. His most regular clients accompanied him, and the procession would stop in front of various
shacks where loyal supporters resided. Other families in the
neighborhood looked on, asking what was happening, who were
the smartly dressed gentlemen, and how come they knew so
many bad people.

Yet despite these evident signs of active client-patron
relationships, they play a relatively minor role in the lives of
these people. In the survey there were several questions
designed to elicit respondents' relationships with people of
middle and upper status. Despite the tendency of poor Guatemalans to cite relationships with influential superiors as evidence of their own status, there were few respondents that cited
relationships with such people. Also, respondents were asked to
cite any visits they had made to people in the previous month
and, in this question again, there were very few responses that
cited visits to middle- and upper-status figures such as lawyers
or military officers.

These survey data bear out the field observations of instances
of relationships with superiors. In the field work, it became
clear that, although families occasionally talked of the advantages of having patrons and cited concrete examples, very few
of them actually had relationships they could call upon in time
of need. I had many opportunities to put this to the test when I
encountered families having evident difficulties in finding
employment or getting welfare aid. I gave what advice and help

I could and also checked informally to see what means they used to get help. In only one case of the perhaps twenty or so I observed did the family use a patronage relationship, and ironically a local priest and an official contact of his were unable to do anything—in this case to secure the release of the son who had been imprisoned for a juvenile misdemeanor.

The cases of relatively stable patron-client relationships are those involving concrete political exchanges. In subsequent chapters, we will see further examples of these as party officials or professionals agree to act on behalf of someone; but their services are provided in return for the work of political organization. Likewise, the most apparent advantage of patronage relationships came to families that were in no particular need, but that had served the right patron at election time. To support a successful candidate did have considerable advantages, and I estimated that perhaps twenty families in San Lorenzo benefited through jobs or concessions as a result of successful political action on behalf of a candidate. Yet, these advantages did not continue and could not be called upon at times of need, until another election period drew near.

In these respects the advantages of the patron-client relations are specific and not diffuse. Rewards are received for services given, but the transaction does not continue expanding through the recurring adjustments of obligations and payments. It is this that makes these urban patronage relationships distinct from those that might be found in the provinces; for the esteem and compliance of clients are only on occasion visible to the patron in a large and busy city. Also, amid the complexities of urban politics and administration it is difficult to identify with certainty the source of any favor. Under these conditions the patron has no guarantee that clients are constant in their support for him; clients are uncertain as to whom they are indebted for the favors they do receive and are reluctant to commit themselves to one patron. The patron-client relationship is thus not a means to continue and expand relationships when there are not specific services to be exchanged. Patronage, like kinship and friendship, cannot be used to consistently organize at either the individual or the group level, and like these other relationships, is but one possible recourse in coping with urban life.

The Emergence of Locally Based Groups

There is a recurrent theme in the description of the various personal relationships found within the neighborhoods: most relationships are essentially dyadic, and what is exchanged is specific to the pair interacting. A wide range of exchange relationships enables individuals to cope with the problems they encounter and provides them with the opportunity to manage their environment in their own favor. This argument parallels Foster's description of the way peasants in a Mexican village organize their social environment.[14] He stresses the precariousness of peasant life, its economic insecurity, and their lack of power or influence. Consequently, existence depends under these conditions on tapping as many as possible of the sources of help and security that are potentially available to villagers. Since these Guatemalan families live under similar conditions of insecurity, it is not surprising that their behavior should be similar to that of the Mexican villagers. This comparison between the procedures of poor families in a large city and that of peasants in a small village is another indication of the dangers in making too clear a distinction between urban and rural styles of life.

If our argument is correct, we should expect those that are without a spread of such relationships to be more inclined to substitute for them by intensive interaction at the local level. Thus, the aged, the poor, those in unstable occupations, and those without kinship ties in the city are likely, if the opportunity presents, to enter into inclusive, locally based associations.

In both neighborhoods, one of the main attractions of the

[14] George Foster, "The Dyadic Contract: A Model for the Social Structure of a Mexican Peasant Village," *American Anthropologist* 63 (December 1961): 1173-1192.

small Protestant sects is precisely that they provide such security to their members. Families with no other relatives in the
city, women whose marriages are broken, and people whose
occupations expose them to exceptional uncertainty, such as
the small self-employed craftsmen or traders, are disproportionately found in these churches. One other striking feature of
these churches is that their active members are females. Given
marital instability and the greater difficulty that women experience in making and maintaining social relationships, the Protestant churches do offer a milieu where females can easily form
relationships and where family cohesion is emphasized and
strengthened through constant interaction in the various church
activities.

The Protestant churches are organizations that emphasize
constant interaction among their members with frequent meetings and with visits to each others' houses, to churches, and to
Protestants in other parts of the city. Indeed, Protestants distinguish between fellow believers and between outsiders in the
same way that other families distinguish long-term friends and
acquaintances. They speak of only being able to trust Protestants and come to their fellow believers for most of the serious
emergencies of life, including illness. They interact with non-
Protestants but speak of them as people with whom a Protestant has to be careful, as being unpredictable. The intensive
interactions of Protestants are noticed and commented upon in
the neighborhoods, and Protestants are often condemned for
being exclusive—for not participating in neighborhood and city-
wide activities. In fact, their church activities extend not only
across the city but also into the provinces.

The only other group that could be similarly characterized is
the Catholic Hermanidad in San Lorenzo. Despite radically
different doctrines and practices, the Hermanidad has some
striking similarities to the Protestant sects. It, too, was dominated by women and by women who were either separated
from their husbands or who could expect little support from
them. These women interacted frequently, both in the organiza-

tion of religious activities and in political activities and recreations. They helped each other out in small and large emergencies and cite few friends outside the group of the Hermanidad. They are the only group of Catholics that worship as a locally based community.

The relation between joining such an intensively interacting group and being relatively isolated is brought out by the case of María. When I first met her, she was a constant visitor at the house of Pepe. She was in her early thirties, had two small children, and had been abandoned by her husband. To make a living she did occasional washing and ironing for local families and at one stage worked as a laborer for a dollar a day, putting in drainage pipes in San Lorenzo. However, she had a bad reputation in the neighborhood, had a sharp tongue, and various imputations were made about her other sources of income. Her friendship with Pepe appeared to be her main relationship in the city, and she had no relatives or long-term friends. Pepe helped her a little with loans, getting her jobs like that on the drainage project and ultimately by getting her a sewing machine from the Social Welfare Agency.

However, it was also clear that this relationship was not sufficient for María's needs. Pepe was not prepared to keep providing help without hope of return and, though María was vociferous in her praises of him, he also suspected that she said different things behind his back. By the time of the second period of field work, the situation had changed completely and María had joined the Hermanidad. Despite her reputation, she was now one of its most active and vociferous members. To add a certain piquancy to the change, the leader of the Hermanidad had obtained for her a job selling candles to the faithful as they entered one of the city-center churches. Her spare time was spent with Hermanidad members, who helped her with loans, aid in illness, and kept an eye on her small children. In return, she became an active campaigner for their secular as well as their religious purposes, including a vitriolic opposition to one of their main enemies—Pepe.

The Significance of an Extended Span of Relationships

The data on social interaction indicate the difficulties these families face in their attempts to reduce risk and uncertainty in their urban environment. The quality of information they are able to obtain about their immediate social environment is reduced by the diffuse pattern of their interactions. Most of the relationships they use to cope with urban life are not based on the neighborhood, though the difference between groups in their attachment to locality is certainly an important element in our later analysis of the divisions in neighborhood organization. Also, the relationships they do maintain are not well-integrated; people known in one situation are not often associates in other situations nor are associates known to each other or bound together by a common set of experiences or skills. Instead, most families maintain relationships with dispersed sets of kin, friends, and possible patrons. While an adequate means of coping with their environment, these associates are not easily combined to consistently organize it.

This segregation of relationships implies that these families cannot generate the completeness of information in their encounters that comes from interacting with and observing the same set of people in different situations. This is underlined by contrasting their situation with that of the Italian families that Suttles described in a south-side Chicago slum.[15] In this Italian neighborhood, personal relationships, recreation, and commercial transactions are concentrated within the neighborhood. The relationships that develop between families are highly personal and take full account of personal idiosyncracies. An individual is judged not by whether he meets the public standards of outside society, but by whether he acts as his acquaintances expect. Suttles characterizes the form of order maintained as provincial, and it enabled families to effectively and informally organize to minimize internal discord and to obtain favors from outsiders.[16]

[15] Gerald Suttles, *The Social Order of the Slum*, pp. 99-107.
[16] Ibid., pp. 223-224.

Possessing dispersed relationships does not improve information about those others outside their neighborhood with whom these Guatemalan families have complementary social or economic interests. We have seen little evidence of them forming enduring relationships on such bases as occupation, ethnicity, or common provincial origin. The relationships of these families appear, in fact, to be quite specific in terms of situation and services exchanged. This is the dilemma: people have neither the intensive interactions that generate trust, nor are there present the identifiable credentials that allow people to readily form and use relationships with strangers. An individual or a group has no constantly available means to establish social credit and cannot be sure that the help of others can be called upon at will. This means that they cope with their environment by using specific exchanges in the different situations in which they become available. In these ways, these families illustrate the difficulties of those who are neither part of a social order based on locality and intensive interaction, nor of one based on membership in recognized social and economic interest groups with organized representation by party, union, or association. They can use neither formal nor informal means to consistently represent their interests.

Possessing relationships that are diverse and unintegrated means that an individual is exposed to inconsistent and, at times, conflicting expectations of his behavior. He has relationships with people who vary in their experiences and present social positions; since these others rarely know each other they do not accommodate any conflicting expectations of his behavior. This is how inconsistency of behavior serves to characterize the situation of underdevelopment. People appear fickle in their political, social, or economic allegiances because they are not encouraged to think that pursuing a consistent course is possible, and they cannot be sure that others will behave in a way that makes their own consistency worthwhile. They must balance short- and long-term advantage or individual or group strategies without any consistent reinforcement from their associates.

This discussion indicates some of the limits for the elaboration of group organization based on trust and social exchange. The absence of conditions favorable to social exchange does not exhaust, however, the possibilities of group organization based on other forms of transaction. In particular, a group may become organized through an emergent differentiation of power within it. Where, for example, people receive more favors than they can return, continuity in the transactions rests upon a differentiation of power, where some provide needed services in return for the esteem and compliance of others. These transactions, when extended over time, can generate, like trust and social exchange, the legitimacy that allows the creation of a stable but stratified social organization at the level of city or nation.[17]

The unstable conditions of Guatemala City appear, however, to preclude the extension of organization based on the differentiation of power as well as of that based on social exchanges between equals. This possibility was evident in the discussion of patron-client relationships, and it will be explored further in the analysis of neighborhood political organization. The analysis of social interaction thus suggests that there is no secure basis for any form of enduring group organization among the mass of the population. They are not likely to combine effectively to further their particular interests, nor do the conditions of their life appear to encourage them to consistently accept the legitimacy of any form of political organization.

[17] Peter Blau, *Exchange and Power in Social Life*, pp. 115-142. I am simplifying Blau's discussion to contrast the two possibilities of group organization—that of horizontal integration based on trust and social exchange and that of vertical differentiation based on power and legitimacy.

5. External Relations and Neighborhood Organization

In this chapter we take up the two related themes of the impact on the lives of these families of external organizations and of the emergence of formal organization within the neighborhoods. The themes are related because it is through the example and direct pressure of their external relationships that internal formal organization emerges. In this respect, we have already noted that these families have relationships that involve them in activity throughout the city; but the emphasis so far has been on the informal relations, and we must now consider the extent that they are exposed to more formalized and public expectations of their behavior.

This focus has a general significance for studying urban organization because the prevalence of formal voluntary associations is thought to characterize urban milieus. It has been argued that, because a city is a large, complex, and heterogeneous collection of people, personal relationships can no longer encompass all the people and resources needed for purposive action.[1] This perspective is strongly emphasized in the work of Wirth, but the emphasis here differs from Wirth and later studies in that it shows the influence of some urban groups upon the emergence of voluntary associations among others.

To obtain concessions from urban administration or to undertake programs of social action requires people to organize themselves with some formality to ensure that their business is conducted and that funds are assured despite their inability to devote their full time to the endeavor.

Though it is true that formal organizations proliferate in the urban milieu to cope with a variety of social, economic, and political problems, such organizations are not necessarily the most effective means for all groups to obtain their ends; neither is the emergence of formal organization a natural response to urban conditions. When we study the urban milieu, we are looking at an arena in which the actions of any one set of individuals is always conditioned by the actions and strategies of others. It is not sufficient to look at the behavior of a social group in isolation, because this behavior is affected by the strategies of other groups. The presence of organization among one group often relates to the needs and intentions that other groups have in the urban milieu. In particular, we will see that formal organization among the poor is more directly related to the need of other urban groups and organizations to reduce risks and uncertainties in their encounters with the poor than it is to the utility of such organization for the poor themselves. In this way the dependence relationships that develop between low-income groups or neighborhoods and economically superior groups and professional people become a factor in the disorganization and powerlessness of the poor.[2]

---

[1] Louis Wirth, "Urbanism as a Way of Life," in P. K. Hatt and J. J. Reiss, eds., *Cities and Society*, pp. 60-61. More recent studies suggest that the membership of voluntary associations in a complex society is equally prevalent in both urban and rural areas. See Nicholas Babchuk and Alan Booth, "Voluntary Association Membership: A Longitudinal Analysis," *American Sociological Review* 34, no. 1 (February 1969): 31-45.

[2] See Valentine's discussion of these points and his critique of those that isolate

Indeed the urban milieu sees a constant process of negotiation in which the different groups and organizations are attempting to impose upon it their definition of public order. This process is clearly seen in the attempts of outsiders to organize low-income neighborhoods and in the way these families are dealt with by the organizations with which they come into contact or of which they are members. The point is that the process is one of negotiation; however unevenly distributed are the resources, poor families also affect the actions and ideologies of other groups in these interactions. This is extending to the city the type of analysis that Strauss develops to understand behavior in a hospital setting.[3] He emphasizes the dynamic of action created within a hospital organization by the constant process of negotiation occurring between various individuals and groups who by their internal and external commitments (i.e., to a profession) have different perceptions of how a hospital should be run. At a very local level it also parallels Norton Long's emphasis on the process of defining the urban order that emerges from the commitments, strategies, and interplays of groups and organizations.[4]

We will proceed by identifying the extent that these families are exposed to the ideologies and pressures of outside groups and organizations and then relate these interactions to the types of formal organization that emerge among them.

Exposure to Organization

These families are not strangers to the more formally organized activities of urban life. They attend sports, films and frequent public health clinics and government and municipal

---

the conditions of the poor from their wider social and economic setting (Charles Valentine, *Culture and Poverty*, pp. 94-97, 141-153). Equally pertinent are the comments on disruptive effects on neighborhood organization of the strategies of outside patrons in Edward Spicer's "Patrons of the Poor," *Human Organization* 29, no. 1 (Spring 1970): 12-19.

[3] Anseln Strauss et al., *Psychiatric Ideologies and Institutions*, pp 12-17, 311-315.

[4] Norton E. Long. "The Local Community as an Ecology of Games," *American Journal of Sociology* 64 (November 1958): 251-261.

offices. Indeed, the limits on participation appear to be placed more by the nonavailability of organizations catering to these families than by their nonutilization of facilities. The extent and range of their participation is given by considering the following summary indices: fifty-six percent read newspapers at least once a month; 66 percent listen to the radio every day; of families with children in school, 94 percent of the mothers and 52 percent of the fathers have visited the school at least once in the past year; 49 percent of the males have visited at least one urban organization such as the municipality, the Social Welfare Institute, or health clinics in the last month; and 50 percent of the husbands and wives have been to shop in the center of the city at least once in the last month. In addition, the majority of husbands attend sports, and a third of them attend films regularly.[5] The level of participation of families differs in similar ways to that described in the last chapter with respect to their friendship and kinship interactions. Briefly, the poorer and older people participate less; self-employed participate less than the employed, and inhabitants of Planificada participate less than those of San Lorenzo. Migrant status is not clearly associated with participation, but in general those born in the city participate more than migrants.

Many government and voluntary associations that include low-income people in other parts of the world are not available in Guatemala. Social security exists but serves the small part of the labor force registered in large-scale enterprises. A very small minority of this sample of workers are in fact employed in enterprises that enroll their workers with the government social security. Labor unions are available to an even smaller fraction of the laboring population; political repression in the past and the restriction of unions to large-scale work settings have effectively limited membership.

About the only workers in these neighborhoods who are

[5] These aspects of participation are more fully dealt with in my chapter "The Social Organization of Low-Income Urban Families" in Richard Adams, *Crucifixion by Power*, pp. 479-514.

unionized are bus drivers, who belong to a union that provides financial guarantees in case of accident. Since the law imprisons a driver involved in any accident where damage to person or property is involved until financial guarantees are given, this union is an important vocational aid. Workers are, however, expected to obtain an identity card from the municipality for which they pay a tax of a dollar. This card serves as identification for jobs and as evidence of their payment of the municipal tax; their visit to obtain this card constitutes the major formal requirement that government makes on these families. They are not subject to any other taxation or rates; their formal contact with government is only a short visit that requires their signature and a few minutes wait in the modern municipal buildings.

The more frequent institutional relationships develop around public health clinics and schools. The municipality has instituted a free public health service in the different neighborhoods of the city where families can receive medical attention and pay a small sum for the medicines that are needed. Planificada possesses a health facility that is run jointly by the municipality and the university. The university uses it to train its medical students and as an opportunity to experiment and practice in the field of public health. Consequently, this clinic involves itself much more in community concerns than do the clinics located near San Lorenzo.

In Planificada, nurses, a public health inspector, and a social worker are frequent visitors to homes. The social worker is one of the main instigators and supports of the various community betterment organizations, while the clinic owns the building used by these organizations and by the various sporting organizations that also affiliate. The public health inspector is also active in protecting the neighborhood against possible health menaces and conducts campaigns against rabies, lack of sanitation, and other health hazards. The relationships that the clinic develops with its neighborhood become quite complex. It is frequented by a large proportion of the neighborhood, and the stability of personnel allow for some stable relationships to be developed.

These are often reinforced by involvement in betterment associations, football clubs, mothers clubs, and the visits of the clinic's personnel. Part of the medical training program required students to practice social medicine with selected families in the neighborhood, so that every year a different and large group of families came into relatively close contact with trainee professionals.

The involvement of outside agencies is not as extensive in the shantytown, but it is also considerable. Families use the public health clinic extensively and also visit the welfare agency located at the top of the neighborhood. Some families develop quite extensive relationships with the public health clinic involving material assistance to themselves and help in placing children in jobs and schools. The social worker in charge of the agency has an interest in neighborhood affairs, helping to sponsor a mothers' club and encouraging the local betterment committee; she often takes the advice of the committee members as to the needs of families within the neighborhood.

Though personal contacts are important in families' relationships with these various agencies, they still represent relatively formal environments. A visitor to the clinic or welfare agency first contacts the secretary who takes particulars or enters a note on the card that the family already has. There follows a long waiting period in rather drab waiting rooms with a crowd of other mothers, children, and some men. Eventually, the name is called and the client has a short interview with a nurse, doctor, or social worker.

The Exposure to Public Morality

Through their participation in more formally organized urban activities, these families are exposed to expectations of behavior that are different from those they meet in their informal relationships. The expectations they meet in public places take less account of the particularities of the individual; he is more likely to be treated as a case or type. This is a common experience for most urban dwellers, but it is a peculiarly difficult one for poor families because they have the characteristics that mark them as posing problems to the efficient running of urban organizations. They are poor, they dress badly, are ill-educated, and are suspected of vice and dishonesty. They are confronted with standards of behavior that often take little account of their expediencies. They are aware that they are defined in public eyes as wanting in desirable moral as well as material attributes. The attention that they receive from social workers and public health workers is itself an indication that they are defined as a group in need of public attention—a group that is not likely to conform to public standards without such attention. This is reinforced by the reception that I observed these families receiving at the hands of these professional workers, who, often with the best intention, would lecture the client in exaggeratedly simple terms. Afterward the family member would often comment to me that they were treated like fools.

Also, most of these families are avid listeners, and if literate, readers of the mass media. In this media they are constantly identified as belonging to the section of the urban population that is the repository of social problems. In the case of the shantytown population, this is particularly acute since one of the names for their neighborhood has already passed into the local vernacular as a synonym for slum. Most days on the radio, preachers and journalists inveigh against the vice and crime that is supposed to abound in this area and see San Lorenzo's eradication as a solution to all the city's problems. When applying for jobs or welfare assistance, San Lorenzo's inhabitants deliberately give a relative's address to obscure their shantytown residence.

Families also visit the schools in which their children are studying, and in these relationships, too, they are exposed to expectations of behavior that contrast with their own situation. Most visiting occurs on summons from the head teacher or an individual teacher and usually concerns the absenteeism of a child or his improper behavior. Most contacts these low-income families have with the schools are thus in situations in which their behavior is being negatively evaluated. Indeed, so strong is the presumption among families in both neighborhoods that this is the case that one response to the question of whether they visited their child's school was a negative reply, adding that the child did not cause any trouble.

The school passes on to the parent via the child a list of requirements concerning equipment and dress, and parents are also expected to cooperate in special events and festivals. The teachers are aware of the social conditions of the families in these neighborhoods, and in the personal interviews I had with them were able to distinguish quite accurately the varying social circumstances of the children. Sample teacher reactions were "well, it's understandable, he apparently comes from that shantytown down the road," or "well, his mother is separated and cannot look after him properly, so he and his brothers are always a lot of trouble."

It is not that these teachers are insensitive to the difficulties poor families face, but they do not have the resources to cope adequately with these problems. They have an interest in good performance and a receptive clientele, but the facilities and number of teachers available make it impossible to meet all the educational demands that could potentially come from either neighborhood. Though they deplore it, teachers find that low enrollments and a very high absentee rate make their task more feasible and lowers the failure rate at the end of the year. They require from the children defined and quite rigid standards of behavior, and teachers communicate such expectations to the parents.

The reactions that these families meet from public agencies are indeed one of the few bases of common identification they possess. This is especially true of the shantytown and is one factor accounting for the higher levels of interest these families show in neighborhood organization. They feel themselves segregated and looked down upon, and this, in some of the situations described later, serves as a basis for unity in opposition to other urban segments. However, the processes we have been describing earlier entail that in most situations families are permeated by public morality and cannot use their social isolation to buffer themselves from its dictates. By public morality I mean those general tenets of behavior designed to regulate expected behavior among strangers and that make no allowance for individual particularities. Since people are not commited locally and, instead, maintain dispersed relationships throughout the city, they do not wish to be identified with their neighbors and thus segregated from their other contacts. Indeed, it is the particular difficulty of poor families in most urban situations that they inevitably maintain two conflicting positions with respect to public morality. On the one hand they are adjudged wanting as a subgroup within the city, but on the other they are themselves participating members in city life who use public morality to adjudge others and to secure their own environment. This is illustrated in the relationships these families maintain with the police and with their churches.

Police and Churches

In Planificada there is a police station and a municipal court attached. Patrols operate out of this station, and it is also extensively used by families as a place to bring marital disputes, property conflicts, and complaints about crimes. The police station and its court are local institutions that are seen as having positive as well as negative functions by the local inhabitants. For example, it frequently happened during the field work that women who were separated from their husbands, or in the process of being abandoned by them, came to the court to ask the magistrate the procedure for obtaining compensation or maintainence payment. Other families used the court when summarily ejected from their rented accommodations by their landlord. The relation of the police with the neighborhood is less apparent in San Lorenzo. There is no police post in the neighborhood, and for long the police did not patrol the streets. However, the United States Agency for International Development devised, in cooperation with the Guatemalan police, a plan for modern police service for the city and took San Lorenzo and its zone as a pilot project.[6] Police began to appear in the streets, usually in pairs, and there was talk of a small post being erected in the neighborhood. The police are treated with more overt suspicion in the shantytown than in the legal neighborhood. Partly, this resulted from the presence of illegal liquor stills and the belief that the police were looking for these and other illegal activities. However, much of the suspicion arises because families think themselves looked down upon by the police. Many remark on the police going about in pairs, saying that it is because the police regard everyone in the neighborhood as thieves or prostitutes. Even in San Lorenzo, however, families are ambivalent about the police; policemen are likely to live in these neighborhoods and the police career is one of the most common occupations among the families we are studying. There are for example at least twelve policemen living in San Lorenzo. These families are quite familiar with the police as private individuals, and many, if not themselves policemen are related to a policeman.

Families in both neighborhoods expect the police to provide for their safety and that of their possessions. It is a constant complaint among older inhabitants of the shantytown that the police are not as efficient as they had been in the days of the dictator Ubico, when the police made a round of every house and every street, checking on doors and making sure that passers-by had legitimate business. Many heads of family have been robbed or assaulted in the street. Such incidents are common topics of gossip, and, since in both neighborhoods

[6] The Agency for International Development is a United States agency responsible to the State Department that has a number of locally based units charged with examining and suggesting projects requiring development aid from the United States. There is a large AID office in Guatemala, most of whose activities are concentrated in rural development and education. However, in recent years AID has become more interested in urban problems; also the frequent publicity its projects receive in the local press makes it visible to city families of the kind we are describing, who regard it as a possible source of aid. The agency, though recognized to be North American, is in fact regarded as almost a normal component of the Guatemalan government.

families left or returned to their homes in darkness and through ill-lit streets, most feel in need of protection.

In Planificada many fathers will not permit their daughters to go out alone at night because of the condition of the streets and the fear of their being molested. In these respects, families stand in a difficult position vis-à-vis the question of law and order. Their journeys across the city, often into unfamiliar territory, and the uncertainty of relationships within their own neighborhoods make them regard their environment as perilous. For these reasons, they positively evaluate the police or army's role in maintaining law and order. At the same time their own relations with the police are difficult and formal, and they perceive themselves as having characteristics that are negatively evaluated by the police forces.

The relationship of the police to families is, in fact, a difficult one. The amount of mobility within the neighborhoods and within the police force mean that it is difficult for stable and personal relationships to develop between police and neighborhood inhabitants. This is a contributing factor to the apparent uneasiness of their relationships. The police are often summoned by families in both neighborhoods to arbitrate family quarrels, settle boundary disputes between neighbors, and the like. Yet their flexibility in settling these disputes is constrained by the circumstance that they cannot be sure that any informal settlement will be respected by the people concerned. A dissatisfied neighbor or spouse might not accept the arbitration of the police or magistrate and appeal back to the police post or to higher police authorities. This uncertainty constrains the police, and it is evident that though reluctant to take legal action in the petty squabbles to which they are called, they often did so as the safest course. The case of Carmen illustrates the complexity of this situation:

While waiting for the arrival of a priest to bless the new cooperative building, co-op members were assailed by the women of the Catholic Hermanidad who were angered that their priest was not being used. The priest arrived and was almost assaulted by the women and stones were thrown. The police were summoned and talked to both parties, taking the attitude that the best solution was to quiet them down without taking further action. This outraged some members of the co-op; they went to the local police station and reported that the police had not acted correctly and that an important priest had been insulted. Consequently, a police car was sent, and Carmen and another woman were arrested; but on arrival at the police station it was found that the president of the co-op was not prepared to make charges because of the delicate situation he was in personally. The women were released. However, other co-op members reported the whole incident to the lawyers attached to the central co-operative movement who got in touch with higher police authorities who agreed that some action should have been taken. The local police chief was by this time exasperated and worried, and, to culminate the affair, the priest finally and angrily told the police that someone in his position could not consider bringing charges.

The point is that the police were reacting in a way similar to police forces everywhere when confronted by situations that they do not know and where the relationships are not sufficiently cohesive and stable to ensure that informal settlements are respected.[7] Being exposed to legal action and police intervention is thus a common experience for families.

An important consequence of seeing people like themselves

[7] Some of the literature on the relationship of the policeman to his community has stressed the discretionary role he plays as "peacekeeping" officer, so that his actions when faced by any given transgression are not entirely predictable. Banton's discussion of the differences between policemen in Britain and the United States is particularly relevant, since he emphasizes the importance of the density of local relations to a policeman's actions (Michael Banton, *The Policeman in the Community*, pp. 214-242). However, the emphasis that I give follows that of Chatterton, who sees police action as predictable if we take into account factors such as the stability of relationships between policemen and their communities and the likelihood that any action will "feed back" to his superiors. Thus, police who feel themselves in a strange situation do not take the chance of there being negative feedback and cover themselves by taking certain types of formal action. See Michael Chatterton, "Crimes of Violence and the Police."

being treated formally and negatively by the police, but at the same time valuing the protection afforded by law and order is an acceptance of the police's view of neighborhoods like San Lorenzo and parts of Planificada. However, this view is thought to apply to others in their neighborhood and not to themselves. I would often discuss the police and newspaper view of the shantytown with its inhabitants and tell them that from my own experience this view was unjustified. On every occasion, the person I was talking with replied saying that although he and some of his neighbors and friends were honest and hard workers, there were other sections of the neighborhood that were full of thieves, criminals, and prostitutes.

The reaction of the police who live in the neighborhood is interesting in this respect. Those sampled, as might be expected, came out most strongly for law and order and a return to the discipline of authoritarian rule. They cited the lawlessness of people within the neighborhood as examples of the decline of public morality, but were careful to add that their own presence in the neighborhood was solely the result of poverty and the expense of maintaining a large family. In these discussions they were unable to generalize their own condition to that of other families in the neighborhood.

The impact of religion is similar, because the churches, like the police, are working in urban situations where stable and close-knit relationships between them and their clients are absent, and thus it becomes difficult to take particular account of the conditions under which people live. The Protestant churches originate from the work of missionaries and emphasize a morality that deliberately rejects the particular conditions of life under which these families live.[8] It is an imposed morality and does not arise from the prevailing social and economic relationships of the environment.

In formal doctrine, the various sects emphasize an overriding

[8] A fuller discussion of Protestantism, as well as Catholicism, is given in my article "Protestant Groups and Coping with Urban Life in Guatemala City," *American Journal of Sociology* 73, no. 6 (May 1968): 753-767.

concern with salvation through leading a life without sin. Sin is usually described in the concrete forms of alcohol, smoking, gambling, dishonesty, and separation from spouse and children. Poverty is seen as a condition that, while regrettable, is a help rather than a hindrance to leading a normal life. And none of these churches makes any great point of the value of material or even educational self-advancement.

In some of these churches, their view of the proper life includes an extensive detailing of personal deportment, courtesy, table manners, and the like. These are the churches— the Mormons, Jehovah's Witnesses, and Seventh Day Adventists —that are most under United States influence and have North American ministers or helpers. Most of the religious propaganda used by the churches originates from the United States, and the concept of the "good church member" closely resembles the American model.

Though many of these doctrines assist poor families to cope with urban life, they are difficult to maintain in practice. Under the unstable conditions of Guatemala, Protestant families are not notably more successful than others. For some, making a living and the effort they have to contribute to this end become incompatible with remaining an active church member. Very poor people find it difficult to make any financial contributions or even to provide the clothes and hospitality that active Protestantism requires. It is also part of the activities of the churches to visit fellow Protestants elsewhere in the city, and though this costs relatively little, it is an important item in the expenses of very poor families.

At the other extreme, richer families find themselves called upon to make larger contributions than most, and these contributions, together with time expended, often detract from a successful business or other social contacts and prove a sufficient discouragement.

In general, the conditions under which these families live— overcrowded housing, unhealthy conditions, and severe economic fluctuations—make it difficult to maintain a "pure" morality. For example, one of the most ardent Protestants in San Lorenzo, Lisandro, has periods when he goes on drinking bouts and later spends up to two weeks repenting in his home. Two other Protestants in San Lorenzo, in the two years I knew them, left their wives, returned to them, and left them again.

Protestant morality also has its impact on Catholics, who compose 75 percent of families in the two neighborhoods. Protestant services are broadcast to the neighborhoods over loud speakers, and Protestants are deliberately public in expounding their morality to others. Catholics are aware of the dictates of this morality and, though not agreeing with some of its specific mandates such as the prohibitions on drinking and dancing, often refer uneasily to the Protestant morality as a good one. Catholics are more exposed to Protestant morality because their own Church membership is often a personal act of devotion not involving a stable congregation. This instability makes the Catholic church less able to attend to the poor, and the reforming efforts of the church also emphasize the short-comings of these families. Acting through local Catholic Hermanidades and through messages in the churches, local priests inveigh against the vice that alledgedly resides among the overcrowded city neighborhoods.

The local priest of San Lorenzo is a case in point. His main contact with the neighborhood is the Hermanidad. They keep him informed of happenings in the neighborhood and he, in turn, tells them of his desires for neighborhood organization. But the communication is affected by the Hermanidad's desire to show itself as an important element of stability in the midst of vice and corruption and by the priest's readiness to accept this version because it allows him to categorize the many families who are not churchgoers. He conducts tours of the neighborhood for visiting church and secular dignitaries; but knowing only a small number of families, he stops at their homes, extols their virtues, and dramatically interrogates them on the vice that surrounds them.

This priest believes that urban slum neighborhoods are a

direct cause of vice and produce an unhealthy family atmo-
sphere. He sees the solution to the problem as a return to the
stabler environment of the countryside and, failing that, the
establishment of a new neighborhood at a distance from the
city where there is plenty of space and families can farm. He is
actively engaged in such a project, and he told me in an interview that the move to rural surroundings is necessary because
under urban conditions the influence of the church must necessarily be weak. To bolster his case, the priest emphasizes the
immorality of the shantytown and regards those who wish to
stay there as sinful and perverse. The priest has a city-wide
reputation as a radical reformer who spends time with poor
people and is presented as such in the news media and through
his own daily radio broadcast.

Families in the neighborhood are directly exposed to concrete expectations of their behavior. They are identified as
people living immoral lives, and they are offered as a solution
the abandonment of the city. Of course, some of these families
recognize that the priest is using this view of morality to further
his own interests, and I have tape recordings of some of the
more radical members of San Lorenzo inveighing against priests
and their desires to control secular life. However, religion,
whether Protestant or Catholic, is an important reference point
for most families, and to many of them it provides the relationships they need to cope with urban life. So, in this field also,
there is pressure upon them to accept a morality they cannot
easily sustain under urban conditions.

We can note in concluding this section that the situation of
these families with respect to public moralities is more exposed
than that of a black community in the United States.[9] These
latter have, at least, their color and minority cohesion to defend
themselves against the mandates of an externally imposed
public morality. In the Guatemalan situation, low-income
families are highly articulated to other social groups and do not

[9] Contrast Ulf Hannerz, *Soulside*, pp. 177-200. See also Gerald Suttles, *The Social
Order of the Slum*, pp. 124-130.

know each other well enough to consistently apply a personalistic morality that takes account of their own conditions as well as each other's particularities. A personalistic morality is here defined as one that takes account of the qualities of an individual, so that judgment is based upon knowing the conditions under which he acts and the consistency of his behavior. A criminal is not condemned by a personalistic morality if his behavior does not disrupt interaction and if it is in accord with the particular circumstances of his life.[10]

The Dynamic of Imposing External Moralities

Families are thus exposed to moralities that they find difficult to sustain but that they cannot easily avoid through sustaining an alternative morality more suited to local conditions. Part of the problem arises because the external agents who espouse these moralities are themselves exposed to pressures that make them actively intervene in the lives of the poor. The priest and the police have to account for their actions to a wider public and to their superiors, and they justify their existence by emphasizing the problems these families create.

This argument can be stated more generally to define the involvement we can expect from outside agencies in the organization of low-income neighborhoods. When resources are scarce and there are no easy means for differentiating the claims of clients, public and private agencies are likely to play an especially active part in the social organization of low-income families. It is a part that is engendered both by their perceptions of what these families need and by the pressures on the people within these organizations to account for their position. They must actively manage the environment of their clients to obtain a demand upon their services that they can deal with and that allows them to visibly justify their work to others. This interest in managing the environment of the poor extends to others such as politicians who need support but have neither the resources

[10]Ibid. pp. 227-233.

nor the desire to meet the range of potential demands. This management takes the form of concrete attempts to formally organize neighborhoods; the attempts at organization communicate and elicit opinions, values, and techniques that become an important, if often dysfunctional, part of the way poor people cope with their environment.

To explore these propositions we will first look at the activities of the political administration and proceed to those of the professionals working with public health and the social service. The important point to remember is that these neighborhoods are closely linked to urban organizations and external social groups; their articulation is one of the factors that characterizes the position of poor people who live in cities.

The public authority that maintains closest links with both neighborhoods is the municipality, through its system of local mayors. These officials—known as *alcalde auxiliares*—are appointed by the city mayor, usually from people who have resided in or have close contact with the area in question. Each zone of the city thus has its own mayor whose major responsibility within the muncipal system of government is to act as a liaison between the local neighborhoods and the central administration. The local mayor acts as an intermediary, explaining municipal policy to local areas and passing back local complaints and projects. He also has some independent authority in settling minor disputes, arranging local festivals, and maintaining such municipal property as parks and meeting halls. Chiefly, however, he acts as a kind of local ombudsman and is assisted by a committee made up of representatives from each neighborhood. The local mayor encourages the work of local betterment committees, coordinates their activities, and lends his prestige to their search for funds and other support. The local mayor is the best-known representative of urban government in both neighborhoods, and the relationship that families maintained with him is often their only relationship with that government.

The local mayor is basically the bottom rung of the urban

administration, and successful performance in that role leads to promotion in the hierarchy or, if unsuccessful, to dismissal. The local mayor's position is consequently insecure and partly depends on the way he handles his superiors' instructions. He is also a local representative, and to the extent that he can marshal local support, he can use it as a bargaining position for his own, as well as his community's, aspirations. Aspiring candidates to the city mayoralty make a point of cultivating local mayors and of placing loyal supporters in these positions. The local mayor thus has an interest in actively developing relationships within neighborhoods and in managing these neighborhoods so that he can both present a local base of support and ensure a degree of compliance with edicts from his superiors.

In the following chapters, we will see many instances of the balancing acts performed by the local mayor of San Lorenzo, Carlos, as he attempts to keep the neighborhood tied to his own interests and maintains the necessary compliance with the instructions of his superiors, whose interests are often opposed to the desires of neighborhood inhabitants. This position makes him a strong proponent of the ideology of community self-help. He undoubtedly believes in it quite sincerely, but his belief is reinforced because community organization allows him to generate support and to obtain some compliance with directives from above, while acting as a filter to reduce the demands to those he can satisfy.

This strategy was strikingly illustrated in a meeting that he summoned when a new betterment committee for San Lorenzo was to be elected. Many neighbors intervened in the meeting to say that they would prefer to rely directly on the municipality and that they saw no point in having a betterment committee that only extracted funds from families and gave nothing in return. These speakers appealed to some of the municipal officers present to give direct help by sending construction workers and engineers. The local mayor then intervened to criticize these suggestions, pointing out that unless neighbors organized themselves they could expect nothing from the municipality. He made a great point of stressing that the municipality was inundated with requests from neighborhoods the city over, and that consequently inhabitants of an illegal neighborhood could not expect to get any help.

This encounter is interesting because not only does it show the local mayor stressing community self-help, but it also shows him passing on a defined public morality. Once again these families are publicly identified as being outside the recognized organization of the city; to obtain recognition they must, by their own efforts, show themselves capable of organization. The legitimacy of these families is thus questioned: it must be achieved and is not innate by reason of their citizenship. In numerous small instances, public officials put across this ideology in their relationships with these families.

The people themselves recognized, and to some degree accepted, this definition of themselves. The local mayor, for example, got widespread applause for his speech. When composing delegations, men in both San Lorenzo and Planificada are quite explicit in wanting to include professional or other high-status individuals. Pepe gave me this account of a projected delegation.

It would be better to include yourself, the *alcalde auxiliar*, a priest, and one of the lawyers [specific name given of person Pepe had met recently at a meeting]. Then we would get some attention. Otherwise it's no good and we would wait in the mayor's anteroom and be treated as nobodies. But with professional people it's different; then they show respect and something is done—that's how it is in Guatemala.

In this respect, the situation of these families with regard to the various political parties that compete for their votes is quite similar. None of the political parties, with the recent exception of the Christian Democrats, maintains a permanent organization for the mobilization of low-income people.[11] Before election

[11] At this time, there was an officially constituted Christian Democrat party in Gautemala that took part in the elections of 1970. However, this party operates through a series of decentralized organizations charged with such matters as peasant organization, the cooperative movement, labor unions, etc. These organizations and the party maintain that there is no formal connection between them, and this

time, the middle- and upper-status groups that compose the parties' ruling organization establish relationships with leaders of local neighborhoods throughout the city. These are approached, as we have seen, through their work place or through kinship, religion, or common regional origin. These local leaders are then expected to establish committees in their neighborhoods on behalf of the political interest group, recruiting in the neighborhoods through their own personal ties.

Here again, low-income families are managed from the outside. Their political demands are not self-created and self-organized but are injected into their situation by the activity of a plethora of political groups originating outside the neighborhoods. The political organization imposed upon the neighborhoods is highly formal. Committees are rapidly set up with officers such as president, vice-president, treasurer, secretary, propaganda secretary, and disputes secretary. Membership lists are opened, and often party cards are issued. Occasional meetings are held to hear speakers brought in from the outside.

The form of organization enables the political parties to account for their activities on a city-wide basis and makes the creation of a city-wide organization feasible in the absence of full-time organizing staff. It is not, however, the basis for concerted political action at the level of low-income neighborhoods. To justify themselves to the party hierarchy and to enable them to make claims on it in case of victory, local organizations recruit mechanically, without trying to convince the people of the justice of their cause. Multiple memberships in parties are tolerated, and the whole operation is regarded as a recurrent game played between low-income people and urban middle- and upper-status groups. One side attempts to extract as much as possible for nominal support, and the other promises

---

allowed the various organizations to pursue their work even during periods when politics was prohibited by martial law. This decentralization is however, more than a political strategy, and some of these organizations such as the Central de Servicios and MONAP saw themselves as public welfare organizations that often developed strategies not necessarily in accord with the interests of the party.

and gives just as little, while still gaining that support. In these relationships, the ideological content is pragmatism. Such practices serve to reinforce the widespread belief in the instrumentality of political allegiance.

Professionals and Their Clients

In the case of the professional workers in contact with these neighborhoods—the health and social welfare personnel—they, too, are in the position of finding ways to justify their role, but, at the same time, to reduce the demands made upon them. Their task is not only to give defined services but also to make their activities accountable to themselves, the sponsoring authorities, and the public with whom they are in contact.

This is a particularly important task in Guatemala, where the time and resources available to these agencies make even the performance of simple services appear to be a socially worthless enterprise. The clinics treat people with a variety of medical problems aggravated by malnutrition and unsanitary living conditions. The treatments required are usually either too expensive or are futile within the social context of the patient (e. g., it is impossible to eat clean food in the conditions of either San Lorenzo or Planificada). Consequently, the clinics give ameliorative treatment through injections of antibiotics and refer patients to hospitals in serious cases. They help, of course, in anticipating illness and, especially in the case of children, make very positive contributions to the health of the community. Yet, for our purposes, the interesting feature of their work is that it shows few visible returns to those who receive its services.

A person comes for a course of injections when he is already seriously ill, and, given his living conditions, it is unlikely that treatment produces lasting positive results. Under these circumstances, many families turn to folk remedies and folk curers— the *curanderos* of rural Guatemala who have migrated to the city with their clients. These folk remedies to illness are used interchangeably by low-income families with the medical services of the clinics. Families do not deny the efficiacy of modern medicine but complain of poor treatment in clinics and the expense of medicine. Few of the clients justify the work of the clinics, and the professionals rarely see the benefits of their work. In contrast, the work of the hospitals is more dramatic and more visible. Especially in Planificada, clinics pay a lot of attention to organizing neighborhoods in ways that provide justification for their work. Different forms of health campaigns and community betterment services are stressed alongside the routine work of the clinic. From these are derived stable relationships with the neighborhood and statistical accounts that serve to justify the record of the clinic.

The social work agencies face similar problems, given the extent of poverty and social problems. They, too, are drawn into the task of managing the neighborhoods so that they are faced with a selective demand that can be met from their resources. They need a clientele, but one that they can help. The involvement of the personnel of these agencies in neighborhood organization becomes for them a necessary part of their job, because it enables them to reduce demand by encouraging self-help projects and provides formal leaders, who help to select and channel the remaining requests. Consequently, they are in a position to encourage people to use their services and thus justify their work to themselves, to their clients, and to their superiors.

It was clear that the personnel of the agencies serving the two neighborhoods desired to serve as the main channels for communicating social problems and grievances to government authorities. They look with suspicion at any other organization that sought to mediate between the neighborhood and the different urban organizations, asking neighborhood leaders to bring their problems directly to them. This desire to serve as a unique channel of communication is understandable in terms of the ideologies and strategies of professionals working in urban situations anywhere. In Guatemala, these are given a sharper edge by a definite pressure from the governmental social welfare institute for local agencies to provide concrete evidence of its community betterment work.

Local social workers are expected to provide the names of responsible community leaders and the projects being under-taken locally to the government institute, and courses for these leaders are arranged. Some people within the shantytown regard this practice as a form of governmental control over their activities, whereas the agencies interpret it as encouragement to community self-help and responsible community leadership.

As part of its training program, the Government School of Social Work also attaches trainee social workers to neighbor-hoods throughout the city. Both Planificada and San Lorenzo have such trainees working every year. Working in close liaison with the local welfare agencies, the task of such trainees is to promote community organization through encouraging such activities as sporting clubs, mothers' clubs, and community betterment work organized by a community betterment com-mittee. These trainees spend a considerable amount of time in the two neighborhoods and maintain frequent and often close relationships with families in both neighborhoods. They thus provide further relationships connecting families in the neighborhood with the professional organizations in the city, and their work of organization complements that of the welfare agencies.

The Content of Communication

Social workers, both trainees and professionals, are not only concerned that neighborhoods organize themselves, but also that they organize themselves in the right way. They are active in speaking with and encouraging individual families, and they hold meetings and courses designed to point out the advantages of community self-organization. These professionals emphasize that families should do the work of organization themselves and should not be directed in a paternalistic manner. But this entails the professionals insuring that families adopt reasonably democratic procedures with elections, office holding, accounting systems, and periodic referendums.

To convey the sense of the communication occurring, we can look at the following description of a course given by the government social service institute to selected leaders drawn from the shantytown communities of the city. Our particular shantytown—San Lorenzo—had between four and six representatives attending the course, which took place in the offices of the official School of Social Administration.

There was a crowd of about a hundred people from the various shantytowns of the city. The participants received a lecture by one of the school's resident social workers, outlining the requirements of democratic leadership, which stressed the need to allow participation, to encourage discussion, and to put matters to the vote. After a period for refreshments, the social-work trainees presented a sociodrama depicting a meeting directed by an authoritarian leader, where the leader spoke most of the time and prevented anyone from disagreeing with him. It was presented partly as a satire and evoked considerable amusement. The participation of the shantytown audience was requested by asking them to comment on the sociodrama and the lecture. Individuals rose to their feet, identifying themselves by name and neighborhood. Most of the comments were praise of the course, and straight repetition of some of the points made earlier, especially concerning the need to encourage participation and to let others speak. The representatives from San Lorenzo seemed to know those from other neighborhoods, and there was much public handshaking and loud greetings. Each of the San Lorenzo representatives got up to make a point—even though it had usually been made before.

Two days later at a second meeting, a lecture was presented on the task of organizing a committee. This was a simple outline of the formal procedures that were necessary, such as appointing officers of various types—president, vice-president, treasurer, secretary, and various committeemen with different responsibilities. Again, the need for democratic participation and vote taking was stressed, as well as the need to define responsibilities clearly. This talk was followed by a sociodrama of a democratic meeting in which each person made his point slowly, clearly, and without animosity; everyone waited until a speaker had finished. Votes were taken at appropriate points.

At this meeting there appeared to be more restlessness among the participants than at the first, though there was about the same amount of audience participation, again remaking in a reasonably accurate way the points made in the course. As I accompanied the representatives from San Lorenzo out of the course, one member commented that the talk had been a word-for-word imitation of the form of meeting described in the United States Information Service booklet that was issued for community organization. Others members concurred and said that this was an example of the influence of propaganda.

At the third meeting, the talk was more specifically on the work of a betterment committee: how to draw up an agenda, the kinds of issues that should be put on it and the scope of the committee. Less participation was encouraged, but at this meeting some of the audience questions were more critical in tone. Some questions were practical, concerning the laws that were involved with committee work and how to get money for the work. The questions still emphasized the need for democratic participation, but some questioners were not satisfied when they failed to get concrete answers to their practical inquiries and repeated their questions. Then followed a film that was about thirty years old, issued by the United States Information Service, which depicted community problems of an industrial town of the United States. The U.S. town had a gigantic steel mill and a powerful labor union. The union leader, whose efforts at community organization were the subject of the film, had a fairly luxurious house and his major problem was a road-safety campaign. The representatives from San Lorenzo appeared happy with the film, their chief comment being that it was enjoyable.

At the next meeting, a rural social worker gave a lecture on how to organize a community project—first investigate, then estimate the resources needed, find out where they could be obtained, estimate whether a long- or short-term project, enlist community cooperation, and, finally, evaluate its success and decide where to go next. Again there was considerable audience participation, with more critical comment than in the previous meeting. These comments centered around the need for more concrete information about how to get money and resources and the need to take political considerations into account. Various members of the audience pointed out that, under Guatemalan conditions, politics constantly interfered in community projects. The social worker made a strong plea for committees to be nonpolitical, since politics confused and divided people. Some shantytown dwellers thought this unrealistic, while others echoed the social worker's words. The representatives of San Lorenzo made a plea for nonpolitical committees; these pleas were followed by bursts of applause.

The discussion continued during the break, with the San Lorenzo representatives citing examples of how their involvement with politics and political figures had interfered with community reorganization. After the break, the audience was invited to tell about their experiences in organizing projects. One man told of his lack of support in getting a sports field going. Various shantytown representatives got up to say that unless he got support he should give up the project because he should not have a one-man project. The San Lorenzo representatives then told of their community development achievements—notably the drainage system. The account was highly positive and neglected to mention the difficulties this project had encountered. They were questioned by other representatives about turnover in the committee—whether, for example, there were periodic elections—and how the money was handled. The San Lorenzo people stressed that there had been frequent elections and that the committee never handled the money but left this to someone outside the committee to avoid suspicion of their motives. The account was greeted with wide-spread applause and was publicly approved by the social workers.

The final meeting of the course was started with a speech on human relations by one of the school's staff. The social worker stressed the need to be cheerful and to greet people with a smile, to recognize differences in peoples' social backgrounds, aspirations, interests, beliefs, customs, and abilities. Leaders should behave with tact, always say thank you, please, be impartial, and use people's names when addressing them. Mimeographed sheets were distributed that amplified the above points and laid down common rules of courtesy. Audience response appeared favorable, though there were few questions.

The course closed with a vote of thanks from the floor—with representatives from each colonia rising continuously to compliment the school, to say that they would like more courses, and to wish for more contact between leaders of the different neighborhoods. The director of the school replied, picking up some of these themes and suggesting that neighborhoods should invite each other to their fiestas or inaugurations, exchange impressions, and stimulate each other's activity. Diplomas were issued to those who had been consistent attenders, and each gave a short speech of thanks.

This extended account has necessarily condensed the verbal content and interactions of the course, but it attempts to convey the points made and the audience reaction without violating the contextual circumstances. The professional ideologies presented are those that inform the training of Guatemalan social and health workers and were repeated on the many occasions when I observed them interacting within the neighborhood context. They are not presented here to indicate their inappropriateness or their shortcomings; from many viewpoints they might be deemed quite unexceptional. Their presentation indicates the kinds of ideologies that impinge upon neighborhood families as they seek to organize themselves. These are the viewpoints they are exposed to in community betterment projects, cooperative projects, sporting clubs and mothers clubs; they are exposed to them whether the participating professional is a government worker or one employed by a private organization.

Certain characteristics of these ideological perspectives will figure prominently in our subsequent discussion of the process of community organization. These professional ideologies stress formal organization; they require these families to pursue formal democratic procedures, the appointment of officers to fill posts that have specified responsibilities, and the planning of change with division of labor and with specified sequences of development. Moreover, they put heavy stress on consensus: neighbors must agree on the project, every effort is to be made to explain it to them, there must be periodic reelections, and the interaction style of leaders is one to promote good feeling through management of human relations.

This ideology suits the practical concerns of social workers in neighborhood contexts by providing visible community organization that selectively channels demands to the agencies. However, it is an ideology that to a large extent is foreign to the concerns of neighborhood families. It was clear during the course that participants were concerned with practical matters such as where to get money and what to do about politics. Their reaction to the ideology is to listen to it but not to fully comprehend its significance; in their questions, participants often parrot a new language. Their own experiences—and this is certainly the case with the San Lorenzo representatives—are fitted to the ideology rather than letting the complexity of those experiences refine the ideology. To the participants, the course did appear as a good thing, the kind of experience to which neighborhood leaders should be exposed. It was seen almost as a *rite de passage*—a qualification for neighborhood leadership—and many of the representatives cited the course in subsequent neighborhood meetings as evidence that they had the credentials for leadership.

Because of their social characteristics, families in the neighborhood do not easily operate according to formal criteria; in undertaking action they prefer to rely on personal relationships. Their relationship with social workers and outside agencies thus takes on the aspect of a constant negotiation in which the participants' definition of the exigencies of the situation is being modified by and is modifying the professional ideology of community action.

This process is to be an important element in the later account of the attempts of low-income families to organize themselves, because they are particularly susceptible to ideologies coming from outside their communities. Neighbors do not know enough about each other nor are they bound by constant interactions, so there is no informal guide to the kinds of people or the kinds of procedures suitable to achieve the neighborhood's purposes. The formal procedures suggested by the professionals are thus seen by these families as useful guides.

The Emergence of Formal Organization

We have been observing two processes at work among these families. One is their further segmentation by being exposed to moralities that make their common identification both difficult and undesirable; the other is the active presence of outside groups and agencies interested in organizing these families to reduce the risks and uncertainties in their own environments. On both counts, we can expect formal organization to emerge among these families. On the one hand, it provides standardized procedures and formal roles that reduce the insecurity of acting with others who are adjudged to be untrustworthy and are, anyway, comparative strangers.[12] On the other hand, formal organization is the type that best suits the interests of outside groups because it is predictable and easily made accountable. The one circumstance that has not emerged from our discussion is whether such organization does respect the needs of these families by allowing them to manipulate their urban environment in their own, not in others' interests.

[12]Compare Gerald Suttles, *The Social Order of the Slum*, pp. 175-188.

In both low-income neighborhoods there is a considerable amount of formal organization catering for the special interests of the families. At first sight, the number and range of these associations would put to shame the most community-conscious North American middle-class suburb. There are the agencies of city-wide organizations such as the local churches, the clinics, local municipal and judicial offices, social welfare agencies, and schools. However, it is the voluntary associations that are of interest to us, and in both neighborhoods there are community betterment associations that meet regularly and discuss projects of neighborhood improvement and sponsor social events. In addition, there are sporting associations, of which the most important are the football clubs, but which also include basketball and other athletics. There are mothers' clubs, where wives meet for sewing and cookery classes or just sit and chat. Consumer cooperatives exist in both neighborhoods and are run by the families themselves; there is one small producer's cooperative in Planificada. Also in Planificada is a mutual benefit association providing insurance in case of illness or death; one of these is in process of formation in San Lorenzo. Both Protestant and Catholic churches have attached to them several associations of wives, adolescents, and husbands that, apart from religious functions, also organize social and recreational events. In San Lorenzo, there are at least three formally established committees supporting established national political parties, and I obtained the names of two such formally organized committees in Planificada from the offices of one of the major national political parties. Separable from all these activities and also formal in their constitution are several groups of young men who come together to form a musical combine and an entertainment show. These hire themselves out both inside and outside the neighborhoods for dances and festivals.

Despite their number and impressive range, these various associations are often not well attended and function less than perfectly. They enable us, however, to explore directly the relation between the emergence of formally organized voluntary associations and the interests of external groups. We will first look at the betterment associations which serve the evident and pressing needs of the population.

In both Planificada and San Lorenzo the setting up of formal betterment associations directly relates to the immediate pressures on the neighborhoods to negotiate with external agencies.[13] The issues in Planificada were those of negotiating with the city administration and with the administration of a nearby town over the provision of urban facilities for the neighborhood. These had long been pressing problems for the inhabitants and had been handled by deputations and informal pressures on both administrations, since it was unclear under whose jurisdiction Planificada fell. With the establishment of a university and municipal clinic in Planificada, the issue came to a head. The clinic became interested in obtaining a new and well-equipped building and discovered that nothing could be done until the issue of jurisdiction was resolved. The establishment of the first formally organized betterment committee came at the instigation of the professionals in the clinic who saw that such a committee was necessary to negotiate with the two municipal authorities.The city administration had already indicated that it was prepared to recognize formally constituted committees of neighbors as a means of local self-improvement and took the position that negotiation with such committees was the correct procedure. When delegations from local areas come to the municipality they are often asked to show their formal credentials—an identification card with photograph that states their position on the local committee.

In San Lorenzo this process is even sharper; since its conception, informally organized groups of neighbors have cooperated

[13] Contrast Stinchcombe's discussion of the social environment of organizations and his stress on the accessibility of a primary group as a variable in the level of their organization (Arthur Stinchcombe, "Social Structure and Organizations," in J. G. March, ed., *Handbook of Organizations*, pp. 142-193). The more homogeneous a group in terms of its culture or relationships, the more likely it is to develop its own organizations (ibid., pp. 184-191).

to improve the community. The establishment of a formally organized betterment association came when, in the course of their informal efforts, they contacted a local politician and, through him, obtained access to the Agency for International Development. The agency did not insist on formal organization to handle the work and the material they provided; but both agency officials and the local politician made it clear to neighbors that such organization would guarantee success of the project and the possibility of further help. Both these outside agents were quite explicit in stating that such formally organized committees made their own work easier. It provided the agency with formalized accounting and other procedures that could be incorporated into the agency's own reports, and it gave the local politician—the local mayor—a means to visibly organize the neighborhood and reduce his own problems of maintaining order.

The present argument becomes stronger if we relate the level of formality of ongoing voluntary associations to the closeness of their link with external agencies. In this respect, it is less interesting to determine how these associations are established than to determine whether, once established, they differ in the extent they have continued to be formally organized. In fact, all of them were established by outside initiative, and it would be surprising if, among poor and ill-educated families, the work of initiating formal associations is done entirely by themselves.

A problem in this analysis is that the data collected on these various associations are only partially adequate to assess the level of their organization. This, in itself, is an indication of the informality of some of the associations; their existence is so insubstantial that I had difficulty in locating them at the times they met. However, some elementary data that indicate the level of formality are available for all these associations.

To see if the persistence of formal organizations is related to the pressures of outside agencies, we need to take indicators of the extent to which such agencies are involved in the particular associations. The two most direct measures of this involvement are the presence of a representative of an outside agency at meetings of the association and the dependence of the association on the outside agency, as measured by whether it is a branch, has delegated responsibility, receives help, or is completely independent of outside connections.[14]

As data on the level of organization, we can use the extent to which the association has specific officers with specialized duties, the existence of formalized rules of procedure (including those for electing or selecting officers), whether minutes of meetings are kept, and whether there are regular meetings. These are mainly outward signs of the extent that these organizations are formally run, and even in those that are highly formal by these criteria, the proceedings are far from those of efficiently run bureaucracies. However, they define minimal levels of organization that are likely to provide continuity in attaining the goals of the association.

Before looking at the results, it is necessary to remember that one important variable has, so far, been left out. This is the complexity of the task that the association faces. Other things being equal, we would expect the formality of organization to depend on how complex is the task being undertaken, with more complex tasks requiring more formal organization. This variable thus threatens to intervene between the posited relation of the interests of external agencies and will be taken account of in the subsequent discussion.

Looking at the array of associations in the two neighborhoods, it appears that there is a correlation between outside involvement and the persistence of formal organization (Table 25). There is one obviously deviant case—the Welfare Association in Planificada. But comparing, for example, the betterment associations of Planificada and San Lorenzo and the sports associations of both, it is clear that the extent to which they continue to be formally organized is associated with the level of

[14] The political committees are branches of national parties and are formally established to further the interests of the national party. Less dependent but still closely articulated are groups like the betterment association, to whom the *alcalde auxiliar* has delegated some authority in return for compliance with his directives. Other associations receive financial aid from outside agencies but are otherwise free to act as they will.

Table 25. Associations and Their Level of Organization in the Two Neighborhoods

Name of Association	Level of Organization					External Articulation		
	Office-holders and Duties	Rules	Minutes	Regular Meetings	Total	Representative Present	Dependence	Total
Welfare Assn. (Planificada)	2	2	1	1	6	0	0	0
Betterment Committee (P)	2	2	1	1	6	2	2	4
Co-operative (Lorenzo)	2	2	1	1	6	2	3	5
Sports Association (P)	1	1	1	1	4	1	1	2
Betterment Committee (L)	1	1	1	1	4	1	2	3
Political Committees (P and L)	2	1	0	0	3	1	1	2
Mothers Club (P)	1	1	0	1	3	1	1	2
Mothers Club (L)	1	1	0	1	3	1	1	2
Street Assn. (P)	1	0	0	0	1	0	0	0
Hermanidad (L)	0	0	0	0	0	0	1	1
Sports Assn. (L)	0	0	0	0	0	0	0	0

Scoring Procedures:

Officeholders: 2 = those who act on behalf of association, hold specified offices, and have specialized functions; 1 = some of those acting on behalf of association who do not have specified office and offices not clearly specialized in function; 0 = few if any specified offices. No specialization.

Rules: 2 = written rules and set procedures followed; 1 = some set procedures (e.g., over elections) but follow precedent or advice rather than set rules; 0 = no evident consistency in procedures.

Minutes: 1 = minutes kept; 0 = minutes not kept.

Regular meetings: 1 = meetings regular during period of study; 0 = meetings not regular.

Representatives: 2 = a representative (usually a social worker) always present; 1 = representatives occasionally present; 0 = representative not present.

Dependence: 3 = branch of outside agency (e.g., political party, co-op movement); 2 = has delegated authority (e.g., betterment committees from local mayors); 1 = receives help (loans, etc.) from outside; 0 = no regular aid from outside.

outside involvement. The political committees are also interesting because their formal organization obviously serves the formal demands of the party's central organization, which takes little active part in neighborhood work. None of the three political branches in San Lorenzo operating during my field work was holding regular meetings, and even during the election period their activities were irregular.

Further evidence that formal organization is a product of external interests rather than internal needs is provided by associations not included in the table—the Protestant churches in San Lorenzo. They, too, are relatively formally organized associations designed to achieve common objectives. The three churches do, however, vary in the extent of formality in their organization. The largest church, which is a branch of a large and well-organized sectarian denomination, has a pastor who lives outside the neighborhood. It is this church that is most formal in the number of its services, of officeholders and extra-service activities. Both the secretary and treasurer of the church keep formal records that are regularly inspected. By comparison, the other two churches are more informally organized. They, too, have a range of activities and officeholders, but these are not as regular as in the largest church. Indeed, the activities of the other two churches are more personally controlled by dominant members; organization and financial affairs are more likely to be settled through informal visits to each other's houses rather than in formal meetings. These two churches are both neighborhood churches in the sense that both their pastors and their congregations are drawn from the neighborhood. Also, their links with other churches of the same sect are less formally organized than those of the first church.

It is also evident that the complexity of the task facing the association is not the only explanation for the formality of organization. For example, the betterment committee in San Lorenzo undertakes a greater range of activities than is the case with the Planificada committee. The San Lorenzo committee has a greater responsibility for maintaining order in its environment, is actively engaged in a series of community projects, and is supposed to oversee the work of other local associations. In contrast, the Planificada committee is less active and its major function is lobbying on behalf of neighborhood improvement. However, the case of the Hermanidad in San Lorenzo is perhaps a clearer indication that an association can have complex tasks with hardly any formal organization.

The Hermandad organizes the festivals for the neighborhood saint's day and for the national holiday. It also organizes special services for deaths, weddings, and christenings, instructs local children in the catechism, and is charged by the local priest with the distribution of welfare milk. Some tasks involve raising money from the whole neighborhood to pay the expenses of the priests, flowers, and so forth, and delegating a large number of people to take care of the various aspects of the services—the procession, the flowers, and cleaning the church. All these activities the brotherhood has accomplished without serious problems. In fact, the members pride themselves on their success and cite this to prove that they do not need a more formal organization with elections and wider participation. Though it is closely allied to the local priest, he is too busy to take an active interest, and he handles contacts through the visits of the leading women to his home. The brotherhood has been under pressure from some external interests—notably the local mayor—to develop a more formal organization. This pressure was strongest in 1966 when, for political reasons, the local mayor wished to bring the brotherhood under the close supervision of the betterment committee.

The Benefits of Formal Organization

We thus come to the final part of this exploration of the significance of formal organization: its feasibility under urban conditions that do not promote trust among neighbors. There is little evidence from this study that formal organization enables strangers to cooperate. It is true that of the formal associations I observed closely—the San Lorenzo betterment committee and the cooperative—it is the cooperative that had the easiest acceptance of formal organization, and the cooperative was initially composed of people who knew each other less well than did members of the betterment committee. Yet the persistence of formal organization is clearly related to the supervision of the professional organizers, and one of the problems encountered by the co-op is members' unwillingness to differentiate their organization further, because it weakens their personal supervision over officeholders.

We can extend this argument by looking at the deviant case in Table 25—the mutual aid association in Planificada, which is formally organized but appears not to be articulated to outside agencies. Although it was originally set up through the intervention of social workers in the neighborhood, it has persisted without their or any other outside agency's active interest. However, this mutual aid association deviates from the other associations found in the two neighborhoods in that it specifically serves a very restricted group of families. The members of the association, some forty in all, are almost entirely skilled or white-collar workers with stable incomes. They are from the elite of the neighborhood and do have many of the characteristics that engender public trust. They also confine their association's activities to the highly specific ones of aid in illness and burial expenses. The contributions are kept in a bank and are regularly audited. I took some leaders from San Lorenzo to a meeting of this association, and the association's officers explained to them the procedures they followed. The people from San Lorenzo were overwhelmed and later, when expressing their admiration to me, they also confided that such an association would be difficult to establish in San Lorenzo because it required people to have such high levels of confidence in other people.

Despite their formal organization, there was also a strong emphasis in the two betterment associations on working through known individuals and with reference to individual qualities that formal procedures could not gainsay. In the

San Lorenzo committee, Pepe is regarded as the man with the qualities best suited to relate to outside agencies and city influentials. Luis is regarded as the orator and organizer of mass meetings and so on. No matter the specific offices that members of the betterment committee held, there was always a tendency for these to be forgotten under the pressure of events.

Pepe was nominally president of the committee for over a year, but in the large meetings it was always Luis or José who took the lead and organized the meetings and subsequent discussions. Pepe regarded this as appropriate, telling me that José and Luis had a way with public meetings. In the Planificada committee a similar procedure is observable, but it is held in greater check by the constant presence of the local social worker. However, many of the irritations that I recorded at the meetings usually arose because of the insistence of the social worker that the officeholders stick to their various offices. Some members regarded this as inappropriate given the known qualities of these officeholders.

Using such preconceptions to divide up responsibilities is a familiar practice among people whose career experiences and education have given them no cause to make any distinction between an office and the person that holds it.[15] Indeed, it is mostly a distinction made, if not always practiced, by professionals and office workers in large-scale organizations. Usually, however, when people see others as having the right characteristics for a job, they have more intimate knowledge of those others than is possible under the conditions of these two neighborhoods. This is one reason why local leaders find it easier to divide their responsibilities than to get such divisions generally accepted.

The inappropriateness of formal organization basically

[15] Suttles (*The Social Order of the Slum*, p. 185) shows how general is the process by which individuals develop enduring identities within a group. In his study of street-corner groups such identities render ineffective any external attempts to formally organize such groups. The unstable groups are, however, those most susceptible to such outside organization.

emerges because these various associations are set within and serve a wider community in which there is no basis for trust. People in these neighborhoods know little of each other and interact little with each other. Furthermore, they are told by the many sources to which they are exposed that the people by whom they are surrounded are untrustworthy and lacking in the desirable moral qualities. Under these circumstances, formal organization aggravates mistrust because it creates the impression that resources are present and being manipulated even where no money or other material resource passes hands. This is reinforced by the close links that the various formal organizations have with external interests. These links are themselves both potential resources and are regarded as potential resources by neighbors. Informal organization, in contrast, has the advantage that its proceedings are only identifiable by those actively engaged in them and thus do not have to extend beyond the actual transactions.

In San Lorenzo, neighbors constantly suspect their betterment committees of misappropriating funds. In very few cases do these committees actually handle money, but the formal procedures they use to obtain and distribute resources occasion suspicion that the neighborhood is, in some way, being cheated. The Agency for International Development directly presented the building materials for the drainage project and no funds were involved, but people from the neighborhood maintained that large sums had passed hands and that committee members had grown rich at the neighborhood's expense.

A similar process occurred over a project to replace the water pipe that provided the San Lorenzo water supply. The existing pipe did not provide sufficient water and, furthermore, it was corroding away in places. The local mayor encouraged the betterment committee to organize the neighborhood to provide funds for the purchase of bigger tubing. To avoid imputations of misappropriating funds, he was careful to insist that the committee give receipts for the money collected and keep full accounts of purchases. However, the collection procedures only served to arouse further mistrust of the committee's motives. Neighbors became aware of a complicated collection procedure and assumed that large sums was being collected. Often they quoted hopelessly inaccurate estimates of the size of the population to justify their claims that the neighborhood had paid more than it received back in tubing.

The emergence of formal association within these neighborhoods is thus part of the wider urban context and is affected both by the strategies of groups external to these neighborhoods and by the perceptions of people within them. Both neighborhoods have been treated in similar fashion, but this should not obscure the differences that exist between them even on these dimensions. Families in Planificada are less exposed to instances of public mistrust than are those in San Lorenzo. Many of them have the types of jobs and income that make them appear publicly trustworthy. We have seen that, in the case of one association at least, Planificada families are able to independently and formally organize to attain common goals. In this respect, we need to note that most of the formal associations in Planificada are run by people who have better than average jobs and education. In the case of the informally organized street committees, their leading members are drawn entirely from the more prosperous homeowners in the neighborhood, and their choice appeared to meet with the agreement of the other families.

In San Lorenzo, the situation is different because no one has the characteristics to escape public mistrust, and, moreover, attempts to organize San Lorenzo are more likely to affect the whole neighborhood. Their situation is a common one, and high density further ensures that organization has some interest to all. Families look on the visible attempts to organize as affecting, possibly negatively, the scarce resources available to the neighborhood. In Planificada, the lower densities and the greater differentiation of ecological situations mean than many of these attempts to organize by-pass families in the neighborhood. Consequently, the neighborhood often appears less organized or cohesive, but evidences less internal strife and rumor. Despite their diversity, it is clear that in neither neighborhood is formal association an indigenous response to the complexities of urban problems.

The City in Microcosm

Formal associations affect in another manner the style of urban participation of these low-income families. They are the concrete expression of their exposure to and exploitation by other urban groups and, as such, affect both their views of coping with urban life and their capacity to do so. Since they involve families in interaction with other social groups, they provide an opportunity for observing in microcosm the transactions that occur between different social groups in the city. It is one of the times when the urban world is sufficiently reduced to be captured, at least in part, within the field of one social situation. The following account of the inauguration of a cooperative in Zone 6 of the city, in which San Lorenzo residents are involved, is intended to convey something of these social interactions and the learning situation that they provide for the people exposed to them.

The Inauguration of a Co-op

The neighborhood is situated near the bridge that takes the coast road out of the city and into the western mountains. The neighborhood is made up of adobe houses and dirt streets, but is legally settled. The street on which the co-op stands had been strewn with pine needles and streamers had been hung from house to house. The signs of MONAP were displayed on telegraph poles and on houses, announcing the inauguration of the co-op. The co-op was established in an ordinary adobe house with the co-op sign outside it, but the shop section was still closed.

The street was filled with children and a few adults who belonged to the local betterment committee. I was introduced to the president of the betterment committee and to the president of the co-op. Julio, the professional co-op organizer, was there helping with the last-minute arrangements, and the second organizer, John, was also present. The assistant to Carlos arrived and came over to chat.[16] Then José and his wife arrived, both dressed neatly in their best clothes. A strong contingent from the co-op neighboring San Lorenzo, Santiago, came led by the president of their betterment committee, all well dressed and bringing a large bunch of flowers to present at the ceremony.

Carlos arrived in his jeep and was shortly followed by a car carrying Miguel Cruz, the general editor of *El Dairio*, and his wife. It appeared that Cruz had provided the loan for the co-op and was due to open it. Chairs were provided by local neighbors, and Cruz and wife sat down and were soon joined by Carlos and the lady members of the Santiago co-op. Carlos began to chat with Cruz. Gradually, the street began to fill with more children, many women, and increasing numbers of men—some thirty adults in all.

The assistant mayor of the zone was also expected and we waited for him, though Carlos seemed to think that political considerations might keep him away. He arrived, however, and firecrackers were used to signal the start of the ceremony. More neighbors arrived, and benches were fetched for other guests, including myself.

Throughout the ceremony there was a lot of noise and bustle in the street. The ceremony started with speeches from the chairmen of the betterment committee and the co-op. Both emphasized the great stride forward that the co-op signaled and how neighbors organizing together could bring a lot of needed improvements. The betterment committee chairman was the orator and went on interminably, whereas the co-op chairman was less practised and repeated himself frequently. The local mayor presented credentials to the betterment committee, emphasizing the municipality's desire to help neighbors and the advantages of neighbors cooperating to help themselves.

[16] Carlos was the local mayor of the zone in which San Lorenzo is located.

A musical interlude by a local band followed. Then flowers were presented to the co-op, and the vice-president of MONAP made a speech praising the enthusiasm of the neighbors and the importance of organizing themselves, pointing to the aid MONAP was giving them to that end. He was a short, very dark-complexioned man dressed in an ill-fitting suit; he lived in a low-income neighborhood to the east of the city. José then spoke, offering congratulations and saying that San Lorenzo would soon have a co-op too.

After more music, a speech by Cruz opened the co-op. He spoke about the importance of neighbors organizing themselves to improve their own lives and that of Guatemala. He was not a powerful orator but spoke clearly and simply. He was neatly dressed in open-necked shirt, sweater, and sports trousers. Since the priest had not yet arrived, the blessing could not be given and the guests ajourned to the Social Christian Library next to the co-op for refreshments.

The guests were joined by members of the co-op and the betterment committee. The men stood around in a circle with Cruz as the dominant figure. Carlos had left in his jeep by this time, but his aide, Ramón, was prominent in the discussions. Cruz spoke about the problems of Guatemala—that the governments had done little, the present one included. Everyone agreed, and someone asked if any election could bring improvement. The question was never really answered.

Guatemalan champagne was brought in, and outside piñatas had been set up for the children, who were busily blindfolding themselves and attempting to break the piñata under the supervision of the professional organizers. There was a crowd outside and inside the co-op, with Julio rushing around to make sure everything was in order. The local priest arrived, but nobody paid much attention. Julio had to clear the co-op shop for the priest to give his blessing. He did this in his vestments while the chatter continued in the street outside and guests continued with their champagne.

Eventually, Julio got some silence in the street, and the co-op was blessed inside and out. The priest then addressed the chattering crowd, saying that the church looks with favor on all attempts of the poor to organize themselves and especially on co-ops. He went on to say that, though some call co-ops the work of communists the church does not believe it. The priest was then offered refreshments and sat with Cruz and his wife and the other guests at a table laid with sandwiches. A few members of the local committee joined them, while the women busied themselves in the kitchen. The men at the table talked generally about the difficult situation in which Guatemala is placed and the value of cooperative action. Then Cruz and priest excused themselves and left. Julio stayed to organize a film showing for the evening. While we were eating, the local band struck up a few more tunes as the children played with the piñatas. The highlight of the performance was a song in honor of the co-op, consisting of about twenty stanzas sung in a cracked voice by the band leader.

This account illustrates the interaction situations that are relatively common for members of formal associations as indeed for many people in low-income areas. In this one, there are represented most of the social levels active in urban affairs. Cruz is rich and from an influential family. Its wealth is of relatively recent origin, and the members of the family have secured their status in the city by participating in public affairs. Absent are the professionals such as lawyers university professors, and doctors, who are often present at such occasions. The priest belongs to this social level, though his position is distinctive. Then comes Julio, representing the skilled, hardworking, but lesser officials and white-collar workers. His style of life is different from the professionals and richer families; he has no car, lives in a relatively small house, and is not university educated. He is not invited to all the social gatherings that the professionals and their wives attend, but he is a valued member of the party and his counsel is taken into account even if he does not participate in decision making.

Carlos is the man that bridges the social world of the white-collar worker and of the low-income families. He lives separated from his family, and his education is rudimentary. He has lived all his life in shacks and small rooming houses in which most Guatemalans live in the city. As a skillful and forceful organizer he has built a position for himself, so that his services are desired by political organizations. His role is seen to be subordinate, and he is expected to follow directions; the party leaders would not think of inviting him to social gatherings to which they might even invite Julio.

Then come the neighborhood leaders who live on low incomes in poor neighborhoods. They are politically aware and active, but their position is precarious. They are replaceable by others, and their style of life remains that of their neighbors; they have little money to spare for clothes, decent housing, or recreation. Their education is often very rudimentary. After them is the ordinary member whose standard of living is similar to that of the neighborhood activists, but he differs in being reticent about engaging in activity.

These distinctions are observable in the interactions of people in the situation. Cruz receives the most attention, people wait for him to speak, and he is seated first. The priest is less important, and people do not leave Cruz to attend to him. Then comes Carlos who is important enough to be seated close to Cruz and to have his utterances respected; but not important enough to be given the prominent role in inaugurating the co-op. Julio is the organizer, and it is accepted without question that what he says about the arrangements for the inauguration should be acted on. He does not participate, however, in social gatherings in which the relative social standing of the people is observable in the deference they give and receive. Julio's position is always a little ambiguous in this respect, for while he is obviously not poor, he does not quite belong to the professional elite. Indeed, the very familiarity that makes him a successful organizer obscures his social status in the eyes of neighborhood families and his professional colleagues.

What is important for our analysis, however, is the fact that such situations and the social nuances that are observable in them acquaint co-op members and others in the neighborhood with the distinctions of socioeconomic position present in the city. Most of these families have come from rural situations in which such nuances are not usually so delicately observed. In the small town the richer landowner, the merchant, and the professional are likely to be of the same family and to interact easily. Though for many low-income people in the city the most apparent social gulf is between rich and poor, interaction in such situations as the one described above alerts poor people to the nuances of social and economic distinction.

However, these families are interacting with the range of social types in the city, and even publishers of national newspapers are not inaccessible to them. These associations thus introduce families to the social complexity of urban life in a manner unlikely to polarize them in opposition to other social groups. In doing so, these associations not only represent the means whereby others in the city reduce their risks and uncertainties in their encounters with the poor, but are also a mechanism for their vertical incorporation in society.

6. The Formation of a Voluntary Association: The Consumer Cooperative

We now turn to a case study of one of these formal organizations in action: the inception and early development of a consumer cooperative in San Lorenzo. This cooperative is especially interesting because it is the neighborhood association that is most closely articulated with the outside and represents a deliberate and planned attempt to use external ideologies to foment cohesion among these families.

Since the cooperative was in the process of formation when the field work was being carried out, the analysis pays particular attention to recruitment, the emergence of leadership, and to the orientations that people bring to cooperative action. These themes enable us to look in microcosm at the effects of the urban processes that we have described earlier. In analyzing recruitment and the emergence of leadership we will be looking at the particular conditions that affect the mobilization of poor families for public activity when most are strangers to each other. Also, the cooperative brings together people of very different social positions, experiences, and perspectives, and in their interaction we see something more of the learning experience that city life involves.

The Background of the Consumer Cooperative

The establishment of the consumer cooperative in early 1968 came mainly through the initiative of professional organizers employed by the Central de Servicios, a semi-autonomous agency of the Christian Democrat party.[1] These organizers began by establishing literacy classes in the neighborhood and opened initial discussions about cooperativism and the possibility of establishing a cooperative. The professional workers had the help of volunteers, usually university students or professors, and had experience in organizing both urban and rural cooperatives. Julio, the full-time worker who spent the most time with the San Lorenzo cooperative, had been in Chile taking courses in cooperativism.

The establishment of consumers' cooperatives is a city-wide policy of the Christian Democrat party, and the cooperative in the shantytown is only one of about six urban consumer cooperatives that were initiated at this time. Not only had the Central de Servicios trained personnel, but it could call upon a considerable amount of teaching material. There existed pamphlets, booklets, films, and other instructional devices that were easily distributed to the co-op members. Also, the Central provided an extensive backing service for the local cooperatives. Some volunteers of the Central specialized in urban wholesale

---

[1] The Central, which is not formally attached to the party, is located in the center of the city in a fairly large house whose various rooms are used by the professional organizers as offices or by the groups dependent on the Central for their place of meeting and organization. For example, MONAP, the urban squatters' movement, meets there regularly, as do some rural peasant organizations. The Central has a lawyer in constant attendance, a social worker, and various trained specialists in organization. It also serves as a center for secretarial and technical services.

and retail prices, comparing the prices asked at various markets and supermarkets; these lists were then made available to officials of the local cooperatives.

It was the Central that negotiated the loans that enabled the cooperatives to purchase their initial stock and the materials for building their stores. Through the Central, each cooperative became closely articulated into a wide cooperative movement receiving newssheets about the activities of other urban and rural cooperatives and information about the cooperative movement in other parts of the world. These cooperatives were frequently visited by national and foreign visitors, and members of the cooperative were themselves encouraged to visit other cooperatives in the city and countryside.

From the beginning, then, those joining the cooperative are made aware that they are not alone in their endeavors and are able to visit ongoing and successful cooperatives. Also, they do not have to construct their organization as they proceed. This organization and the material backing required for its success is handed to them from the beginning. For these reasons, the development and success of the cooperative depends more on the characteristics and orientations of its members than it does on their technical skills. Furthermore, it places members of the cooperative in a situation where, for one of the few times in their lives, they have interests in common with other low-income families, not only in their immediate environment but also elsewhere in the city, the countryside, and even abroad.

These features of its development make the case of this co-op especially relevant to analyzing the possibilities of collective organization among the poor. Co-ops have been historically identified with the efforts of poor people to organize and improve their environment. Moreover, they represent a form of self-help that arises from a recognition of social and economic exploitation and are thus potentially a means of formulating class interests. Despite this aspect of their organization, co-ops can also prejudice local groups in important respects. They can enable national and local authorities to control local production and consumption more effectively; those members who already have the most resources often disproportionately gain from the rationalization of purchasing and marketing. In this respect, co-op organization expresses the dilemma of organization among the poor: they need to organize to express effectively their interests, but organization involves them in external relationships and in internal procedures that expose them to new and more subtle forms of exploitation.

In these respects the San Lorenzo co-op provides a test case of the relevance of externally generated organization to the poor. It is sponsored from without and is part of a larger organization, but it serves the needs of the population and its organizers attempt to promote the class consciousness of these shantytown dwellers. This co-op enables us to see whether outsiders can promote a consciousness of their common needs among poor people or whether such consciousness emerges, if at all, only as a consequence of their own experiences and interactions.

The data will be organized to explore the following possible limits on formally organizing the poor that result from the processes reported in the previous chapters. First, there are inherent limits to the appeal and representativeness of an organization such as this co-op. It seeks to be inclusive, but its potential clientele is not equally accessible and the characteristics of those it recruits necessarily limit and condition its activities. This results from differences among these families in the span of their relationships and in their economic position. Furthermore, the co-op is a locally based organization, and any differences in the local commitment of neighbors affect recruitment. This is an important constraint on the organization of the poor in a city where there are no other extensive and enduring bases for organization.

Second, the effective functioning of a membership based organization like the co-op is limited by the absence of conditions that promote trust among its potential membership. They have neither the stable identities nor the credentials that permit effective collective action, and the absence of trust is likely to confine the organization to simple tasks. The work of the co-op does, however, promote trust to some extent, and we need to see how effective this emergent process is in face of the disorganizing tendencies in the co-op's environment. Finally, it is likely that such an organization advocates orientations that are incompatible with those of its audience. The presuppositions of formal organization with long-term goals have little meaning to people whose experiences are limited by poverty and lack of education.

The exploration of these possibilities indicates the limited success that is likely to be gained from formally and externally organizing the poor, even where the objectives are concrete ones. Concurrent with this investigation, we must pay special attention to another and often unintended consequence of the activities of this co-op: the significance of its providing an ongoing and formally organized dialogue between different sections of the urban population.

The Characteristics of Members

From April 1968, when the consumer cooperative received its official charter of establishment, to five months later when its store was opened, twenty-one members were recruited. This represents a small fraction of the 420 households in the neighborhood, but it was quite typical of the membership of other urban consumers' cooperatives in their early days. The thriving cooperative of the neighboring and larger shantytown, which has sixty members and is growing larger each week, began its first six months with nineteen members. The expansion of membership comes with the opening of the store and the evident advantages to be gained from membership; when the store in San Lorenzo opened, five more people became members of the co-op. The development of a co-op in Guatemala City depends on concrete achievements, not on a large and unsatisfied desire of poor people to engage in cooperative action.[2]

[2] This is not to say that under other conditions cooperatives or cooperative projects do not receive a ready response among poor people. The purpose here is to

Since the co-op is a local organization in a neighborhood in which people have many relationships outside, one factor selecting those who initially join is the degree and nature of their commitment to San Lorenzo. Participation in the co-op requires people to invest time and material resources. Membership is obtained by subscribing to a share worth approximately twenty-five dollars, and the purchase is spread over a series of installments of one and a quarter dollars. The amount of money an individual receives back from the cooperative as a dividend depends on the amount purchased at the cooperative store. Both factors require an individual to stay long enough in the neighborhood to pay for a share and to spend enough time in the neighborhood each day to make local purchases a common occurrence.

Participation in the co-op also involves one in neighborhood-based social relationships. People are expected to conduct their business with the same set of people and in a stable context of interaction. In these senses, joining a co-op is a public commitment involving relationships with other families and committing one's own family to such relationships. It is not an activity that families who are involved in sets of relationships outside the neighborhood are likely to find easy to enter or accept.

One factor, then, in recruitment to the cooperative is the extent to which a family's social relationships are concentrated in the neighborhood. This is measured by the proportion of the kinship relationships that a family has in the neighborhood and the amount of time spent there. On both these counts, cooperative recruits are more heavily committed to the neighborhood than is normal among San Lorenzo inhabitants. Eighteen of the cooperative recruits have close kin living in the same neighborhood other than their own children, and these same families often have grown children also living close by. Fourteen

further demonstrate that what appears to be a similar social position, including such apparently obvious common needs as obtaining cheaper food, is not sufficient to counter the fragmentation engendered by the development of the city and by peoples' perception of their place within it.

of the recruits, including seven of the twelve males, have occupations that are carried out within the shantytown and that involve some degree of interaction with other shantytown dwellers. Two members are firewood salesmen who buy large stocks of wood that are delivered to them in the shantytown and that they sell door-to-door. One of them sells mostly outside, but the other visits every shack to carry out his sales and is well known in the neighborhood. Examples of other locally based occupations are dressmakers and tailors, who often sell to neighborhood people.

Women who, as a category, commit more time to the neighborhood are less numerous than men, but the women who have joined are especially active in the management of their household affairs. Two of them are the heads of their household and another three are in effect the heads because of their husbands' absence for lengthy periods. In the other cases, the women joining are relatively independent partners in their marriages, earning money through small-scale trading or dressmaking. Since joining the co-op means committing a part of the family's budget as well as time that could be spent on family chores, it is not surprising that it is only the more independent women who join. When the husband is interested, he usually joins; the appeal of the co-op is aimed at both sexes, stressing activities in addition to sales of consumer goods, including welfare, educational and recreational projects, as well as possible production activities.

But jobs that commit people to the locality are also those that have little in common with the tenets of cooperativism. Petty traders, small shopkeepers, and even the dressmakers and artisans selling locally live from the neighborhood, from people not having the time or resources to purchase cheaply in bulk or at central locations. In contrast, one principle of cooperativism is precisely that people amalgamate their resources to buy more cheaply and eliminate, as far as possible, the profits of the middleman. People in the neighborhood who own the large shops and even such resources as electricity meters are quite explicit in opposing the inception of the co-op.

It is striking evidence of the importance of being committed locally that not one of these early recruits comes from workers in the neighborhood who have jobs in such large-scale enterprises as transportation or factories, where, through unions or benefit associations, there is already a cooperative tradition.

At the other extreme, families without resources at all do not have the money or the security to keep up the regular payments of co-op dues. The food purchases of these families are so little that the value of joining the co-op is less evident to them. The co-op thus does not include either the very poor, those who work in stable large-scale enterprises, or the most important local entrepreneurs. Instead, it appeals to locally based people of medium resources, 66 percent of whom earn between thirty and ninety dollars a month.

By comparison, an analysis was carried out of the characteristics of members of the larger (sixty members) and longer established co-op in the neighboring shantytown. Because many members had joined since its initial period, the analysis is not strictly comparable with the San Lorenzo co-op. However, it is striking that the characteristics of members of the larger co-op exaggerate the tendencies reported for San Lorenzo. There are many more women in the co-op in Santiago (the neighboring shantytown), 84 percent of members, but of these women 25 percent are heads of their families and the majority (54 percent) have jobs of their own. This suggests that with longer establishment more women become active members, since the members who established the co-op in San Lorenzo were predominantly male. Of the women who do not work, the large majority have husbands who are either self-employed or employed in small-scale service or craft activities (watchman, carpenter). Taking all members of the co-op who work, both male and female, 85 percent are self-employed and 10 percent work in large-scale enterprises. The men are usually traders or job laborers, while the women are traders, food peddlers, or take in ironing and washing. Only a very small minority (15 percent including husbands of those women members not working) are involved in a work situation that is likely to encourage or present opportunities for cooperative activity among people of like situation.

Neighborhood co-op activity is not an extension of activity learned elsewhere but serves the particular needs and problems of a certain section of neighbors. Under the conditions of this city, neighborhood co-ops basically appeal to those with few work-based relationships and who are dependent on the neighborhood for support. In this respect the characteristics of members are similar to those of Protestant sects, and it is likely that the co-ops, like the churches, have the attraction of providing available and relatively secure relationships for those whose urban position requires them to have such support.[3]

The Nature of Commitment

We can explore the characteristics of recruits in San Lorenzo from another direction using data on contributions to a water tubing project and answers to a government questionnaire about housing.[4] These data provide concrete examples of recruits' commitment to the neighborhood. The water tubing project was organized locally to collect enough money to replace the neighborhood's aging and inadequate system of tubing that brought water from the main supply. Each neighbor was asked to give $1.25. Since each contribution had a receipt, I could obtain a list of all who contributed—some 48 percent of the families in the neighborhood. Even when we compare recruits to the co-op with people whose social characteristics are

[3] Bryan Roberts, "Protestant Groups and Coping with Urban Life in Guatemala City," *American Journal of Sociology* 73, no. 6 (May 1968): 753-767.

[4] This questionnaire was administered in July 1968 by the government agency in charge of housing to everyone within the three shantytown neighborhoods sharing the same ravine. Its explicit intention was to map the social characteristics and aspirations of inhabitants in order to plan their removal to other housing. The questionnaire was administered at the weekend by specially selected high-school students who had to visit each shack according to a plan and maps previously drawn up. The questionnaire detailed the number of the shack and when I was given permission by the agency to look at the completed questionnaires, I was thus able to identify those people who fell within my own sample. This proved an additional and valuable source of data, since it provided some check on my own data and also became an effective "test" of families' commitment to the neighborhood.

positively associated with payment (higher income, education, or being long-term residents of San Lorenzo), they are more likely than other neighbors to have contributed to the project, with 78 percent contributing.

The nature of their commitment is clarified by their responses to the housing survey, which was attended by much publicity and purported to be a preliminary to concrete action. It asked for a considerable range of personal, financial, and social data and also included specific questions about their existing housing, their preferences for a zone of resettlement, and their means of financing new housing. Only a small minority of people in the neighborhood (5 percent) said they would not consider the possibility of moving elsewhere; both the public reputation of the shantytown and the living conditions there are bad enough to make families at least think of moving. Most families also said that they would be able to pay small monthly installments and make a down payment as well; between them, they cited a range of urban zones to which they would be prepared to move. The exceptions to this general reaction fall into two classes: those who depend economically on their location by having a business there and those who are so poor that they do not consider any prospect of paying money for housing.

Though the co-op includes people who work locally, the general response of its members to the survey is as favorable as that of the neighborhood as a whole. The average downpayment cited (twenty-eight dollars) is slightly higher than the neighborhood average of twenty-four dollars. There were, however, two members who were more reluctant to leave—the owner of one of the firewood businesses and one of the shoemakers who worked in his house, both of whom cited business reasons for their reluctance. Apart from these two cases, there is no evidence that co-op members feel an especially strong commitment to their physical location. Indeed, one member is in the course of purchasing a lot elsewhere in the city, and in several meetings members discussed the possibility of the co-op extending its activity to a co-op housing project. Members of the co-op have, in fact, about average length of residence (60 percent have eight or more years) in San Lorenzo, and there is no suggestion that the co-op makes a special appeal to those who first settled in the neighborhood.

These data imply that the nature of members' commitment is to a set of relationships that help them to cope with urban life. They are people for whom a local base is important, but who are not irrevocably committed to it by poverty or by a special economic or family attachment.

Although neighborhood leaders helped to establish the co-op, are committed to the locality, and have experience of organization, they are with one exception—Luis—not active in the co-op. The absence of the neighborhood leaders underlines another important characteristic of members of the cooperative; they are predominantly people whose orientation can be described as a local and passive one. We will see many illustrations of this orientation as we discuss the process of forming the cooperative. In the course of field work these members stand out by their concentration on immediate issues, their willingness to let others organize for them, their desire to avoid conflict of any kind, and their relative insensitivity to the socioeconomic differences present in the city.

Looking at the life careers of cooperative members indicates nothing likely to disrupt such orientations. In comparison with the neighborhood leaders, the cooperative members have experienced less pre-urban and intra-urban mobility, and their job careers have been relatively stable. The large majority of members are migrants from villages extremely close to the capital, and some are born in the capital; the cooperative does not include the long-distance migrants or those with highly discontinuous careers.

These differences in orientations between co-op recruits and local leaders are not accidental, and in my observations in other co-ops in the city a similar pattern emerges. Whereas the leaders of the particular neighborhood would be highly articulate and relatively sophisticated in their analyses of events, the cooperative officials would usually find difficulty in public speaking and would always orient their speeches and conversations to immediate and practical issues. In the large cooperative in the neighboring shantytown, the cooperative officials are quiet people who find it difficult to express themselves or to link their activities with broader issues of neighborhood and city organization. Consequently, many of their meetings are dominated by local activists, especially the president of the betterment committee, who would use cooperative celebrations to propound the strategies and ideologies of the Christian Democrat residents' MONAP movement, of which he is a leading member.

It became quite feasible to predict the types of speeches that could be expected at the inauguration of the urban cooperatives. The president of the newly formed cooperative would give a hesitant, low-key speech expressing many thanks and emphasizing the local benefits to be gained. He would be followed by the president of the local betterment committee or by a zone official who would, with fervor, deliver a relatively sophisticated political speech and link the cooperative to the widest possible social reform.

These differences are explicable by the character of the organizations in which the two groups are involved. Though both sets of organizations are closely articulated to external interests, there is an important difference in the focus of their activities. Betterment committees, branches of political parties, and even religious associations are basically involved in relating internal and external environments. This task involves their members in active public relations and makes them aware of the intricacies of manipulating the city's economic and political structure.

By contrast, the co-op is an organization mainly concerned with internal neighborhood issues. The external environment of the co-op is taken care of by its professional organizers and affiliates such as the MONAP organization. The co-op has recruited people oriented to short-term neighborhood issues, whose careers have been relatively continuous. It demonstrates that even the character of the membership of local associations is influenced by the nature of external relations.

Networks and Recruitment

We can extend the analysis by examining how the co-operative members came to be initially recruited. The location of cooperative members suggests a first explanation. The members are grouped into three distinct residential clusters, with the largest concentrated at the bottom end of the neighborhood ravine. All the people within the clusters are linked to each other not only by living within a few yards of each other, but also by a customary exchange of small services; some are further linked by kinship. The initial recruitment for the co-operative was carried out by José and other leaders of the betterment committee acting on the special request of the organizers from the Central de Servicios. In theory, they went from house to house explaining the purpose of the cooperative and attempting to interest neighbors in it. In practice, however, they spent most of their time and persuasion with people they already knew.

In José's case, all the people he recruited from the bottom of the neighborhood are close neighbors, interact frequently with him, and exchange services with his wife, Alicia. Some of these he urged to join the co-op by remarks about their aloofness from neighborhood affairs. The two Protestants—Isabel and Olga, mother and daughter—were teased about the refusal of Protestants to take any part in nonchurch-based activity. Such verbal interchanges were backed, however, by the commitments of these families to the neighborhood and the need they had to develop relationships based on the neighborhood.

The second group was recruited by the very strong links of friendship they have with the members of the betterment committee living nearby. One of these committee members, Efraim, joined the co-op but never attended, and another, Luis, is a constant attender. The third group was recruited because they work in the neighborhood and are highly visible to others. In the past, some of them have been called upon to help with community affairs. Apart from knowing each other, two of them have strong kinship links with other recruits.

The clustering of co-op members occurs because these clusters define small groups of people who are known to each other and whose existing relationships strengthen their new relationships based on membership in the co-op. They encourage each other to attend meetings and to make the payments; nine of them have kin within the co-op. None of the groups is isolated; they are all strongly linked through friendship or kinship. Before these people were recruited to the co-op they were known to each other by exchanges of services—even if through one other person—for at least four years, and none of them are strangers. Moreover, though the neighborhood is divided by internal factions, none of the recruits are linked by relationships of hostility. By this I mean that no one has a strong and positive relationship with someone in continuing conflict with another member of the co-op. The relationships existing among the co-op members are, at the time of their recruitment, basically in balance.

This is in itself an interesting datum because two of the groups (2 and 3) are closely tied to the two main opposing political factions in the neighborhood. In both groups, however, those who come to the co-op are marginal to the conflicts of interest of the factions. With the exception of Efraim, who does not attend the co-op, and Luis, whose propensity for joining available organizations had become a neighborhood joke and has made him less of a target for hostility, leaders of the political factions do not join the co-op. We have already noted one explanation for this, but the process is also a straightforward one, with both members and nonmembers being quite explicit in citing hostility or lack of trust as a reason for some not entering the co-op.

The recruits are not, however, a homogeneous group. Though known to each other, their relationships are in different areas of the neighborhood and are based on different grounds. Some are related by kinship, region of origin, or religion, while others are related by propinquity and exchange of favors. There are thus potential lines of fragmentation, and these are important in our later analysis of the reaction of co-op members to neighborhood events.

The Limits on Co-Op Recruitment

When organization is based on territory and the relationships therein are segmented by different interests, experiences, and timetables, organizations appealing to the common interest of poor people are still unlikely to recruit members whose characteristics are a random sample of those found among the total group. This means that, over and above any difficulties such an organization meets as a result of the hostility of the external environment, it faces problems arising from the particular characteristics of its members.

Three basic conditions appear necessary if such organizations are to expand and encompass others of similar social and economic position. First, a situation must be created where the development of relationships among people of similar position becomes more advantageous than maintaining or developing relationships with people in different social or geographical position. Second, the extension of relationships among a wider group must have advantages that outweigh any losses involved in reducing the intensity of relationships among a small group of intimates.

Finally, conditions must be appropriate for people to interact frequently with each other and not be hindered by a diversity of movements in time and space. This is the more necessary if officers and specialized sections of the organization are to undertake activities without demands for their constant supervision.

These conditions, which are also the conditions for the development of trust within a group, provide a means of evaluating the difficulties with which the co-op is faced. The process of organization to be described is, in part, an account of members' attempts to proceed to meet these conditions.

Leaders and Followers

The emergence of trust facilitates the delegation of responsibility within an organization and the acceptance by members of a stable differentiation of power. This provides the dynamic that enables organizations to achieve their goals and to take on more complex tasks.[5] For these processes to occur, however, requires that an organization is stable and autonomous enough to separate extraneous events and opportunities from the internal transactions of its members. The significance of this condition for the effectiveness of a co-op working amid unstable urban conditions is seen in the transactions of leaders and followers in the early months of the formation of the San Lorenzo co-op.

The situation within the co-op at its inception was a fluid one in which a group of neighbors had been gathered together by outside initiative, but in which the recruitment process did not define the leaders. This was also part of the ideology of the professional organizations that instituted the co-op. They emphasized, through their professional workers and through the pamphlets and booklets that were distributed, that leaders must be freely chosen by all members and that all members should attempt to partake in office.

The first months of the co-op's existence were taken up with courses of instruction given locally and at the party's office, during which members were to learn their rights and responsibilites and be introduced to the wider significance of the cooperative movement. This was also the period in which the

---

[5] This is a summary statement of Blau's analysis of the conditions of effective leadership and legitimate authority that are further explored in the next chapter (Peter Blau, *Exchange and Power in Social Life*, pp. 200-223). To quote Blau, "Power is the resource that permits an individual or group to co-ordinate the efforts of many others, and legitimate authority is the resource that makes possible a stable organization of such co-ordinated effort on a large scale" (p. 222).

formal organization of the cooperative was established by electing officers specifying duties, and developing specialization in the various branches of cooperative activity. It was thus the period during which a leadership had to emerge out of the relatively undifferentiated group of neighbors that had joined.

We thus have an excellent opportunity to look, in a non-laboratory situation, at the general factors governing the emergence and effectiveness of leaders. Such an analysis will, in fact, be the concern of both this and the next chapter, where it is extended to include leadership at the neighborhood level. In making the analysis, it will become clear that a vital condition is, initially, that these people have none of the attributes that enable suitable leaders to be readily identified. This is to re-introduce, in another context, the problem of organization among people that neither know each other well enough nor possess the relevant public symbols to be able to identify the presumed capacities of others.

In fact, it is common in many voluntary associations that I observed in "low-income" areas for people such as teachers and social workers to be nominated for and to serve as officers in local associations; this illustrates the ethnography of the general statement that leaders are selected by their possession of the relevant public symbols. San Lorenzo is an interesting case because it is exceptional in not possessing either of the habitual criteria for selecting leaders.

The first meetings of the cooperative were entirely dominated by the professional organizer who gave talks about co-op organization and outlined the procedure to be followed. There was little participation from people in the neighborhood, and those most active were the betterment committee members who had helped initiate the co-op. They issued the list of invitations to join, visited houses, and did most of the talking at the early co-op meetings. These neighborhood leaders began to drop out of the twice-weekly meetings, and by the time set for the election for the administration of the co-op, they had, with the exception of Luis, ceased to attend.

The first election was conducted without competition, with an evident sense that certain people were fit for the posts. Proposing of candidates was carried out easily, with no sense of rivalry or hostility. One of the evident procedures was for people to propose those who had lost a previous contest, and this appeared to be done as much to preserve good feeling as because of the merits of the candidates. Luis, the one member of the betterment committee present, tended to dominate, nominating someone for each post and usually backing the winning candidate.

Only one election—that between Antonio and Fina—was really contested. The others resulted in overwhelming votes for one of the candidates with the other candidate getting little more than the vote of the person who had proposed him. The one contested election was between candidates who, in a certain sense, could be described as qualified for office. These were the only two, with the exception of Luis, who had the education and the capacity to initiate discussion.

The candidates who won by overwhelming votes were deemed to have evident qualities that facilitated choice. These qualities were not related to their capacity to run a co-op but to their position and reputation in the neighborhood. Age and span of relationships counted more in this respect than did education or even the possession of useful resources. This should not surprise us, since in these first weeks of the co-op's existence the dominance of the professional organizers meant that members had been given little chance to perceive the relevance of other qualities.

Luis's position as a leader within the co-op essentially depended upon the services he could provide as someone knowledgeable in the ways of organizations and their politics and upon the links he maintained with external organizations— especially the betterment committee. What Luis could not offer was either material resources or the time to devote to the work of the co-op. Luis had an unstable income from tailoring eked out by his work for outside political groups, and this meant that his available time was consumed in work for these interests. Since effective leadership depends on offering services that others need and cannot return in kind, we can expect that an important dynamic of Luis's actions within the co-op was his attempt to persuade members that the services he can offer were the vital ones for the co-op's progress and survival. Likewise, the weakening of his leadership occurred the more it became apparent that it was concrete services that the organization needed and not those of a skilled politician.

We can now follow the emergence of leadership in the co-op to illustrate these principles in action. The early meetings of the co-op were necessarily taken up with intricacies of organization and the question of the relation of the co-op to its external environment. In these meetings, Luis dominated and used every opportunity to define the problems of the co-op in a way that stressed his own importance as someone with experience of how to promote such organizations. In the first meeting in which members participated, Luis made the only two interventions to say that a subscription of twenty-five dollars was easily within neighbors' resources when paid over a year and to argue that the sum in fact should be higher to demonstrate their enthusiasm. The next meeting was the election, and again Luis was the only neighborhood speaker, getting up unasked at the end of the election to enthuse about the idea of a cooperative and the necessity of progress and development. At the following meeting, when Antonio for the first time took up his office as president, Luis intervened almost immediately to make a correction to the way Antonio presented the results of the election, saying that it was important for it to be clear that all were elected by the general assembly of the co-op. Luis was also the only member who intervened when the professionals present from the Central de Servicios read out the formal document of incorporation of the co-op, making the point that the zone and not just the name of the neighborhood should be mentioned, since there were various neighborhoods of the same name.

The situation began to change, however, when the space for building the shop was obtained and the co-op was faced by the urgent task of getting money and building materials to do the job. The officers of the committee had by this time received further training at party headquarters on how to run the co-op and its meetings and they began to show a firmer grasp of proceedings. This was especially true of the president, Antonio, and was made easier for him because he could now talk about his own trade—construction—in reference to the co-op. It was also becoming evident that, despite Luis's oratorical gifts, he was lacking in both time and money that the co-op now needed. The influence of these leaders thus varied with their ability to carry out the tasks of the organization, and their capacities in this respect are likely either to be specialized from the beginning or to become specialized during the process of organization.[6] Noticeably, their influence was based on concrete services and did not generate authority that could be used as "credit" when they are unable to provide such services. In Luis's place, Antonio and Fina, the vice-president, emerged as leaders capable of making decisions and having them respected by other members of the co-op. Both not only had the highest offices in the co-op but were contributing substantially to its current activities. Fina helped through loans, organizing the collections of material, and gathering of labor. Her brother substituted for her on the manual work of building the co-op. Antonio was the most consistent worker, using his construction experience to direct the building of the shop. He also loaned substantial amounts to purchase building materials and provided the contacts that were necessary to obtain them. At this period, Antonio's position was strengthened in an unexpected way when he lost his job and dedicated himself full

[6] There is a similar emphasis in small group research on the differentiation of tasks within these groups that corresponds to the different functions needed to organize them for action. Some leaders specialize in coercive organization, others in engendering support. See Philip E. Slater, "Role Differentiation in Small Groups," *American Sociological Review* 20 no. 3 (1955): 300-310.

time to co-op activities. He now had the time and took on more and more of the daily activities of the co-op.

The growing influence of Antonio and Fina were indicated by the number of decisions they took without consulting others, and their ability to get the members to accept these. Lists of people to work on the shop were drawn up, the loan to establish the co-op was finally negotiated, and the secretary was reprimanded for failure to deliver her books when absent. At the meeting subsequent to these actions, no one, including Luis, made an issue of them. Although there was a little grumbling from some of the affected parties, the various decisions were accepted. Leadership became unsettled again, however, as events outside the co-op influenced its internal activities through the attempt of one of the neighborhood politicians to use a technicality to subordinate the co-op to the local betterment committee.

Luis met this challenge on behalf of the co-op in face of Antonio's evident inexperience. Luis defined the situation in such a way that the kind of service he had to offer appeared vital to members of the co-op. In face of the external threat, Antonio's work and contributions appeared to members as less important than Luis's ability to stand up to external manipulations threatening their autonomy.

In the weeks that followed, the leadership of Antonio, Fina, and Luis was balanced. Luis's intervention was listened to and acted upon in co-op meetings, but Antonio was also making decisions and getting the other members to agree. Antonio's continuing importance as the chief worker and one of the main sources of loans for the building compensated for the loss of influence he suffered from the affair of the attempted takeover.

The course of events that has been described also involved more intense interaction of co-op members with each other, their increasing material and personal committment to the cooperative, and the development of exchange relationships among themselves. Coming together in meetings or engaging together in a co-op activity meant that they used these opportunities to help each other in other ways also. Whereas, in the beginning, relationships were segmented in the clusters described, by this period exchanges had developed throughout the group as a consequence of their common activity. Also, members had been made more aware both of the intricacies of co-op organization and of the types of relationships it maintained with the outside as rival leaders brought them in to help on a particular problem.[7] By this time, co-op members were no longer relying on their leaders or the professionals to interpret events.

The members remained uneasy about the fact that they were engaging in joint action with relative strangers despite the ties that linked most of them. They were suspicious of the practices of the officers, especially of the secretary and the treasurer. On one occasion, there was trouble when members asked the secretary (a Protestant) to leave her books when she went on vacation. This request was seen by the secretary as an insult, and she commented to me that it was only among Protestants that there was trust. Likewise, the treasurer was ultimately removed because she did not attend regularly and was hard to find. Working out of the neighborhood as a servant, she was not visible to members and this caused anxiety about the funds. Some members complained to the professional organizer of the danger of her absconding, and he decided that to quell suspicions the treasurer should resign.

In meetings at this period, members were reluctant to expand and differentiate their organization, saying that to create special functions meant that they would be harder to oversee directly. They resisted the organizer's attempts to extend the organization by placing different people in charge of the various

[7] To analyze a similar process Bruce Kapferer argues that it is imbalance in the exchanges between leaders and followers that potentially creates group cohesion through the processes of competition for allegiance that articulate members of the group. The suggestion is that the significance of an external "threat" for group cohesion occurs through the mechanics of intensifying interaction and negotiation within a group as its established pattern of leadership and goal attainment is disrupted by the redefinition of its situation. Bruce Kapferer, *Strategies and Coalitions*.

branches of purchasing or in charge of study groups and the like. To the organizer, however, this specialization was necessary to introduce more formality into the organization and to make members recognize their responsibilities.

We can capture something of these different processes and the impact of the wider social setting upon them by considering the following description of the co-op's inauguration and the events subsequent to it. The inauguration is particularly interesting since it provides a social situation in which the role conflicts of people variously involved in co-op, neighborhood, and city are "acted out."[8]

The Inauguration of the Co-op

Antonio, Fina, and Olga (the co-op secretary) met with a group supported by the Hermanidad, which rivaled Luis and the reestablished committee, to reach agreement on the festivities and the procedure for inaugurating the co-op.[9] They did this at the suggestion of the professional workers, some of whom were also advising this group, and of a co-op member who belonged to the Hermanidad. One of the agreements made in order to secure some support from this group for the co-op and thus unite the neighborhood behind it (the reestablished committee and Luis were already publicly committed to the co-op) was that the local priest should bless the co-op and, in return, the Hermanidad would organize the religious part of the inauguration.

Luis was hostile to the suggestion and tried to persuade the co-op members not to involve the local priest. Both he and Antonio talked individually to the members, but eventually

[8] This is the use of an analysis of a social situation made familiar by Gluckman to analyze the ambiguities of the positions and statuses of whites and blacks with the colonial incorporation of a community (the Zulus) into a wider social system (South African society). See Max Gluckman, *An Analysis of a Social Situation in Modern Zululand*, Rhodes-Livingstone Paper No. 28.

[9] It is enough to note here that the betterment committee was reestablished to oust José from his authority, and he in turn sided with the Hermanidad and its allies in the neighborhood to challenge the leadership of the reestablished committee.

Antonio obtained the agreement of almost all to invite the priest. However, when the priest demurred over the suggested time, Luis succeeded in persuading the others including Antonio, that another priest should be invited and the Hermanidad be told that their priest was unavailable. Luis was strongly backed in this by some members of the reformed committee who had joined the co-op or reactivated their membership in an explicit attempt to ensure that their rivals did not gain influence in it. However, the majority of the existing membership, regardless of their allegiances, were worried by these developments; they visited each other and told me that they wanted to avoid trouble.

Trouble indeed came when the Hermanidad amassed in force with sticks and stones in front of the neighborhood on the day of the inauguration to prevent the stranger priest from entering. Luis came into abusive contact with them and tried to force a way through; but finally the priest himself decided to retire to avoid further trouble. The police were called, and the two women leaders of the Hermanidad were arrested. The whole neighborhood was full of little groups discussing the events, and wives and mothers were anxiously trying to find where their husbands or sons were so that they can be kept out of trouble.

Antonio was in a difficult position, since the police called upon him as co-op president to make a charge, and he himself was deeply disappointed at the turn of events. Despite Luis's urging, it was clear that the other co-op members were deeply opposed to a charge being made. Fina, Olga, and the woodcutters and their families, as well as some co-op members who belonged to the Luis faction, were telling Antonio to avoid further trouble. He refused to make a charge, and Luis disappeared from the scene to avoid becoming involved with the police with whom he had had previous brushes. The other co-op members appeared unanimous (with the exception of the committee members who had reactivated their membership) in condemning Luis for provoking trouble; they pointed to the exposed position of the co-op if neighbors decided to harm it.

There was also some criticism of Antonio for his weakness. Fina acted as intermediary, talking to members as well as to Antonio and consulting with the professionals from the Central.

The co-op was finally inaugurated, with a small crowd present and speeches from various functionaries of the Central and from Antonio. Luis and some of the betterment committee then proceeded to take over the meetings using the microphone to denounce the Hermanidad. Gradually the affair began to degenerate into drunken incoherence. However, the members of the co-op kept away from these proceedings. Antonio eventually got the microphone from Luis and quieted him down, but attendance inside the new shop was noticeably composed of members of the betterment committee and their friends. Luis attempted to take the affair further the next day, attempting to get lawyers from the Central to make a formal charge; but finally this failed and the lawyers would not pursue it because they did not wish to antagonize the various factions within the neighborhood. They told me that the story they got from Luis was different from that of the other co-op members, citing Fina in particular, and they were not prepared to press the matter.

Antonio, with the aid of Fina, now became the chief and unquestioned organizer of the co-op, superivising the purchase of commodities, the daily organization of produce, and allocating the various tasks to members. In meetings he directed proceedings with the help of the professional organizer and kept Luis in check; on one occasion Antonio told him he should not talk so much since he did so little work.

At the end of field work however, there were signs that the situation might change. As a result of the incident with the priest, the Hermanidad was opposed to the co-op as a Protestant organization. Also, members of the betterment committee were trying to gain influence in it as they prepared to challenge the Hermanidad and its allies in a neighborhood contest. Members were still confident in the leadership of Antonio, Fina, and Olga, who were by now clearly the dominant figures. But, ominously, Antonio was becoming involved with external contacts. He received a job through the help of one of the lawyers attached to the Central and was also becoming interested in supporting one of the candidates for mayor.

This description of events indicates both the weaknesses and the potential strength of the co-op as an organizing force in the neighborhood. The co-op was quite remarkable among the many organizations I visited in that over time it created its own leadership from poor people who had been hitherto somewhat passive members of the neighborhood. In so doing, it both added to the stock of potential leadership among poor people and did so by adding people with characteristics different from those of normal neighborhood activists. In their usual jobs, in their span of relationships, and in their life careers, both Antonio and Fina are more representative of the urban poor than the other activists described in the next chapter. The co-op also appears to have generated participation among its members over concrete common interests and to have provided some basis for an emergent group organization cutting across division of kinship, religion, and politics.

The relationships among the ordinary members impose some restrictions on the leaders' capacity to use their organization for their external purposes. Leaders must take account of this potential cohesion if they are not to be replaced by rivals; both they and ordinary members are thus more committed to the success of the co-op. Simple transactions have become expanded into more complex ones involving not only money but also the organization of a shop and its activities. There is thus an emergent basis for trust that is evidenced by members' increasing likelihood to turn to each for advice or help even in such potentially divisive events as neighborhood faction fights.

The effectiveness of the co-op is limited, however, because it cannot define its sphere of operation so as to enclose itself from the factions of the neighborhood. Consequently, it does not provide a stable and relatively enclosed situation to facilitate the development of trust. This is shown not only by the co-op being dragged into local hostilities and its members being divided by them, but also by the way Antonio begins to segment his activity, participating both in the co-op and in city politics. His various relationships undermine one basis for the emerging trust in which he is held by members that of his total commitment to the co-op. Under these conditions co-op organization remains a matter for personal supervision with little extension or differentiation of organization; members literally demand to keep their eye on what is going on and do not trust to fellow members to effectively carry out delegated tasks. In fundamental ways, then, the effectiveness of formal organization is limited by the absence of those common understandings and trust relationships that underlie stable transactions. They cannot be created within the organization because it can neither be totally inclusive of members' activities nor are its members able to distinguish sufficiently the services provided from those they can find elsewhere in their urban environment.

The Interplay of Orientations

In this section, we will explore the orientations the members bring with them to the co-op and examine them in relation to the avowed intent of the co-op organization to encourage a spirit of self-help through cooperation. Orientations are often independent factors in peoples' use of and reaction to social and material resources. Their examination complements that of social interaction and underlines the peculiar problems facing those that seek to organize people of different life experiences. The life careers of most co-op members are continuous, and their orientations to present action are likely to be local ones. This gives us the opportunity to look closely at the importance of people's perception of their situation, for their readiness to engage in joint action when "objectively" their situation places them in a position common to that of people of similar social and economic position and in opposition to other social groups.

At the very first co-op class, the professional organizers began to introduce members to the ideology of the co-op movement. This they did quite systematically, using a small textbook and the formal statutes of a cooperative society. These early meetings were teaching sessions in which the professional or an assistant would sit in front of the group, read out a section from the book, then put it into simpler language with illustrations drawn from the local conditions of the neighborhood. He would then ask for questions and attempt to stimulate discussion among the members.

The following account gives the outline of the proceedings of the first meeting I attended.

The Dialogue of a Co-op Meeting

The organizer, Julio, explained what a co-op is and what some of its rules are. As an example, he told the meeting that the profits that the co-op makes are not all divided among members, but that by law 10 percent must be put away as capital and that it was also wise to put aside another 5 percent for education and 5 percent for social welfare projects. He went on to point out that the rich always exploit the poor in Guatemala, and for that reason it is important to organize into a cooperative to get the best value for their money. He spent a long time explaining why a co-op cannot buy on credit because that is a sure way to lose money with interest rates so high. He emphasized that they must rely on themselves and on their own forces and not rely on those of higher social position and that this was the surest way to improve their position.

He tried to get his audience involved in a dialogue by asking whether the weights that shopkeepers used in the neighborhood were exact. There was little readiness to reply, and most appeared embarrassed by the question. He kept this up in a semijocular way for a while, teasing some of the women who were themselves traders. He then asked if they thought it was necessary to start a co-op in the neighborhood and all agreed that it was. Julio then started asking questions about the nature of cooperativism. He asked about the difference between a co-op and a shop. The first answer was that there is no difference, since they both sell. Then after a wait and prompting, another member said that a co-op sells for the benefit of all. Julio then asked if an owner of a large store could be a member of a co-op and several people replied quite quickly that he could not, since he would have interests opposed to the co-op. Julio then asked them what was necessary if people were to become members of a co-op, and they replied that people must be willing to cooperate and that they must be consumers. Julio then made sure that they all understood what a consumer is, and he asked several people to define it. Then he prompted them a little further with hints, until someone added that another essential of a member is that he understands what a cooperative movement is. Julio then emphasized that cooperativism has nothing to do with communism. He terminated the meeting by pointing out to them that people living in shantytowns like theirs have more values and worth than those in Zone 1 or Zone 10 (rich zones) and that they are good people.

The aim of the organizer is to encourage people to have confidence in themselves and in their capacity to work together for their own benefit. He also tries to avoid the implication that the cooperative has political ends, which is especially important given that the country is under a state of seige and political activity is forbidden. Julio also tries to avoid the political faction fights common to neighborhoods that had entered the co-op movement. To the members, however, the co-op is mainly seen as a possible means of saving money and as an opportunity to spend their time in the company of others. When I talked with members later, they could not remember the talk and confessed that they would be more interested when something concrete happened.

These kinds of exchanges occured in all the co-op meetings in which the professional organizers attempted to impart the ideology of the co-op. The pattern of dialogue was that the organizer put the idea of the co-op into general perspective using elementary concepts and simple vocabulary, and then tried to get the members to repeat these ideas in response to questions. The answers, however, always focused on concrete issues having to do with the buying and selling aspects of the co-op, such as correct weights, fair prices, and saving money. Members could always be prompted into answering more generally, but their first responses referred to the concrete and individual advantages of co-op membership.

The only exceptions to this were some of the neighborhood committee members who occasionally attended the co-op. Luis constantly talked in ideological terms with reference to group action and distinctions of social and economic position. However, the others, even the best educated and vocal ones, talked mainly in concrete terms. One set of exchanges in which Manuel, a supporter of Luis and the committee and a relatively well-educated person, answered the organizer went as follows:

Q: What is the difference between a co-op and a shop?
A: Well, members are in control of the co-op, and it has a social purpose.
Q: It also serves educational purposes, and why should that be?
A: [Silence]
Q: Education ... so that owners know how to run the business.
A: Yes, it is important for the co-op to have correct weights.
Q: Why is that possible in the co-op ... because all members are responsible for looking after the co-op. Would you prefer to be clients in a shop or owners of a co-op?
A: [A period of silence] As owners of a co-op, we can learn more.
Q: How can you learn more ... in what ways is it better?
A: Well, we get a profit from the co-op at the end of the year.
Q: Do any of you know any syndicate or organization that defends the rights of the consumer against the ambitions of traders?
A: [Long period of silence] No, don't think so.
Q: Does the co-op harm traders who are honorable and just?
A: No, the co-op will not harm them, because if they are just then their prices will be same as the co-op.

This exchange is representative of not only an actual

exchange but of the many exchanges that occurred in the co-op meetings. The replies of members were always short, and they did not elaborate on any answer. In searching for an answer, which was what they were in effect doing for most of the time during meetings, they constantly returned to the concrete advantages that the co-op offers.

The issue is not just one of vocabulary differences between the professional organizers and the semiliterate members of the co-op, but also the unwillingness on the part of members to include certain frames of reference in their thinking about their environment. They do not think in terms that imply possible conflicts that result from their joint action. They endeavor to overlook or minimize the possible conflict with local traders. They do not talk in terms of conflict with other social groups or organizations, and their questions, answers, and informal conversations assume that others will be benevolent to them. At the same time, they rarely talk about the value of cooperation and trust among people like themselves. Their thinking, when it comes to issues involving cooperation, stresses the concrete and individual advantages that accrue.

These are ways of thinking that are understandable given the careers and environment of members. These have given members a set of experiences in which they have learned to trust to intimates and to see their interests as tied to such relationships, rather than to the progress of broad social and economic categories. They have not been in situations where it is apparent to them that their treatment is linked to their membership of a social or economic category. Cooperation among strangers or even opposition to broad groups of strangers are relatively novel concepts. They hear them, but do not understand them in terms of their own experiences. Without such meaning, the outcome of any such cooperative action is regarded as unclear at best and positively dangerous at worse. They may learn the social meaning of such concepts in the course of events, but at present they translate them into the concrete terms of their own experiences.

To illustrate some of the problems of communication that occur and to provide an idea of the issues discussed in the co-op, I list the words and phrases that I most frequently recorded from the utterances of the two professional organizers and from the replies and interventions of the co-op members. The terms are ordered by their rough equivalence; that is, the ways in which members most frequently replied to or tried to express the terms of the organizers. The organizers, of course, took care to express these terms in simpler ways also, and it is through their probing that many of these equivalents emerged.

Organizers	*Members*
Exploitation, special interests, personal interests	To have an interest or business
Social Position	To be poor; to be in a group like professionals
Organization	Participation
Cooperativism, cooperation	Confidence among neighbors or members; to be united
Communism	Agitators, politicians
Private property	To have money or resources
Social isolation	To have no kin or friends
Industrialization, industrial countries	Rich countries, United States; leaving the land
To be in an economic situation; to buy a share	To have ready money
To be impartial in politics and religion	To avoid trouble
Continuing education; to be educated in affairs of co-op.	To be smart; to buy carefully; to be good housekeepers
To keep a reserve for educational and social welfare purposes	To keep money safe, in a bank.
Discussion of themes	So much talk and no action

Many of the terms used by members are reasonable and not unexpected translations of those of the organizers. The problem is ultimately not one of understanding, but of placing the concepts in a social context that members have experienced and to which they can relate. Their own equivalents of the organizers' phrases are not only simple translations but also transformations of meaning, emphasizing day-to-day activity, immediate concerns, and individual qualities and relationships. Yet, one of the most important aspects of the list is that the terms used by the organizers are those whose dynamic for action depends on their being placed within a very different context to that in which members place them. In some cases, the implications of these terms depend upon their being placed within a societal context, and in most cases their interest to the organizers is that they refer to stages in an *achieved* process, such as the existence of a large-scale cooperative movement exercizing pressure on government or to a more integrated and prosperous society. They thus refer to a planned process of social change in which concerted action brings the foreseen results. This is the basic problem of communication, because such a conception was completely foreign to the co-op members' intellectual and personal experience.

The dilemmas of this situation are brought out by looking at the exchange that occurs at one meeting between Tin, a large store owner opposed to the co-op, and one of the organizers. The meeting is a regular one to instruct members further in the principles of cooperativism, but the younger organizer came in place of the more experienced one, and this encouraged Tin to come to the meeting and intervene. Tin's intervention is as follows:

The co-op is going to harm traders because it gets people together and tells them false things, and the co-op will harm small shops. A co-op is better in a large neighborhood and is not right in a small neighborhood like San Lorenzo. The co-op is in fact the work of agitators. Only the owners of businesses are likely to work honorably, for they work with their own money. In a co-op, people will steal money. [Organizer intervenes to say that co-op will be supervised by its members.] No, you will never get proper supervision, and the co-op will never work in San Lorenzo and is bound to fail because there is not enough business and there is too great a risk. This is especially so since a group of people is running the co-op and thus there will be less confidence. [Intervention by organizer to ask what consumers are to do if prices are too high in shops.] They can do nothing because this is up to the government. [For first time other members intervene, saying that consumers can exert some pressure.] The organizer here and those that give these courses have political ambitions and they support a political party. Some people from the neighborhood are already in this party, and their names are well known to everybody.

Tin is one of the neighborhood activists who is most local in his orientation. He rarely, if ever, talks in terms other than those of individual interest and about local matters and personalities. In this speech, he is talking in terms of a local orientation and appealing directly to what he thinks are shared beliefs between him and the members of the co-op.

The correctness of his estimate is borne out somewhat by the inability of any member to disagree with him and by the absence in some subsequent meetings of several of the people who had attended this meeting. When these people were approached to find out why they did not come, they talked about Tin's intervention and their desire to avoid trouble. The members I talked to did not question Tin's premises, and their disagreement with him was based rather on his interpretation of their motives. Thus, it is worthwhile to look a little more closely at some of the premises of his speech.

An important one, a premise that on many occasions poor families are ready to accept, is that people have a right to make a profit from their neighbors provided they do not actually cheat by giving false measure. This premise was to be accepted in later co-op meetings when the issue of lighting was discussed, and they agreed about how much they should pay for one light socket. The charge of two dollars was seen as exorbitant by a social worker present, who complained that the owner of the meter was making a large profit; but this profit was defended and accepted by members on the grounds of risk taken and service offered.

A second premise, which we have referred to many times in our previous discussion, is that a group of people are unlikely to be able to work together well because there can be no trust between strangers. Trust, to Tin, occurs when someone is looking after his own interests with the help of a few kin or friends. A third assumption, which has also been apparent before, is that politics is an illegitimate enterprise, the work of agitators, and is only designed to cheat families.

Tin's speech demonstrates the essential difficulties that the co-op organizers face in convincing members of the ideologies of cooperativism. Members saw the making of profits in the co-op as legitimate and as contributing to their individual welfare. They did not, however, see this as incompatible with other people, such as small traders, making profits. The co-op was seen as their means of getting what they can from the environment, and its future implications for widening the scope of joint action were not considered.

Finally, because members reacted negatively to any suggestion of politics they were reluctant for the co-op to engage in any activity designed to lobby for its own or its members' interests. To members of the co-op, politics mean factionalism and the advancement of individual interests. This was the way they had experienced politics in the neighborhood and in their life careers. One member, for example, has been in jail as a result of an innocent involvement in political squabbles in the rural area, and the eldest son of another had spent a long period in jail for his activity in a labor union. To members of the co-op, the people who benefited from politics were middle-class professionals, while those who were harmed were people like themselves.

In contrast, the organizers were thinking in terms of a wider context, of the experience of other countries and of the possibility of long-term changes in Guatemala. Although they are cautious in their political activities, the organizers consistently attempt to get members to recognize the importance of engaging in group political action. Yet, as we have seen, members do not recognize that *as a group* they have rights that should be respected and need to be defended.

The Field of Orientations

We have, so far. posed the problem of the difference in orientations between organizers and members, recognizing that even members are not entirely uniform in their orientations. However, we must now look at this question from a somewhat different angle by recognizing that, in the course of their membership in the co-op, these low-income families are in contact with a range of orientations and life styles. Membership in the co-op means participating in an organization that includes much of the social diversity of urban life. From this viewpoint, a co-op is one of the places in which the various participants in urban life meet and verbally interact. This process of interaction is one in which different orientations come face to face and accommodate to each other. This is not to say that the accommodation is necessarily a permanent one; it is one that affects the situational behavior of participants.

The first condition of these interactions is the high degree of articulation that they entail between co-op members and the life styles of other social groups both national and foreign. Their coming together in this one situation is an example of a defining characteristic of urban life for the poor—their permeation by external groups and organizations. But it has the immediate significance of bringing co-op members to adopt somewhat different orientations. The interactions affect the other participants also, but our main interest here is to suggest that their impact on orientations is the greater because members are in a situation where they have to take them into account as part of defining their own participation and actions.

First, we can consider the range of interactions that are occurring. One organizer has completed secondary education and has been a long-term worker in the various agencies of the Christian Democrat party. In the course of his work, he has traveled in other Latin American countries and to Europe and the United States. He is attuned to events outside Guatemala and often refers to them in his talks with neighborhood families. On the day of Robert Kennedy's assassination he was visibly upset, blaming it on a conspiracy of the rich in the United States and seeing Robert, like his brother Jack, as someone who was really interested in the welfare of Latin

America. Through him, co-op members learned about the politics of the United States and a little about the significance of the assassination.

The other organizer is an American Friends Service Volunteer, a black American who has completed college. His own experiences were also introduced into co-op life. I was regarded as a participant in the course of events in the co-op. In my visits to other co-ops in the city, accompanied by members of the San Lorenzo co-op, I would be called upon to speak as someone originating from England where the legendary Rochdale Pioneers had lived, and I would have to tell assembled members about the organization and fortunes of the English cooperative movement.

My visits to the neighborhood co-op and to others in the city were some among the many visits made by local and foreign people of professional status. At one co-op meeting in a dimly lit shack of a neighborhood shantytown, there were present (apart from the professional organizers) myself from England, a priest from Switzerland, and a photographer from France, as well as two Guatemalan professionals who were high-ranking officials of the Christian Democrat party. Admittedly, the president of the co-op was unable to distinguish the nationalities when these were told to him and took the easy way out by introducing us all, including the Guatemalans, as visitors from the United States. Yet these contacts with people of a very different social and national status are an important component in the way co-op members view their world. For example, in thanking me for a speech about the Rochdale Pioneers, the president of a shantytown co-op replied by saying: "I thought it was only in Guatemala that there were humble people like us, and it was a revelation to learn otherwise."

Co-op members were constantly exposed to the organizers who saw members frequently and visited their houses as well as coming regularly to co-op meetings. It became expected by most co-op members that they would account frequently for their activities and see them placed within broader issues. This occasionally emerged in a somewhat forced manner as co-op members, whom I had known two years earlier as quiet and uncommunicative people, would make a point of showing me that they had some knowledge of the intricacies of local and international events.

One apparent effect of the co-op was to make it a more normal practice ior members to take stock of themselves and of others. The visitors and other external people with whom members came into contact also served as reference points, evidencing to co-op members the interest of others in their activities and the possibilities open to them in the wider national and even international sphere. As a result, members became noticeably more confident in themselves over time, explicitly recognizing that they had problems in common with people outside their neighborhood and that outside agencies and groups were sympathetic to their situation. They began to feel more secure against the attacks of the people opposing the co-op. It was noticeable that, after Tin's speech, members began to attend regularly again after a period of visits from the outside.

However, it is important to remember that we are talking about a process of accommodation in which members interpret their new experiences with the aid of the familiar. This alters the intended impact of the ideologies to which they are exposed. They interpreted the range of interactions in terms of the personal advantages to be gained and began to bring the outside reference points into their personal as well as co-op calculations. One family needed a loan and spoke to me of the possibility of getting it from one of the Guatemalan dignitaries whom they had heard about at co-op meetings. This same dignitary, a newspaper publisher, was cited in co-op meetings as one able to guarantee the financial security of their enterprise. The co-op opened a range of possible contacts, especially to the officers, and this led members to further interpret their organization as a link in a patronage chain as well as a base for group organization. As we have already seen, Antonio got a job through one of the professional contacts and began to be interested in supporting a political candidate for mayor.

However, within the co-op, members came to terms with external ideologies in a way that they never had in other local situations. They showed, for example, little interest in the content of the speeches of city politicians. Nor did they pay attention to the speeches of neighborhood activists, who were often sophisticated exponents of ideological slogans. Luis, both within the co-op and outside it, constantly spoke in terms that contained more ideology than those of the co-op's professional organizers, frequently using words such as patriotism, nationalism, imperialism, and foreign exploitation. Luis and the other political activists were, however, identified by families as politicians, and their words regarded as normal preambles to any concrete suggestion that they had to make.

Ordinary families and local activists never negotiated over the meaning of concepts in the way that co-op members had to negotiate with those they came into contact with in the co-op. In the co-op such practices were necessary to enable the everyday affairs to be conducted with some security; members had to know what organizers and visitors expected, and these in turn attuned themselves to the local emphases. By contrast, activists were mainly interested in political support, which they mobilized by offering the prospect of concrete services, and learned little from talking to neighbors. Conversely, neighbors had heard what the activists had to say before, and their words carried little effect beyond that of a signal for political support.

Furthermore, the process of organization in the co-op led members to become more closely linked and more likely to react as a group. This process meant that cooperative orientations began to penetrate members and they became used to talking of group action and group decisions. The group was still composed of the same set of friends and kin, but the advantages of its actions as a group became, over time, more readily recognized, even though the aims of group action were still seen in purely concrete and material terms. The orientations of the organizers were also being affected by the dialogue. For Julio, the main organizer, it was a process to which he had long been exposed. Its outcome was an increasing emphasis on small concrete gains together with an increasing impatience with what he called the theoreticians of the party who spoke in sweeping and, to him, inappropriate terms. Though an employee of a political party, Julio became, in fact, one of the first to de-emphasize the wider political implications of what he was doing, justifying this on the ground that the first essential was to get neighbors to recognize the value of working together. Indeed, one of the central characteristics of the co-op was that people were being exposed to a series of perspectives and having to accommodate to these at different times and in different fashions. It did not imply that co-op members emerged with a consistent ideology, but the fact that they came to accept diverse orientations was an important contribution of the co-op. Consider these comments by Félix in reply to a question about the cooperative during the tape recording of his life story. Félix had always been a very passive member of the neighborhood, and on previous occasions I had found it difficult to get him to make any general statements about his life or expectations.

Here [in the capital] it's becoming so that it's a gathering; all united. Here in the capital, let's say, when we are united, then we go to the cooperative, and we have made a little group, which is the thing I have worked most in. We live together, and we are some ten of us. It's the cooperative and we are taking part in it, coming and calling to the community to unite themselves with us, so that we can have a betterment among our very selves here. So me, for example, I operate in this fashion. The co-op people, both the members and the chiefs, they talked me into it. Now that I am in a group, well now they came to ask me if my daughter could take part as the co-op salesgirl. I acceded to her. Now they are talking in the co-op that they are going to pay her a wage and that they think a lot of her and will look after her for me. In few days there's a lot of people who want to get into the gathering and join us. So I figure that shortly we will have some more people; more strength and we will have more goods in the shop to satisfy the demands of the community, so that we can make more sales and supply all within the co-op. The co-op is the first group I have joined. I also helped the people in the old committee [betterment committee]. When they were here I helped them, but I did not take part. I would not have joined the co-op, but my wife kept on talking about it for days. I wouldn't have joined because coming from my work, well I was resting and would go and lie on the bed. Then one day I went to hear a talk, and so I entered and we have worked a lot in the co-op.

I have not joined other groups because they cause a lot of problems. They talk a lot about you. Even here being a member of the co-op the people talk. But the point of it is to take a greater part in the community, so that we are united, that we are all alike, so that the co-op comes to benefit all, not only to the benefit and strength of us who are running the co-op. No, we want all to take part and all to have a benefit. With time they will have some benefit. Many of them think that we keep our money in our pockets, but it is not true, because the money goes to the bank. So many will say that they make good use of the money, and it's going to happen, we have already taken the first step, we have opened a shop. Now many want to join too, and we await them with open arms. I have a lot of relations with people in the co-op as the group of the co-op keeps growing. I have few relations with people at work. They are from all over the city. There are only some two who live nearby and they are friends, and they told me that they would take part in the co-op too.

What we see in Félix's comments is the combination of the various perspectives to which he has been exposed with his own orientations deriving from his career experiences. Interestingly, his use of the term "community" probably reflects his own origins in a relatively solidary Indian community. The communidad, which is the term he uses in the tape recording, has a social meaning as referring to the body of property and custom that constitutes traditional Indian organization. Félix consistently interpreted city life in terms of a local orientation, emphasizing the value of local organization and the goodwill and patronage of those outside. Here, he is translating the remembered rural ideologies to take account of what is essentially a novel and urban organization. But this organization becomes translated into familiar terms and in the course of doing so both his traditional definition and the organizers' definition undergo subtle but important changes. The translation is literal, and the apparent *non sequiturs* and free associations represent his own efforts to recount to me his experiences and perceptions. He is not consistent and wavers between pride in group action and fear of committing himself to the company of relative strangers. He defends his decision partly by emphasizing the value of cooperative action and partly by emphasizing the smartness of the way in which the co-op organizes, using their banking as an example. He is concerned both with personal gains, such as a salary for his daughter, and with the broader benefits for the community. These orientations are not incompatible, and Félix sees nothing inconsistent in what he says. They do, moreover, define some of the achievements of the co-op. Through the course of exposure, someone who has remained essentially an illiterate peasant has begun to see his environment in more general terms than ever before. Indeed, his views are also evidenced in his acts, and in the last months of my acquaintance he became more active in community affairs than he was in the previous years.

The co-op is then, one of the few situations that introduces families to something of the social complexity of urban life, and it does so in a manner that does not discourage them from participating. This happens because it presents a situation in which general perspectives are imparted through a concrete activity that is to the immediate interest of participants. This in itself conditions the impact of the co-op, emphasizing the short-term advantages to be gained from correctly manipulating the environment. It does not make for action that is broadly based on the interests of social and economic categories, and, indeed, it may contribute to an emerging stratification based on special and local interests whose articulation is vertical rather than horizontal.[10]

[10] The small-scale processes we are observing here are one means to assess the mechanisms by which people are grouped and see themselves as grouped across socioeconomic categories as well as within them. The literature on these themes is extensive, but especially relevant to this argument is Torcuato di Tella, "Populism

In this respect, encouraging members to recognize the small but significant differences that their efforts make to their position and giving them greater confidence in their own respectability encourages group action less than it encourages individual participation such as making educational investments on behalf of their children, committing themselves to joint action with neighbors, and giving stable support for organizations. The co-op and the situations it provides is thus one means whereby people with local orientations are brought to accommodate the possibility of long-term and gradual social improvement. But it is an improvement conditioned by the definitions of social change advocated by external, socially and economically superior groups.

---

and Reform in Latin America," in Claudio Véliz, ed., *Obstacles to Change in Latin America*, pp. 47-90.

7. The Organization of a Neighborhood

This chapter will examine the differences in peoples' readiness to become publicly active that are produced by their varying career experiences and by their exposure to the moralities and strategies of other urban groups.[1] We are dealing with local-level politics and define this to include any activity designed to determine public goals and to affect the distribution of scarce public resources. Local-level politics is primarily the work of organizing people to define and implement common goals; at this level there are rarely clearly stated ideologies or organizations specialized for this task.

We will thus be looking at both formal and informal political processes and will find that this distinction is often blurred. Though formal political organization is a factor in the changes occurring within San Lorenzo, it is conducted through personal

[1] See Marc J. Swartz's introduction to *Local-Level Politics*, pp. 1-2.

relationships, which are influenced by factors other than its explicit purposes and ideology. Also, political activities are carried on in groups and associations that often appear remote from formal politics. Betterment associations, religious associations, and groupings of kinsfolk are important political instruments in local-level politics.

Politics extends outward to reach urban economic and administrative organizations and to involve other people and other social groups. A study of local-level politics is incomplete without considering the crucial involvement of external interests.[2] This involvement is not, however, a one-way process, and the plans of important government agencies and influential politicians are often conditioned in unforeseen ways by the events to be described.

Few data were collected on the ways in which these people cooperate outside their neighborhood in such organizations as labor unions and recreational associations. This restriction is, however, one that reflects conditions in the city. The neighborhood is the main basis for political organization among low-income families, and outside the neighborhood there are scarcely any bases for cooperative association with people in like situations. The economic and political organization of the city discourages labor unions and, as we have seen, neither class, ethnicity, nor their own position in opposition to urban administration offers a solid basis for city-wide association among poor people. The organized activities of the poor are, in fact, locally based, and in most cases this means based within an administrative neighborhood. It is to these boundaries that churches, urban administration, local betterment committees, and sporting associations refer when they establish a local basis. For most low-income people, their only experience of organizing to further common interests is within a neighborhood, usually on behalf of neighborhood concerns. This localism is itself an important condition in the pattern of politics we find among low-income people.

[2] Ibid., p. 1

When we talk about common interests, we refer to two somewhat extreme possibilities. There are those issues that are of common interest to all people in the neighborhood and as such are likely to represent the lowest common denominator of neighborhood concerns; for example, the provision of more adequate urban services. Second, there are the very broad, though also very apparent, interests that these families have in opposition to the advantaged urban groups. In the division between rich and the poor, all these families are clearly and expressly classed among the poor. One of the difficulties of neighborhood organization is precisely that these two sets of common interests are difficult to combine on any practical issue under the informal urban conditions that have been described.

The Factors Affecting Participation

In this section we will consider the set of factors that determine those who become publicly active, defining as public any activity that is expressly designed to further goals of relevance to others, whether they involve improving facilities or campaigning for a political or religious ideology. The analysis will test our previous conclusions that it is not the incapacities inherent in such individual characteristics as poverty or illiteracy that basically prevent people from engaging in activity with those around, but differences in their perceptions of their interests and their reliance on private arrangements to secure their environment. A crucial difference between this analysis and that using a culture of poverty thesis is that the problems and factionalism of the poor are attributed to their interaction with other urban groups and not to their being encapsulated in a set of characteristics and attitudes that make them unwilling to participate and hostile and suspicious of each other. This is not to say that poverty and the characteristics associated with it are not contributing factors to their fragmentation and the passivity often found among the urban poor, but they are aggravated by the involvement of external ideologies and interest groups. The shrewd calculations and skill in manipulating urban organization that these Guatemalans show, or their relative success in securing their personal environment, appear to have no counterparts in Lewis's account of the types of participation associated with the culture of poverty. Yet he is talking about families and situations (San Juan and Mexico City) that, in his own terms, should be less embedded in the culture of poverty than these "marginal" people of a much less developed country.[3]

It is important to distinguish between an individual's ability to cope with his urban environment and that of the categorical group of which he is a part; the apparent disorganization of the poor does not necessarily imply that the life space of a poor person is insecure. It does mean, however, that groups with common interests such as the urban poor, concertedly exercise power and affect the distribution of resources when these common interests are not just based on a similar economic or residential position but are also based on a similarity of careers and prospects and on a relatively high density of social relationships. This is the more necessary when their evident characteristics do not permit them to readily trust each other or to identify each other's likely behavior.

The factors that are likely to determine whether a person becomes publicly active are those that give people the locally based social relationships that make them available and visible to others and provide them with some means of trusting those with whom they cooperate. Such factors are different from those that are normally associated with such political activity as voting, and they give the politics of these families their peculiar character. The distinction I am making is that between public and private political behavior.[4] The point of the distinction is that our assessment of political change is often based on indices of private political behavior (voting, attitudes in questionnaires) and that this behavior does not involve continuing relationships with others. However, it is the political activity of mobilizing

[3] Oscar Lewis, *La Vida*, pp. xiv-xlviii.

[4] Bryan Roberts, "Urban Poverty and Political Behavior in Guatemala," *Human Organization* 29, no. 1 (Spring 1970): 20-28.

people for collective action that is more significant for enduring change; such activity does involve continuing relationships with others and is determined by different attributes than private behavior. The significance of this distinction is the sharper because the 1966 voting statistics in Guatemala appeared to herald a period of stable reformist governments with urban residence positively associated with voting for a civilian government of the center left.[5] That this did not last is due to the dynamics of public political activity partly documented here.

The Activists

In the course of the three years, approximately forty people took an active part in organizing events within a neighborhood of some eight hundred adults. Often they held formal positions within one of the many committees established for political, social, or recreational purposes, but often they were active in more informal ways and in more informal groups. Obviously, the distinction between the active and those who are not active is, to some extent, an arbitrary one, especially when there are considerable differences in the level of activity and when the distinction is often based on an assessment of informal position. These forty are widely recognized by others in the neighborhood as active organizers; they are, in most cases, visibly active in directing and organizing within the neighborhood. Their names, with unfailing regularity, are put forward by neighbors in the general assemblies held to organize new projects or to set up new groups. People divide into factions in support of one or another group of active organizers, but the disagreements are always about the same sets of people. Also, in my own observations of neighborhood groups at work within and without the neighborhood, it is always people from among this set that act as leaders, directing people in how to lay communal drainage tubes, addressing assemblies, and organizing delegations or protest marches.

[5] For the voting distribution, see Kenneth F. Johnson, *The Guatemalan Presidential Election, 1966.*

In their work they recruit the help of others, usually neighbors, kin, or friends, so that considerably more than forty people engage at one time or another in public activity. However, it is only at times of neighborhood meetings and local elections that much larger numbers are present such as, for example, in the election for a new betterment committee in September 1968, when a total of 268 votes were cast for the various candidates.

It also appears that those presently active include the main core of those active from the neighborhood's inception. It is difficult to obtain accurate information on those active in the period prior to this study, but the names cited in neighborhood records and by various informants are those who are most important in present activities.

The distribution of occupations among the active is by no means in accord with that of the neighborhood as a whole. There are many more self-employed workers than in the whole neighborhood (55 percent compared to 33 percent), and the jobs are mainly in the more unstable sectors of the economy such as construction, trade, and services. The data also suggest that activists have unusual characteristics. They include a higher than average percentage of migrants (78 percent compared to 75 percent for the whole neighborhood), and the five cases of activists born in the city are, with the exception of José, people on the margin of neighborhood activity. Activists are also those with higher incomes and education. Whereas the majority of family heads in San Lorenzo earn under fifty dollars a month, 76 percent of activists earn more, and of these some 38 percent earn over seventy dollars a month. There are fewer illiterates among the activists. Only about 28 percent of them have second-grade education or less, but the majority (65 percent) have not completed primary school.

To begin to make sense of these statistics, we can compare them with those on individual participation in local and national affairs. At the local level, financial support for community projects is an indicator of individual participation that does not involve public activity, and at the national level voting is a similar index. Though higher income and higher education are positively associated both with voting and financial support of local projects, being a migrant or being self-employed is negatively associated with such participation. For example, those most likely to contribute to the neighborhood's project to replace its water tubing have higher than average incomes and higher levels of education, but they are also more likely than average to be employed in large-scale enterprises. These differences indicate the importance of an individual's social relationships for public activity; it is these relationships that are partly being measured by a person's job or his migrant status. To explore further this relation, we need to consider more generally the characteristics likely to be associated with local activity. This we do under the headings of commitment to the neighborhood, availability for organization, resources, and orientations.

Commitment

Commitment to the neighborhood varies in two basic ways. Families are so committed if most of the social relationships that serve them in their daily life are located in or near the neighborhood. Families whose near kinsmen also live in the neighborhood or whose close friends are located there are more likely to have an interest in what happens to the neighborhood than those whose social relationships are mainly located elsewhere. Action on a neighborhood basis is likely to be more meaningful for such people because it involves others who are relevant; the people with whom they are cooperating are their kin and friends.

Second, commitment is engendered when the neighborhood presents the best and only feasible way of coping with urban residential problems.[6] Partly this is a life-career variable, for as

[6] The type of commitment referred to here is somewhat different from that described for co-op members; while they are primarily committed to a locally based set of relationships, there is some evidence that activists are committed to physical location also. This differentiation is quite important for the flexibility people show in considering changes in their environment and indicates how even formal associations marginally but importantly appeal to different types of people.

families grow in size it becomes less feasible for them to think of moving to bought or rented accommodations elsewhere. Some families, especially where the head is a separated woman, find it difficult enough to make ends meet in the shantytown. People who are not committed in the above sense are people whose social relationships lie mainly outside the neighborhood; these have steady jobs, are in the early stages of their family cycle or have children who are adult, and thus envision the possibility of moving to another neighborhood to rent or to purchase homes.

One important determinant of activism should be degree of commitment to the neighborhood. Comparing the activists with other heads of family in the neighborhood, it is clear that on both counts—the concentration of relationships and stage in life cycle—activists are more highly committed than those who are not active. Of the forty activists, 75 percent have their own kin living in separate households in the same neighborhood, whereas 56 percent of San Lorenzo male heads of family have no relatives living even within the same zone. The recreation and friendships of the activists also appear to be more locally based. It is usual to see members of the committee faction talking together, and they go as a group to bingo or some other amusement. Since many of them are self-employed, the neighborhood is their work location also. Likewise, groups of the radical faction spend a lot of time in each other's company, and common origins also serve as a basis for their interaction with a number of other neighborhood families. Indeed, members of another intensively interacting local group—those who have come from the small town of San Antonio de la Paz—are being increasingly drawn into activity as some of their members become involved in the cooperative.

In terms of their family cycle, activists are also highly committed, having, on the average, 4.1 children compared with 3.1 for the neighborhood as a whole; those falling below this average are in most cases the exceptionally poor, such as María or Daniel, or those who are in a stage of their career where they need to reserve their resources because they are not finding stable employment. Activists are those who can least afford to move to other accommodations. Their reluctance to move is demonstrated quite concretely in their attitudes to the Housing Agency survey that was cited in chapter 6. Despite the fact that activists sampled had above average incomes for the neighborhood, the average deposit they cited (nineteen dollars) in the survey was below that of the neighborhood (twenty-four dollars); in almost all the cases, it was well below what these families could afford even with a small amount of saving. One group of activists formed a committee that was explicitly named the Committee on Behalf of New Housing from the Agency of Housing. Yet the replies of the activists sampled from this group were also below average and certainly below what could be afforded.

The commitment we are describing is not unchanging but varies with stages in an individual's career. As children grow older and move from the neighborhood, so too the commitment of their parents to the neighborhood, is likely to diminish. Likewise, as individuals accumulate urban contacts beyond those with their neighbors, they become more likely to think of moving elsewhere. A change of job often has similar effects as the necessities of the new job require investments of time or money that make it convenient to sell the shack in the neighborhood and move elsewhere. Changes in the composition of the activists are to be explained by these career factors rather than by competition for their places. Some of the activists left the neighborhood completely after changing the nature of their jobs and because their children became less of a financial problem as they grew up.

Justo was a committed activist, but this commitment diminished as his large family grew up, and he finally left San Lorenzo when he obtained stable employment with the government. Similarly, Pepe is now considering selling his shack in the neighborhood, although he has been consistently active from the time of the invasion of the neighborhood. His children are now living apart, and his recent venture into a dry-goods business requires money that he can get by capitalizing on his shack. This venture has increasingly involved him in non-local relationships. For some activists such as Efraim F., their activity has sharply diminished as their families have become less centered on the neighborhood.

Availability

Commitment alone, however, is unlikely to be sufficient unless individuals have the types of jobs and social relationships that make them available for neighborhood activity. Because of the neighborhood's close contacts with external groups and organizations, one aspect of availability is the extent to which people are visible to organizers working outside San Lorenzo. These are likely to recruit people who have jobs that put them into frequent contact with a range of people outside the neighborhood. Conversely, people are willing to be recruited if their jobs allow them the time flexibility to be useful in organizing but without incurring prohibitive costs to themselves. These conditions are best filled by those who are self-employed or who have jobs that have very flexible timetables. Moreover, people in such jobs are also those most likely to be able to benefit from external contacts by putting to use their favors. A self-employed worker, especially those in trade or services, turns such favors to advantage by obtaining trading concessions or licenses, and by getting a little extra work or perhaps a more stable job.

Consider, by contrast, the position of an employed factory worker. If he has a stable job, he will be working long and regular hours with his free time concentrated mostly in the evening and the weekends. He is unlikely to have contact with people of different social position, except for the occasional contact with the factory owner or supervisors. In Guatemala these contacts are infrequent and day-to-day administration is carried out mainly by foremen and low-level managers. Also, contacts with social and economic superiors are less likely to be useful to him, since the potential favors they offer, like getting a job or influencing the city or national administration, are less relevant to someone with a regular and relatively well-paying job.

Everything thus conspires to make it likely that activists recruited by external agencies are in a very particular occupational category—people whose work brings them into contact with higher-status people and are sufficiently flexible in work routine to offer and receive services. If the jobs of the forty people listed in the chart are categorized by these principles, we find that at least two-thirds of them have jobs that both bring them into contact with people throughout the city and have flexible timetables, so that small cost is incurred by the work of organizing. All the self-employed are in this category because, apart from those mobile as part of their job such as traders and salesmen, the self-employed craftsmen move about to purchase materials and sell their wares.

Two of the leading organizers shown in the chart, Angel and Justo, are barbers who through their work came into contact with city professionals and politicians; they can also arrange their time to devote to organization. Likewise, Pepe and Efraim G., even though not self-employed, have timetables that allow them time in the day to organize. As bus inspectors they work alternate morning and afternoon shifts, and their mobility puts them in contact with many outside the neighborhood.

Commitment also becomes a factor in availability, because recruitment proceeds by those already active bringing in those with whom they have continuing and relatively binding relationships; these are the people that leaders among the activists find trustworthy. Relationships with close kin or fellow townsmen are of this kind when they live close together and when these, through recent arrival, age, or separation from their families, have few other resources in the city. It is this process that accounts both for the presence of a disproportionate number of migrants among the activists and for those activists who are unemployed, extremely poor, and illiterate.

The left-wing political group associated with Pablo became composed almost entirely of people from the same village who were united by kinship and who depended upon each other's help in obtaining loans and getting jobs. This grouping was widely identified in the neighborhood as being the most politically radical. It supported communist and socialist candidates at elections, and members of it claimed that they had contacts with urban and rural guerilla groups. In conversation and at their meetings, the ideology put forward was one condemning imperialist intervention and private property, and advocating the need for revolutionary rural and urban reforms. It is interesting and ironic that it is precisely this group that became identified with the essentially conservative and religious activities of the Hermanidad. As we will see, this is to be understood in terms of the inconsistencies to which they are exposed by their social relationships and by the nature of the neighborhood's external involvement.

Some of the women in the Hermanidad are separated from their husbands, have few relatives in the city, and depend on its woman leader for advice and small amounts of material assistance. Although they dislike taking part in public activity, they are occasionally recruited to help their leader. Likewise, several members of the betterment committee were recruited through their debts to some of its existing members; one because he is unemployed and depends on some of the activists for odd jobs and contacts to get employment; another because Pepe and others look after the interests of his aged mother and younger brothers and sisters when he is away at work; and yet another because of his legal trouble that had been resolved by a lawyer friend of the leaders of the betterment committee.

Treating political activity as strongly influenced by the nature and availability of social relationships is necessary under urban conditions where time is valuable and ideology is imprecisely defined. To engage in activity means that individuals forego other possible uses of their time, including earning money, and the gains in terms of satisfying ideological ends are not clearly established in the absence of coherent political programs and in face of the suspicion, and often hostility, of other neighbors.

Resources

We have already seen that activists have higher incomes than nonactivists and that these are necessary to meet the expenses involved. The incidental expenses of neighborhood organizing, though small, are large relative to the budgets of these families. Organizers often take buses on neighborhood business, and on three separate occasions during the field work, the president of the betterment committee hired a taxi to get to an appointment. The writing and sending of letters, the purchase of light bulbs for community meetings, the payment of electricity bills, and many other incidentals are met from the pockets of the organizers; no contributions are levied from neighbors and none are provided by the outside organizations. The benefits that organizers obtain from their external contacts are long-term ones, and from my observations a person earning much less than sixty dollars a month finds it difficult to meet the expenses and has only a distant prospect of return.

However, the source of their income is also important, since those are most likely to participate who derive their income locally and thus are committed to the neighborhood by, for example, the ownership of a neighborhood shop or workshop. Such resources also make people visible and, to some extent, predictable to others in the neighborhood. Neighbors come to small shopkeepers for favors, usually credit, and know they can easily be reached when needed. Four of the most consistently active people in the neighborhood (Hector C. Barnabé, Lisandro, and Efraim G.) are owners of light meters from which they extend up to twenty subsidiary lines to other neighbors for a payment of about one dollar a month. These meter owners are constantly in contact with a range of neighbors, either collecting their dues or mending a fixture. Their visibility ensures that their names are always suggested for offices at community meetings.

Although their "exploitation" of neighbors is often the occasion for critical comment, especially when a light fails, it often happened that someone angered at this situation would soon afterward be citing his meter owner as a friend or "good leader." I pressed several people to explain this apparent inconsistency and always got an answer equivalent to "well, at least I know him." The large shopkeepers and workshop owners in the neighborhood are similarly placed, and neighborhood activists do, in fact, contain a disproportionate number of those with resources of this kind. Eleven of the activists own important neighborhood resources such as a large shop, light meter, or workshop.

Orientations

So far we have looked at the activity of heads of families mainly in terms of the factors in their present situation that predispose them to take a part in organizing the neighborhood. Yet these families are also differentiated by their experiences and by the perceptions that these experiences give them of events around them. A further dimension on which activists should differ from nonactivists is that of the orientations they bring to cooperative activity. An individual's commitment, his availability, and his resources are themselves sufficient explanation of activity, but the style of activity or, for that matter, of nonactivity is directly influenced by people's perceptions of the purpose of neighborhood activity. The orientations we speak of are thus distinct from values; orientations are defined as those dispositions to act that emerge from the conscious effort of individuals to make sense of their past experiences and to mold their futures in accordance with these interpretations.[7]

[7] This I take to be one of the central points emerging from ethnomethodological studies of individuals and their careers. One of the main dynamics of action is an individual's constant, though often unconsidered, attempts to create an identity for

As part of this endeavor, individuals may iterate and hold to certain norms of behavior and overriding values, but these norms and values are always interpreted in terms of an individual's ongoing efforts to impose meaning on his environment.

Among the families that are being described, norms and values do not refer to fixed and clearly defined prescriptions, but to guidelines that are being constantly reinterpreted as an individual attempts to manage his environment. However, this is not to say that these families react only to situational stimuli, and the purpose of emphasizing orientations is to indicate that their attempts to follow a consistent path as they are confronted by different situations is one of the dynamics of change in the urban environment.

In the second chapter, we observed the way in which Angel's career is interpretable in these terms; his experiences made him sensitive to his social environment but provided him with no consistent social identity. He is orientated to actively establishing such an identity by gaining local respect and by showing himself capable of manipulating the complexities of urban politics. He seeks out the type of public activity that is least controversial at the local level, but which allows him to extend its significance to the city and national level.

The two occasions, separated by over a year, on which he became highly active were when he saw that neighborhood events have a clear significance for social and economic change within the city and country and involved him in the minimum of controversy. He became an officer in the local campaign of the civilian party that was supported by most of the neighbor-

---

himself that he can present both to himself and to others as a viable one. The importance of stressing orientations is that they represent the very process of individual "stocktaking" and rationalizing, leading one to select from the present behaviors those that contribute to the identity that is being presented. Since I am dealing with large numbers of people, my analysis is conducted crudely and without the necessary sophistication that attends a proper explanation of such processes. I merely wish to emphasize that it is possible to make certain significant distinctions in the manner in which people undertake this process. See Harold Garfinkel, *Studies in Ethnomethodology*, chapter 5.

hood in the 1966 election. But he ceased to be active after its victory when its work subsequently became locally controversial. In the intervening year he took little part in organization, even when it was not controversial, saying that he was thinking of moving elsewhere. He again became active when he was persuaded by the Christian Democrats that a new and non-controversial betterment committee was urgently needed and could be linked to a wider but nonpolitical social movement. After he was elected president of this new committee, he continued to insist to me and others that his interest was not in factional politics and that his public activity would only continue so long as it did not involve him in controversies. In my last days with him, he was already noticeably upset at the hint of controversy emerging within the committee.

Angel's case illustrates the difficulty of systematically relating orientations to action. Such an attempt not only requires fairly complete data on the attitudes, experiences, and actions of an individual, but also involves the hazardous enterprise of interpreting these data. However, in the case of ten people, including Angel, the data are reasonably complete and allow us to approach the task; since these cases were deliberately selected to overrepresent those active in neighborhood organization, they can be used to draw some general conclusions about the types of orientations that are present.

Apart from the situational pressures that induce people to local activity, we can expect an additional motivation to be that of recognizing the value of organizing others. Certainly there are activists who put no such value on their activity but are attracted by the individual benefits they can derive. For many of the activists, however, the time they spend and the controversies in which it involves them would not be sufficiently compensated by possible benefits. The most successful and shrewd entrepreneurs in the neighborhood are careful to steer clear of activity, emphasizing to me in private that their time is more valuable spent in their businesses.

It is possible to distinguish two prevailing orientations to the value of activity. Some positively value activity because it entails cooperation with others and an attempt to change the current distribution of social and economic resources. In this orientation, such changes are seen to depend on extra-local as well as local organization. By contrast, other activists derive their orientation from the long tradition of community organization in Guatemala that emphasizes not only the value of such organization, but also that it is both an obligation of the more important community members and a sign of their importance. In this last orientation the interest is less in the extra-local significance of organization than in the responsibilities of local leaders to look after the welfare of their neighbors.

These two orientations cut across the factions in San Lorenzo and lead people to interpret events differently. Those more interested in purposive social change always attempt to link local happenings to the wider political processes of the city. Also, though people with this orientation use contacts with professionals and social superiors, the use of such contacts is seen as part of the strategy of changing the distribution of resources in the city. By contrast, those orientated to the value of traditional community organization use these outside contacts more as patronage resources, as means of linking the neighborhood to the power interests outside. They claim that they avoid politics in their local work, and to them the term "politican" is synonymous with deceit and corruption. Pepe, who held to this second orientation, always assured me that he and his committee avoided politics and kept it from entering the neighborhood even at election time. He knew that I knew this to be patently untrue and that I thought it anyway undesirable; but he was communicating to me his belief that local activity has a value but that its wider significance has undesirable and perhaps dangerous implications.

These two orientations, which I call cosmopolitan and local, are related to the career experiences of these families.[8] In

---

[8] This distinction relates to that made familiar by Merton and Gouldner. See Robert Merton, "Patterns of Influence: Local and Cosmopolitan Influentials," in

closely analyzing the life histories of six of the prominent activists (Angel, José, Luis, Pablo, Pepe, and Fausto), their different orientations appear to relate to the extent to which their careers (a) were sharply discontinuous and (b) gave them experience of the necessity and value of cooperating with others.

Each of the three who in neighborhood affairs are likely to emphasize the wider significance of local organization—José, Luis, and Angel—has experienced quite severe discontinuities.[9] José left the city several times in search of work, was a labor organizer at one of the ports, and lost his land for political reasons; Luis was active in labor unions in Arbenz's time and lost his job through these activities; Angel, as we saw in the account of his life, came to see the point of cooperating with fellow workers during his dispute with the Malaria Control. All three have obtained work through their own initiative and have had occasion to confront, in company with fellow workers, the interests of their superiors. All three, in their life histories, interpret their past experiences as a constant effort to improve their own and others' situations, and they see their efforts constantly frustrated by the actions of social and economic superiors.

Pablo is an interesting intermediate case. He has experienced

---

Social Theory and Social Structure, pp. 387-420; and Alvin Gouldner, "Cosmopolitans and Locals: Towards an analysis of Latent Social Roles," *Administrative Science Quarterly* 2, no. 3 (December 1967): 281-306. My use of it does not imply that all the components of these roles are present, but that even the life careers of the poor do significantly differentiate behavior along these dimensions.

[9] I am extracting from orientations only those aspects that appear most crucial to participation in local organization. In the case of Angel it is clear that, though he is classed as a cosmopolitan, there are many individualistic elements in his approach to community action. However, his dominant style is to place local events in their broader context, and in this he contrasts with those I call individualists, whose dominant style is to think first of the individual significance of events. Angel is interesting because, as a moderately successful entrepreneur (he has two barber shops established in good locations in legal areas of the zone), it is not in his personal interest to engage in politics at the local level since it consumes time and might antagonize clients. He is drawn into it because he has come to interpret his own career as an individual expression of the difficulties the poor face in improving themselves in Guatemala, and he acts because placing local events in a wide context is consistent with and helps to reinforce the view he has of himself.

sharp discontinuities as he moved around the provinces and was for a time a labor organizer in a large plantation. But he also served for many years in the army and police and puts great store on the value of the ordered life he led there and on his loyalty to his superiors. He contrasts with his brother Hector, who also worked and organized on plantations, but had no experiences of government work. It is Hector who is the most consistent in placing a wider significance on local events, being the active organizer of their left-wing political group. Pablo participates at Hector's prompting, but he is also a member of the Hermanidad, which is tied to the conservative interests of the local priest, and is thus less consistent in his interpretation of local actions.

The other two activists—Pepe and Fausto—operate on different principles. They are not unaware of extra-local events, but it is clear from their accounts that they see local organization as being both their duty and an indication of their status. Pepe has changed jobs, but with the help of friends, and he has always been active in local sporting and religious associations. He sees himself as a respectable ladino whose position is to help others in local work. His career has helped him sustain this image, and his contacts with social and economic superiors have been entirely of a patronage kind. Fausto comes from a provincial town where his ladino family has long dominated local organization. He himself has come down in the world, spending his time peeling carrots for his Indian wife to sell in the street. But he constantly sees himself as guiding neighbors in their problems, citing his experiences in his home town and as a secretary to various provincial municipalities as evidence of his worth. He, again, though not uncritical of social injustice in Guatemala, primarily interprets extra-local contacts as patronage resources.

Similarly, we can expect those who are not active to be also differentiated by this dimension. It is evident that there are many families in the neighborhood who hold to a traditional definition of community organization; they do not become active because they do not see themselves as having the characteristics suited to such activity. In Félix's life history, a constant theme is his Indian background and the value he places on life in the city because Ladinos and Indians cooperate to improve their position. Although he has experienced social injustive (losing his land) his prior experiences confirm his faith in the benevolence of locally based city organization. However, he emphasizes that his poverty and illiteracy disqualify him from active organization and says he trusts to the competence of the local leaders. He treats Pepe, for example, as an esteemed and respected confidant. Likewise, Prudencio, recently arrived from San Antonio de la Paz and helped first by relatives and then by his employers, sees local organization as necessary but as something reserved for other people. When pressed on the performance of local leaders, he replies that their work is good, though of course there are always problems and people always talk. He is not aware of extra-local politics, and his life revolves around his local Protestant church and their activities.

There are neighbors whose careers have been sharply discontinuous, but for whom such discontinuity leads them to devalue the benefits of cooperation and to emphasize the need to look to the welfare of the individual and his family. This orientation, which can be labeled individualistic, is present among both activists and nonactivists. Among activists it characterizes those for whom local organization is primarily an opportunity to defend or advance their own interests, and among nonactivists it characterizes most of those whose commitments orient them outside the neighborhood and makes them skeptical of the purposes of local organization. Either these people have had experiences that disrupt their faith in traditional community organization, or they have had little experience in it; at the same time they have no experience of cooperating with others against social and economic superiors. Lisandro, for example, has remained on the margin of local activity, and, though he has all the characteristics that should draw him into persisting activity (he has a local business, is self-employed, has a young and growing family, has other relatives in the neighborhood, is literate, and has resources) and is always named at local meetings, he resists all but the occasional service.

His life history is one of separation from his kin, making his own way in the city, becoming an alcoholic, and thinking several times of suicide. He became a Protestant at the instigation of his wife, and this helps him retain some balance despite occasional lapses. He has never experienced the traditional benefits of local organization and sees no particular prestige in community service. At the same time, as a self-employed shoemaker, he has had no positive experience in cooperating with his fellows and no bad experiences with superiors. When interpreting his past, he recites the deceptions of fellow workers and the sin abounding in the city. This suits the ideology of his church, but it also means that he interprets all local activity as primarily intended to cheat neighbors. He is indeed one of the most frequent sources of rumor about local misdoing and gives priority to his work and his family's interest over that of community projects. Another leading Protestant, Isabella, is similar. She too, has characteristics that make people suggest her for local organization, but unlike her daughter, who is also a Protestant, she rarely participates. In her life history, she emphasizes her experiences of individual interests breaking down the traditional cooperation of provincial society and exposing her many times to direct exploitation. She was subsequently abandoned in the city by her husband and reared her children in considerable poverty. Her eldest son got into political trouble and was imprisoned at a time when he was one of the main breadwinners. These experiences have made her avoid wider political implications of organization, but she has little confidence in the value of purely local organization. She is, for example, highly skeptical about the beneficence of external interests and sees them as ultimately geared to her own and others' exploitation.

These differences in orientations are direct consequences of the diversity of careers that have led to the neighborhood under the present conditions of the city's growth. Isolating them illustrates something of the present significance of these careers and helps us to estimate the future of locally based organization in face of the current trends in the city's development. The kind of career that develops local orientations becomes more infrequent as provincial society becomes less self-contained and as personal relationships are less crucial as a means of organizing urban life. As more migrants come direct to the city from smaller towns and villages, and if the urban economy continues to be composed of small-scale enterprises, there is also less opportunity to develop cosmopolitan orientations. Those presently attracted to locally based organization are likely to be replaced by people with more pragmatic and individualistic orientations. In one sense, this development is likely to make local organization more consistent, reducing it to a denominator understandable to all and eliminating the misunderstandings and consequent mistrusts arising among those stressing distinct orientations. However, it also means the weakening of a major impetus for self-organization among poor people in Guatemala City.

Differences in orientations have the immediate implication for our analysis that, when politics is based upon people with different types of life careers, we must take symbolic negotiation into account as an element in neighborhood organization; people must present actions in ways understandable to the orientations of the different segments. This is to be an important dynamic in our analysis of the sequence of organization in the neighborhood.

The Direction of Activity

The various attributes that we have identified reinforce an individual in his local activity, but it is also the case that activists differ in the extent to which they possess these attributes. To understand the significance of this for action, we can rank the factions by their possession of these various attributes.

If we assign the activists to the three groups that are evident in local politics, it is clear that they are sharply distinguished by their time flexibility and by their resources. Whereas the committee faction is highly committed, flexible in

Table 26. Attributes of Activists by Faction (Percentages)

	Highly Com- mitted	Flexible Time- tables	Suffi- cient Resources	Possess all Three Attri- butes	Orientations		
					Local	Cosmp.	Indiv.
Committee faction (16 members)	72	87	87	56	38	23	39
Radical faction (19 members)	80	58	39	16	39	45	16
Uncommitted (5 members)	60	25	60	–	40	40	20

"Highly committed" means those with at least one kinsman in a separate household in the neighborhood. (In all cases, my field notes also suggest that the friendships of the committed are also locally based.) "Flexible timetables" means that the individual can arrange his day to spend time in work of organization. "Sufficient resources" is defined as having incomes over 60 dollars either through work or through additional sidelines such as a shop or a meter.

its timetables, and possessed of adequate resources, only a minority of the radical faction is flexible and has sufficient resources (Table 26). Only one of the uncommitted has a flexible timetable. In the fourth column of the table are those who possess all three of these attributes, and the distinction between the three groups becomes sharper. Over half the committee faction possess all three attributes and, consequently, there is a substantial nucleus readily available for local organization. In contrast, only three of the radical faction possess all three attributes, and one of these, Justo, has left the neighborhood. None of the uncommitted possess all three attributes.

We thus have one explanation for why, despite all its vicissitudes and political defeats, the committee faction continues to dominate the local betterment committee, which is the only persisting formal expression of neighborhood organization. They are the only ones continuously available for such organization. In contrast, the radical faction, though active informally, is unable to provide candidates for posts in the local betterment committee. This is observable in the various meetings to elect new committees when members of the radical faction launch extensive criticisms of the committee's work but excuse themselves from serving on a new committee because of lack of time or money. When, at the end of the field work, members of the radical faction were finally elected to replace the committee faction, the most active member and president was Angel, one of the two of the radical faction that possesses the three attributes.

From these findings, we can derive a further important condition of formal neighborhood organization; it is that only a certain segment of those publicly active are available for it, and these have characteristics, such as being self-employed, that make it likely that their other concerns will influence the conduct of such organizations. The implications are evident when we consider the dominant orientations of the two major factions. These are extracted from field notes of conversations and from statements and speeches at public meetings. There are no sharp differences between the two factions, but it is clear that the committee faction contains more individualists and the radical faction more cosmopolitans. The committee faction contains a large number who are, and have long been, self-employed so that while their careers may have been discontinuous, only a few will have experienced cooperation with others of like situation, and are likely to have individualistic orientations.

This means that one element in the style of local formal organization is the presence of those who emphasize the individual advantages to be gained and take advantage of links with external groups to further these interests. The wider implications of local organization are more frequently expressed by their opponents. These identify local organizations such as the betterment committee with exploitation and help to reinforce neighbors' lack of confidence in the possibilities of such organization.

The Conditions of Dependency

I intend to analyze the sequence of events in terms of the constraints placed upon local organization by the transactions occurring within the neighborhood and between the neighborhood and external groups and organizations. This extends our previous analysis by showing how events internal to the neighborhood are themselves an independent dynamic in influencing the activities of external interests and places local activity within a set of transactions occurring throughout the city.

I will claim that, despite the apparent flux of political activity among the poor, it is basically organized in a recurring pattern that insures their continuing fragmentation and their inability to act to change the distribution of resources in society. This pattern is produced by the interplay of three sets of conditions, and their presence among the families we are discussing, or among the urban poor elsewhere, limits the capacity of poor people to organize for themselves.

These conditions have been implicit in our previous analysis, and I restate them summarily before specifying them in terms of the political events inside and outside San Lorenzo. They are (1) the absence of bases for effective leadership, (2) the recruitment of leaders from those who are particularly accessible to external influence, and (3) the informality of the urban environment.

Effective leadership emerges from transactions in which the services of one or several members become so apparently useful to others that to obtain them they are willing to comply with directives.[10] This continues as long as followers receive what is regarded as either a fair or a going (the best available) rate of exchange. The services received may be of several kinds, such as monetary rewards, technical aid, or physical or moral security. The point of specifying this process is that it implies that a leader is constantly spending and replenishing his ability to get others to comply. Every directive he issues that requires extra effort from followers consumes some of the "credit" he has gained through past services. Effective leadership, especially when it is not institutionalized or backed by coercive force, is thus constantly being achieved. This is one important condition

---

[10] This analysis of leadership depends heavily on Blau and is the specification of the implications of his analysis in an informally organized environment. Peter Blau, *Exchange and Power in Social Life*, pp. 118-122, 201-205.

on the operation of local-level politics, indicating that the securing of effective leadership is an independent factor in local events. This becomes more evident if we look at the theoretical conditions for obtaining the compliance of others. First, leaders exercise power over others to the extent that they are able to provide needed services. Furthermore, their power is greater if there is no other source of the services needed and if those who need them are unwilling to do without these services. The last condition suggested by Blau—that those needing the services are unable to use coercion to obtain them—does not concern us here.[11]

In local-level politics, there is likely to be little basis for continuing and effective leadership. There are no services within the capabilities of members of the neighborhood that are habitually needed there; the number and span of external relationships is in this sense both an alternative resource to neighborhood exchanges and a reason why families are not likely to be interested in services offered locally. There are some neighborhood groups that intensively exchange services, but these exchanges are in part dependent on the smallness and isolation of the groups. Most neighbors have many alternatives to neighborhood-based services and are not constrained to give compliance for services that they may be able to obtain at a better rate elsewhere, for example at work. Also, we have noted that one characteristic of a low-income neighborhood is the diversity of orientations among families. There is no common standard placed on communal action, and its benefits are regarded as illusory by people holding certain orientations in the neighborhood.

Those who wish to organize others are thus faced by evident difficulties in trying to obtain their compliance. They cannot use qualities of leadership or know-how that are not apparent to or particularly valued by the majority; instead, they are increasingly forced to supply specific material services. Given their poverty and the nature of the services needed in a neighborhood, they are likely to turn to external groups to help them

[11] Ibid., pp. 118-119.

provide such services. This extension has its own dynamic requiring local leaders to offer something in return, usually their services in the political organization of the neighborhood on behalf of the external group. This further consumes the local credit of leaders and adds to instability and the likelihood of competition over their position.

The second condition—that leaders are recruited from those whose jobs make them particularly accessible to external favors and patronage—creates a situation in which it is easy for neighbors to mistrust leaders, especially when they administer formally organized services. No matter how hard the leaders attempt to provide services, neighbors see them as personally benefiting from the resources formal organization appears to command. As far as neighbors are concerned, there is a constant imbalance in their exchanges with leaders. This increases the problem of establishing effective leadership, especially when, as in the case of the betterment association, competition for leadership and lack of confidence in leaders is not resolved by others taking over. Consequently, suspicions about the private interests of the leadership group and the unintended consequences of their other commitments undermine both the credibility of leaders and the possibility of local organization.

It is, however, the informality of the urban environment that encourages locally competing groups to include a range of external interests in local organization. The nature of this process is clarified by making use of the concepts of arena and field.[12] By field, I mean the set of relationships involved in the issue in question. This depends on participants' own definitions of what is relevant to their action and is subject to negotiation and redefinition. A local controversy involves a field that includes its instigators and those other people, social groups, or organi-

---

[12] These are discussed in Swartz, but the definitions given here are intended to emphasize the dynamic of the relation between arena and field. The concepts are significant because they suggest that the flexibility of defining fields of action within a given arena is a characteristic of local-level politics under informal urban conditions. March J. Swartz, *Local-Level Politics*, pp. 8-18. Cf. Kapferer, *Strategy and Transaction*, chap. 4.

zations that are actively defined as relevant to the issue. It is clear that a property of a field and its advantage in conceptualizing political processes is its fluidity; its composition changes from issue to issue as new people are brought in and old ones contract out.

Apart from the field of relationships involved, there is, however, the wider arena in which the action takes place. This can define the total structural and cultural context of participants, but for our immediate purposes, it will be confined to the city and its economic, social, and administrative organization. The value of distinguishing field and arena is, first, that it enables us to relate the particular sequence of action to its wider context. Second, and more important for the present analysis, it enables us to see that a further vital condition of local-level politics is that the participants can use the arena to redefine the particular field of action to include other individuals, groups, or organizations (other social loci) that are presumed to favor them. Minimally, redefinition serves to exclude from the field of action social loci that favor the competing interests.

This strategy is more prevalent when the relationship of a particular field of activity to the wider arena is sufficiently unstructured for participants to choose relatively freely the social loci they wish to define as relevant. In contrast, in those cities where the relation of a local neighborhood to welfare and administrative agencies is precisely defined, participants in local politics must often compete within a relatively stable definition of the field of their activity. In relatively formally organized cities, many of the life chances of the poor are determined for them by their evident credentials and characteristics. Getting welfare aid, getting a job, or petitioning for improved services depends on a defined structure of opportunities that allows relatively little flexibility of interpretation. The emphasis, of course, is on "relatively," since in any situation people are likely to find means of redefining the appropriate field to their advantage; but in comparison with the poor in Guatemala their flexibility is low. This means that the poor in informal situations are more likely to be active manipulators of their environment than those in formally organized situations, but at the cost of fragmentation and the reduced likelihood of organizing themselves against evident administrative exploitation. In Guatemala City, the position of local residential units is so imprecisely defined that a variety of external interests are able to be involved in local fields of activity without violating any implicit or explicit definition of the boundaries of action.

Redefining the field of activity becomes a continuing dynamic of involvement with external interests. It is also a process through which the business of local politics continues and expands without a substantial currency of exchange. It is essentially a means of obtaining local support on credit by offering an interpretation of a neighborhood's position that promises future rewards deriving from particular external interests. The credit in political compliance gained by successfully convincing others of a particular definition of a field of activity is then usable to purchase favors from external interests. The local credit can then be repaid.

Our discussion of the conditions of organization among these families can be summarized in propositions that serve to guide the analysis of the sequence of events that follows. First, we can expect local leadership to become less effective the more San Lorenzo loses its identity and the more fragmented and dispersed become the relationships of its inhabitants. Second, the more formally organized the neighborhood becomes the more likely are leaders to be perceived as unrepresentative and self-interested. Third, at the times when the administrative relation of San Lorenzo to the city is least structured, the more successful is the strategy of redefining the field of activity in local-level politics and the more dependent the neighborhood becomes on external interests. Any collective action among the poor is thus more likely to be successful when the group is bounded in ways that exclude outsiders and that give rise to a generally accepted informal leadership.

The Background of Events

We have already discussed the circumstances of San

Lorenzo's foundation in 1959. The neighborhood has pursued an eventful career from this date, at first defending its interests against the antagonism of government and municipality and then becoming increasingly accepted as part of urban administration and politics. The details of the early history do not concern us, but we can extract from the early situation some points relevant to our present analysis.

When the neighborhood was first invaded, families had a common and urgent problem—maintaining themselves in extremely difficult surroundings and in face of the hostility of the authorities. In addition, the occasion for many of the families coming to the neighborhood was their pressing urban needs—needs that were not alleviated by their existing relationships. It was a period when families in the neighborhood could be expected to depend upon each other and when conditions would be favorable for the emergence of a leadership to coordinate activity.

The services this leadership offered were constant and relatively easy to give. They consisted of the protection of inhabitants' rights and the negotiations of minimal urban services. Though there were differences among the early leadership, it is apparent that neighbors did cooperate together under their direction and with some success. Until a year or so before field work began, the most prominent members of the factions worked together on the various projects. This organization was informal and not instituted in committees with set procedures. People in the neighborhood look back to this period as almost a golden age before faction fights and politics entered the situation.

By 1963, however, it was clear that the local leadership no longer found it easy to obtain neighborhood cooperation. The immediate threat to the security of the neighborhood had passed, and the neighborhood was beginning to change its composition, not only through the exodus of some of the original settlers but by the filling of available space with new shacks. The newly arrived often paid a small fee and, according to present leaders, felt less committed to the neighborhood. To this day, anyone who arrived after 1962 is regarded as a recent arrival and as belonging to a category that cannot claim the same rights as the original settlers.

A situation was thus created in which the original bases for effective leadership were weakened, and those wishing to organize consequently had to look for means of providing concrete services to obtain compliance. Those among the original leaders who, because of their orientations or the individual benefits they obtained, wished to continue to organize the neighborhood, became active in the search for external resources.

In the course of these years, it also became evident that a variety of external interests could be defined as relevant to the fortunes of San Lorenzo. Throughout this period, no formal arrangement was made to define its legal position. It came under the successive surveillance of the national government, a committee of government-appointed notables, the municipality, and the local mayor. The church, through the local priest, participated actively in the affairs of the neighborhood. The informality of San Lorenzo's relation with the rest of the city is indeed exceptional, and as such is interesting in the analysis of arena and fields. However, most neighborhoods have no rigidly defined relationship with outside agencies in Guatemala City, and it is common for various individuals and groups to take an interest even in administrative matters within neighborhoods.

At the end of this early period in 1964, the Agency for International Development entered the neighborhood's field of activity through the auspices of the local mayor. As a direct result there was the inception of a formally organized neighborhood betterment committee. To man this committee, the local mayor sponsored people who had been his political enemies in a previous election, because he could find no one else willing to cooperate.[13] These members used their new-found connection

---

[13] The local mayor is my term for the man appointed by the mayor of the city to look after a particular zone of the city. The ethnography of local politics in Guatemala is highly complex. These committee members (basically the core of what I call the committee faction) had in 1962 sponsored a rival candidate for city mayor to

with the local mayor and with the agency to make themselves appear effective leaders and the only formal channel of services and requests. The specific services they provided, mainly a large-scale drainage system, consolidated their leadership, and in the 1966 election their "credit" was such as to lead outside observers to estimate that San Lorenzo voted fairly solidly for the candidate sponsored by the local mayor, Alfonso, and the betterment committee.

These background events set the conditions that impose the subsequent pattern on neighborhood activity, and I will now present some extended cases of political activity involving San Lorenzo in the period from 1966 onward. Remember that the activity to be described is the only continuing political activity that occurs among the poor in Guatemala City. It forms the stuff of political change and, by comparison, voting statistics or attitudes reported at second hand are misleading indicators. Such activity does not have the glamour of the violent clash of men and ideas that is sometimes thought to constitute the politics of the underdeveloped world; but this local-level activity fundamentally determines the political prospects of Guatemala.

The argument must be put this strongly because, in face of the complexity of small-scale incidents, it is easy to overlook the underlying pattern they give to the political process. What I shall try to demonstrate is that the fragmentation of the poor and their accessibility to external interests prevents any stable political development, be it labeled left or right. Everyone, including professional and other high-status people, is caught in the difficulties this entails. Ideology remains a part of these political conflicts and is sincerely sponsored by many of the participants, but their ideas have no stable audience under the conditions I will describe.

---

the one sponsored by the local mayor. They subsequently became allies of the local mayor, Alfonso, and switched their allegiance to his chief and political ally, the mayor of the city. They then became the mayor's neighborhood committee for reelection. The mayor, however, lost his bid for reelection in 1966.

The Search for New Resources

The result of the 1966 election—the defeat of the outgoing mayor and the coming to power of a mayor with links with the Christian Democrats—effectively destroyed the authority of the existing formal leadership in San Lorenzo. In this period, Carlos, a full-time Christian Democrat worker, attempted to organize the city's shantytowns into committees in defense of their residential interests. The issue he used was the threatened takeover by a governmental agency of the land on which San Lorenzo and other shantytowns are located. Despite the apparent saliency of the issue to residents, Carlos's attempts were not successful. In San Lorenzo, neighbors were apathetic and listened to those internal and external groups that advised them to await the coming to power of the new national government.[14]

The next important stage in events occurred with the official appointment of Carlos as coordinator of the neighborhood committees of the zone in which San Lorenzo is located. This appointment came quite dramatically on the day that a delegation of the committee faction was due at the Agency for International Development to petition for more aid to San Lorenzo. Carlos was able to accompany it in his official position, and this proved to be the beginning of a new relationship that the agency developed with the zone. The agency was eager to foster urban development and offered Carlos small amounts of aid, including sending his nominees on traineeship courses to the United States. In return, they continued to receive propaganda for their program. Visiting dignitaries, including in this period a United States Senator, were always brought to tour the neighborhood and its projects.

Carlos's new position also changed his relationships with the committee faction, which had been his political opponent in the

---

[14] This particular event is partly analyzed in my article, "Politics in a Neighborhood of Guatemala City," *Sociology* 2, no. 2 (May 1968): 185-203.

recent election, although Carlos agreed to work with them. The reasons appear to be those suggested in my analysis of activists' commitment. He admitted to me that he had first approached his old supporters, who included members of the radical faction, but that they had no time and wanted only specific rewards such as jobs or municipal favors. Also, most of the committee faction were in situations in which they could profit easily from the services Carlos offered. A municipal job for a son or a trading concession were the favors that Carlos was to use to obtain the support of the committee faction. Carlos needed their support in return. His position with respect to the municipality was insecure; his job had been granted in return for the electoral support that he and his party had given, but the ambitions of both were suspect to the new mayor and his assistants. It thus suited the interests of both Carlos and the committee faction to attempt to reestablish their authority in the neighborhood. The strategies they used to accomplish this are shown in the event set out below, which marked the beginning of the committee faction's renewed authority.

The Emergence of Effective Leadership

A large meeting was called at Carlos's official zonal residence to establish a new committee. This was well attended by about two hundred neighbors. Present at the meeting were observers from the municipality; it was chaired by the municipality's central coordinator of committees. Carlos explained the purpose of the meeting, saying that the mayor wished to work through committees of neighbors. He then individually presented the old committee and read out a shortened version of the neighborhood's achievements and talked about proposed projects, which included a possible donation from AID, a plan to get building materials for neighborhood projects from the demolition of the penitentiary, and further work on the drainage. He then allowed the old committee to resign individually with speeches recounting and justifying their previous work. Carlos emphasized that these resignations did not bar them from being reelected. Except in the case of Oscar, Efraim, and Barnabé, the old committee expressed the desire to go on working and stressed the need for more work in the neighborhood.

The radical faction came in force to the meetings. They talked together before it and sat together. Members of the faction had already been told by their official contacts that the national government had no desire to interfere in the problem of the shantytowns, and four of them had been individually rewarded with jobs. A further background factor was that the local priest was cooperating with the new mayor and was expecting him to help with the plan for relocating the shantytown at a distance from the city.

After the resignations of the old committee, members of the radical faction got up to argue that, though they were grateful to the committee for the work they had done, it was better for help to come directly from the municipality that could provide better technical advice and avoid any suspicion of local dishonesty. The speeches set off bursts of affirmative applause and even dependents of the committee faction rose to talk of the advantages of direct aid. The sense of the meetings after about twenty to thirty speeches was clearly in favor of direct action by the municipality. Throughout, Carlos favored the committee faction, calling on them to speak more frequently than anyone else in order to refute charges of personal dishonesty.

The central coordinator then addressed the meeting, arguing that people must obtain for themselves what they need and not depend on the paternalism of those above, whether it be the government, the municipality, the United States, or Europe. He reemphasized this point by saying that the neighborhood otherwise had no hope of getting help from the municipality, since its illegality made the municipality careful of giving direct aid. Also, he added, though the municipality can help, since people pay no taxes it is under no obligation to do so. His speech was loudly applauded.

Carlos then spoke and made the same points. In the election that followed immediately, the committee faction was easily reelected—fifty-seven to seven, though there were many abstentions. The negative votes came from the most active members of the radical faction. However, because of the resignation of three members and two vacant places, new members had to be nominated. Carlos prevented the committee faction from making any nominations and asked for nominations from the floor. Fringe members of the radical faction put forward a series of names, including all their most active members. Each of these refused to be nominated, pleading work as an excuse. Finally, three members of this faction agreed to let their names stand and were elected. In the meetings of the reconstituted committee, the new members found themselves given minor posts and were infrequently called upon to speak. All three dropped out after the first three meetings of the committee.

This event marked the beginning of the reconstitution of the authority of the committee faction. It demonstrated to neighbors San Lorenzo's newly established relation to the municipality and excluded other possible definitions of their field of activity. In the months following, the municipality did engage in specific projects such as repairing the public latrines and improving the streets and community facilities.

However, the event is also interesting because it illustrates a further stage in the development of local politics. The radical faction desires the ending of formal organization in the neighborhood and defines the field of activity as one in which San Lorenzo becomes a normal part of city administration. They are, however, in a certain dilemma since it is an important component of the orientations of many of their own members that poor people should organize themselves and not trust to the good will of the middle-class politicians that control city administration. The members of the radical faction who take the most prominent part in the discussion are those with local or individualistic orientations. They appeal directly to an important component in local orientations—that of the many families who see their position as being relatively favorable and to be maintained by keeping out of trouble and relying on external favors. For this reason they receive warm applause, even from people closely tied to the committee faction who held to this orientation.

They failed in their attempt because their definitions could not match the evident crystallization of the neighborhood's position as a part of decentralized municipal administration, in which Carlos and his supporters had a key place. The success that Carlos and the central coordinator achieved was emphasized by their securing representatives from the radical faction to stand for election. This was an implicit recognition that they accept Carlos's definition of the neighborhood's position. It further suited Carlos because the new members represented some of the interests that had supported him in the last election, but did not include the most forceful opponents of the committee faction. He thus achieved the appearance of consensus without weakening the position of the group now most tied to him.

This event is also interesting because it shows us external agencies emphasizing local self-help and internal activists pressing for dependence. We have seen the reasons for this, but one of its consequences was to further diminish the credibility of local activists. It defined for many a situation in which local politics was inevitably tied to the interests and favors of external groups.

The reestablishment of the authority of the committee faction meant a period of relative calm in the neighborhood. A series of stable exchanges differentiated the neighborhood, assigning individuals and groups to their various spheres of interest. The various members of the radical faction continued their political, religious, and other activities but in a subordinate position to the committee faction. The Hermanidad was brought into closer contact with the betterment committee and was expected to provide some account of its activities, and there were similar moves to associate the Protestant churches. The various services that were provided for the neighborhood were mainly channeled through the betterment committee.

An indicator of the relative stability of this period was the cooperation of the radical faction over the proposed renewal of the neighborhood's water system. The most prominent members of the radical faction agreed to help collect the money for this and thereby not only aided in a project adding prestige to Carlos and the committee faction but also gave up the opportunity of later being able to accuse the committee of expropriating funds.

Payment for Services Received and the Creation of Internal Imbalances

The authority of the committee was, however, bought at a price. Henceforth the committee and its individual members became increasingly drawn into the wider organization that Carlos and the Christian Democrats were establishing throughout the city. Also, Carlos himself became a member of the San Lorenzo committee, serving as its treasurer even though he himself did not live in the neighborhood.

The members of the committee also received individual rewards for their cooperation. With Pepe and Luis, this took the form of loans to allow them to finance personal projects, and in the case of José, his incorporation as a paid official of the wider political movement. These acts were regarded by Carlos and the committee as binding their relationship.

In Pepe's case, for example, the form of aid established a close working relationship between him and Carlos. Carlos first invested money in a newspaper route, with Pepe organizing it. This proved a failure, and the next scheme was to set up Pepe in the production of popsicles, with Carlos taking a cut of the profits. This enterprise again failed due to unfavorable newspaper publicity concerning the health menace of such popsicles. Finally, Carlos obtained Pepe a stall in the new market of the zone and lent him the money to purchase most of the stock. Pepe was slowly repaying this loan and, in the meantime, repaid Carlos in other kind by acting as a loyal supporter not only on the committee but also in Carlos's various other interests in the city. Pepe served as an organizer in the new market, and, unwillingly, on Carlos's instructions appeared in the leading national newspaper as heading a delegation to attack municipal policy toward the markets. Pepe was also one of the zonal residents who went to lobby on Carlos's behalf when he was attacked in the city press for his machinations in the zone.

In this period, which covers the end of 1966 through 1967, the neighborhood became increasingly organized from the outside. With the help of the betterment committee, literacy classes and the beginnings of a consumer's cooperative movement were introduced into the neighborhood by professionals from the Christian Democrat party. They cooperated with the social worker attached to the neighborhood to launch a concerted campaign to involve families throughout San Lorenzo. The neighborhood also became involved in the city-wide schemes of the party to establish a viable residents' movement with consumer cooperatives. San Lorenzo residents figured with others in national press reports of meetings to lobby government or municipality for improved urban services.

Within the neighborhood, however, these activities generated little sense of identity or cohesion. Residents complied with directives to improve the neighborhood, but few became actually involved in the work of organization. With the increasing penetration of the neighborhood by outside organizations, families increasingly came to regard the services they received as their due. The various works undertaken in the neighborhood were increasingly carried out by municipal workmen, and for many this provided evidence that the neighborhood was being incorporated into the regular system of urban administration. This feeling was reinforced by the increasing practice of selling shacks instead of giving them to friends and kin, and for sums of up to five hundred dollars. There was also increasing evidence of accommodations being rented. Newcomers were expected to make small donations on taking over their houses and came under stronger pressure than long-established residents to pay their contributions to the several community projects of the period. These newcomers regarded such solicitations as a form of tax and interpreted the payment as some form of official recognition of the legitimacy of their occupation. When I first met some of these new families, they would search out the receipt for payment to show to me as proof that they were legitimate residents.

One of the most important bases for cooperative action among these low-income families had been almost totally eroded; their situation was being increasingly defined for them as a regular, if underprivileged, section of the city's residential organization. The activities of the committee and the organizations to which it was linked were, moreover, beginning to create increasing difficulties for the relationships of others in the neighborhood. As the neighborhood became increasingly incorporated into zonal administration, so it jeopardized the relationships of the Hermanidad with the local priest. The priest saw the neighborhood as part of his particular concern and thought it needed to be moved to a more suitable location. As the neighborhood became part of zonal administration, so his influence was threatened and the favors he extended, such as free welfare milk, seemed likely to become part of normal administrative procedures. The Hermanidad, which distributed the milk among its own dependents, was not reassured by the attempts of the committee to bring its activities under surveillance.

Likewise, the attempts to organize cooperatives and the various other associations began to threaten the interests of families who depended on the exploitation of others. The forty small shopkeepers became increasingly hostile to the idea of the cooperative, and those neighbors who made a living by letting out electricity, by giving advice, and so forth, suspected that the external organizations were also aiming to provide these services.

What was basically happening was that the increasing attempt of external organizations to extend their influence disrupted the established transactions within San Lorenzo, especially those among the groups most committed to the neighborhood. They were thus attacking the very groups who were most likely to engage in local collective activity. Those families who were not threatened were those whose relationships were mostly outside the neighborhood and who used it for purchasing commodities and as a place to sleep.

Apart from these processes, the transactions occurring between external interests added an additional dynamic to the local situation. As Carlos extended his own organization throughout the zone, he consolidated his position and made himself less dependent on the favors and support of either the mayor or the Christian Democrat Party. His activities extended the field of action of the neighborhood to include important political foci within the city.

The Emergence of a Local Boss

Carlos had been constructing a powerful local base in the zone, appointing representatives from each neighborhood to serve with him on a central committee and establishing committees of his own to link the various neighborhoods. At this time, he began to be more explicit in his criticisms of the middle-class professionals who were in charge of the various Christian Democrat organizations, saying that they looked down on uneducated people and wanted to run everything their way. In turn, these professionals began to tell me that they were worried about Carlos because he seemed to be looking for his own interests and not to the development of the whole movement. They particularly cited the authoritarian way he ran the various zonal committees. He replied to these criticisms by arguing that the democratic procedures the professionals advocate are merely ways of weakening intermediate officials and strengthening the party's central control.

Carlos began to give active support to a prominent newspaper publisher who was to be a candidate in the next mayoral elections. This publisher was also the party's candidate, but Carlos approached him independently and acted independently as his agent. Publicity favorable to Carlos appeared in the newspaper—the second largest in the country—and Carlos assured the publisher of the support of his extensive network of zonal committees. In this period, Carlos became active throughout the city. He directly approached prominent businessmen for their financial support for festivities and projects.

He also used the municipal beauty queen contest as a means of mobilizing support in the zone and of making contact with other local mayors throughout the city, since each zone offered a candidate for the city election. Carlos's meetings differed from the proceedings elsewhere by having his zone's candidate elected from a competition among representatives from the various neighborhoods. To judge the election, he recruited seven prominent zonal personalities—a headmaster of the school, several important businessmen and landowners, a military officer, and the newspaper publisher. The newspaper publisher donated the trophy and clothes and presented the prizes.

In the election, the judges gave short speeches complimenting Carlos before the assembled neighborhoods, and Carlos in turn gave warm thanks to them, especially the publisher. Carlos sponsored the victorious candidate in the subsequent preliminaries to the municipal contest, gaining, he claimed, valuable contacts throughout the city. Since the city was, at the time, under a state of seige and political activities were banned, beauty queen contests were a valuable and unobtrusive means of politicking. A large zonal festival was organized in favor of the candidate, with a dance and refreshments. Again the publisher presented the prizes and was given publicity by Carlos.

Carlos was also under pressure from the municipal authorities to support their own chosen candidate, a high official of the municipality. Carlos duly squired him around the zone and organized meetings, ostensibly for the official to talk about municipal projects for the zone, but also intended to get the official known to local inhabitants. The official paid Carlos the due compliments at each meeting. Members of the neighborhood committee were drawn into these activities. Pepe became a supporter of the newspaper publisher and began to approach him for small gifts for local football teams.

In the above account an important element in the dynamic of exchange and power emerges: success and increasing power at one level can imbalance relationships at another. As Carlos became more powerful in the zone, he became less dependent on the services of the Christian Democrats; for them to obtain compliance, he expected them to offer him more in return. The particular favor he required was to be put in semiautonomous charge of the party's city-wide residents' movement, MONAP. Likewise, he began to demand more from the mayor in return for supporting the mayor's politics, such as increased municipal support for the zone and positions for his dependents.

As the costs increased, the external organizations became less willing to pay and were increasingly active in seeking alternative means to obtain local support. This implied increasing competition for the support of local residents that devalued the services they received from Carlos and his allies in the committee faction of San Lorenzo. These processes are the product of an unstructured and unstable social environment; they indicate why it is that there can be little consistent political activity in this city.

The City as an Arena

The effect of the imbalances occurring within and without San Lorenzo was to make it apparent that the political position of the neighborhood was fluid again. This happened quite concretely as attacks began to appear in the national press, accusing Carlos of misusing his authority in the zone and questioning his jurisdiction over San Lorenzo and other neighborhoods. The Christian Democrats publicly supported these attacks, and they were given tacit approval by the municipality which, however, did not wish to completely alienate Carlos by dismissing him.

A public advertisement referring to Carlos, placed by

MONAP in the large circulation daily *El Diario* on August 8, 1968, read as follows:[15]

To the Mayor of Guatemala

Open letter of the Movimiento Nacional de Pobladores "MONAP"
Questions:

1. We ask his honor the mayor if it is as his representative and as that of the departmental governor that this official of the administration is carrying out activities promoting social disintegration. [These had been specified in an earlier section.]

2. If he has any authority to do what he has done?

3. If the marginal areas that in the majority contributed to the triumph of [name of mayor] have to be submitted to the arbitrariness of his representatives to improve themselves? Is it not the obligation of the mayor to stimulate the development of the city? If there are indeed *tons* of materials [this had been earlier cited as one of Carlos's promises to the neighborhoods to get their support], does the poor person have to sell himself into bondage to get them?

Finally and respectfully, we demand of the mayor that he does not let his delegates turn the local municipal administrations into little dictatorships that offend human dignity, and we request him to take *immediate* action so that Mr. [Carlos's name] ceases any kind of maneuver against the underprivileged.

The local priest became openly abusive in pulpit and on the radio, attacking Carlos's actions within San Lorenzo and elsewhere as those of a communist. The effect of these various attacks was to encourage several people within San Lorenzo to try again to redefine the political position of their neighborhood. We see this in three incidents that progressively increased the involvement of external agents and organizations in neighborhood affairs.

First Redefinition

After an alleged physical assault by Carlos on the local priest,

[15] The events that are being described all received attention in the national press, and during the summer of 1968 there was frequent publicity for the people involved. Indeed, the photographs of delegations that appeared in the press often helped me to document a network relationship or to follow a lead in subsequent field work.

the Hermanidad became implacably hostile to Carlos and his dependents. They set themselves up as a committee named "On Behalf of Government Housing" and argued that the proper jurisdiction of San Lorenzo fell to the Government Housing Agency, which should have relocated them in alternative accommodations. The agency was at this time negotiating with international development agencies for a large loan and launched a large publicity drive about the problems of shanty-towns. It proposed to conduct a large-scale survey to find out their conditions and to prepare the way for solving the problem. The Hermanidad argued against any community improvement work and attacked the work of the committee and its external links as motivated purely by political considerations. Other families were bewildered by the course of events and cited the uncertainty as a reason for not improving their own dwellings.

Members of the radical faction were also establishing contacts with a national political party. This contact was initially obtained through the local priest and was reinforced by the visits members of the group paid to the president's brother, a military officer with personal political ambitions. Pablo visited him several times in this period, and Maria, who had switched allegiance to the Hermanidad, was also active in keeping up this contact.

Second Re-definition: José and MONAP

José began to split from the rest of the committee as a result of a quarrel with Carlos. He had a paid position in MONAP, which was partly assured by Carlos's withdrawal from the party's organizing activities. José thus became an essential link for the party's organization. José henceforth attempted to expand his personal authority in the neighborhood, working with a section of the committee and attempting to dominate and claim jurisdiction over the cooperative and mothers' clubs. He began to stress the achievements of the movement in other neighborhoods and to use the party's professional staff to provide services for neighbors. The cooperative resisted his attempts with the aid of a Christian Democrat official who constantly insisted to members that they should keep out of factional conflict.

Third Redefinition: The State Government

José and the radical faction learned from some of Carlos's enemies in the Christian Democrat party that the departmental governor had a residual responsibility for the work of betterment committees. Access was obtained to the governor, since he was both a friend of the military officer with whom the religious group had contact and a friend of some of the Christian democrats. The governor received their appeal with interest and summoned members of both factions to his office. The radical faction was accompanied by Christian Democrat professionals hostile to Carlos. The governor listened to their various accusations and counteraccusations, and closed the meeting after a particularly virulent attack on the committee faction by Maria by remarking "sometimes truth comes from a woman." The governor then said he would hold an election in the neighborhood and would regard it as an experiment to see if such proceedings could be extended to other neighborhoods. For this reason, he asked them to be especially careful in their proceedings. He also said that none of the existing committee (the one that Carlos had reconstituted) could stand for reelection to avoid the impression of their being permanently in charge. The factions were asked to deposit lists of candidates in the office of the governor. On the day of the election, an official of the state government came to supervise the election, which was conducted by secret ballot. A total of 268 votes were cast, with the radical faction's slate, headed by Angel, narrowly winning, 142 to 126. The committee faction took their defeat badly. Pepe and the Efraims were particularly emotional about what they regarded as rejection by their neighbors after the work they had done.

These three sets of events basically concern the attempts of local-level politicians to introduce new patrons to their neighborhood, with themselves acting as brokers. Their attempts had some ideological components, and they often talked in terms of the underprivileged and their exploitation. Yet the actions undertaken were not designed to foster class consciousness over particular issues but to stress the evident benefactions to be gained from outside patrons. The choices presented to these people by the urban arena deemphasize the ideological issues by obscuring the cleavages between the poor and others in their immediate environment.

In all three sets of events the initiative for the involvement of external interests arises locally. They show poor people embroiling important external agencies in their affairs. Also, the involvement of these agencies, though often temporary or unsuccessful, has evident ramifications by creating a climate in which other external interests and their local supporters note activity and assume the play of politics. In this way, people in San Lorenzo, and others like them elsewhere in the city, are further increasing the risks and uncertainties of those participating in national-level politics and administration. These higher-level participants do not ignore happenings so close to them and will attempt to secure better information, reinforcing the process of external involvement in local affairs. Though San Lorenzo is an unusual neighborhood in terms of its dense political linkages, this process is repeated elsewhere and creates a highly mobile and uncertain urban political climate, which is the basic uncertainty of political development in Guatemala.

These events have been simplified and conceal the amount of intense political activity occurring within and without San Lorenzo during this time. The various active figures are constantly on the move, using their relationships and calling on their credit to meet what they regard as threats to their position. The intricacy of these movements obscures the essential continuity in the powerlessness of local people. The nature of this powerlessness is illustrated by the effects of the radical faction's success in the election.

The committee they sponsored was made up of the marginal

members of the faction—those who had the attributes for engaging in formal organization. Already before leaving the field, there were problems as the Hermanidad began to suspect that Angel's Protestantism would harm their interests. The election was a narrow one, and the credit of Carlos and the committee appeared still to exist among a substantial segment of the neighborhood, which was to be expected since many had directly benefited from their work. In contrast, the radical faction, using their coalition of very different groups—religious, kinship, and political—mobilized their votes in terms of smaller exchanges and offered no prospect of substantial services. Once in control of the committee, their first task was to find a source of services to consolidate their position. Consequently, they turned to the most available external resource—the Christian Democrat organizers who had already been working with the committee faction. As the next national and municipal election draws near, the cycle will be repeated. As candidates seek local favors, both the relative cost of the services provided by the Christian Democrats and the value of the neighbors' compliance is likely to rise. Other external interests will be brought into local affairs.

Though the cycle appears to continue, its occurence changes the character of local organization. We are reporting a situation in which a neighborhood is being linked with a variety of external social foci and, in the course of this, losing its capacity for independent organization. Though such organization may have been difficult from the beginning, it seemed undesirable to most of these families by the end. Whatever their orientation, they had learned that ultimately they depend on the play of external groups. This being the case they are less likely to distinguish among the policies of these external groups. Indeed, many neighbors remarked to me before I left that it was probably better to have a government that kept things in order and efficiently organized affairs, rather than to have one like their actual government, which talked of revolution but did nothing. In 1970, a military officer of authoritarian persuasion was elected president on the platform of law and order.

8. Reorganization of the Poor in an Urban Setting

The recurrent theme of this book has been the difficulty of collective organization among people who do not have enough information about each other to develop trust and cooperation. The diverse origins of these families, their differing careers, and their mobility within the city have prevented the development of stable identities that enable them to recognize the interests they have in common with others of similar situation. Unlike the situation among ethnic groups in a south-side Chicago slum reported by Suttles, there is no principle of ordered segmentation by which these Guatemalan families can progressively order their social relationships on the basis of sex, age, ethnicity, and, finally, neighborhood.[1] Yet in Guatemala City there are few nonresidential bases of collective identity. Ethnicity is not present to discriminate one group from another in the city, and workers are rarely employed in the same

---

[1] Gerald Suttles, *The Social Order of the Slum*, pp. 4-12, 225-227.

industrial enterprise. Job careers, types of work, and work timetables are factors that differentiate these families, and few workers have common problems of work or of opposition to their bosses.

The local-level politics described in chapters 6 and 7 show just how limited is organization when people do not know or trust each other. Organization develops most effectively at those times when these families are placed in situations that give them a collective identity; such was the case in the early years of the shantytown's foundation or during the stable periods of co-op organization. Usually, however, most of the relationships of these families lie outside the neighborhood; they leave the work of organization to those whose jobs and personal situations most commit them to the neighborhood. External interests permeate and help to fragment both neighborhoods, and the work of organization involves the imposition of ideologies that are not understandable in terms of the experiences of residents. Residents are suspicious of any organization that involves them in delegating responsibility and are fickle in their allegiances to such organizations.

The description of political organization in chapter 7 makes it clear that lack of trust at the local level has significant repercussions for the whole political structure. The absence of a well-established collective identity means that these poor families are active in involving outsiders in their affairs. Outsiders are moved to direct intervention in order to obtain information about the behavior of the poor and to reduce their own risks and uncertainties. This creates a constant imbalance in urban political organization, because the attempts of these various individuals and agencies to secure their own environment threaten that of others and invites further intervention. It is for these reasons that the development of strong collective identities among social groups is essential to stable political development. Their absence means that individual politicians are unable to develop their policies consistently and to build their organization. It is thus in the interests of the middle- and upper-status Christian Democrat organizers in San Lorenzo to secure some degree of political organization and order among the poor. Likewise, the right-wing political groups that have intervened in the two neighborhoods were attempting to develop stable paternalistic relationships with these poor families in order to secure their own political environment. Such attempts are doomed to failure because the poor are not sufficiently cohesive to enable any arrangements to persist. The political anarchy that plagues Guatemala is thus not an accident of culture or personalties, but is founded on the absence of stable collective identities among its population. Since this instability pervades the city, even the actions of a small and unrepresentative sample from two urban neighborhoods illustrate its consequences.

This argument implies that even those political organizations based on the differentiation of power among their member groups and individuals are unlikely to be stable. We looked at this possibility in connection with patrons and clients and again in connection with cooperative and political organization in San Lorenzo. These cases indicated that only in very limited circumstances could what Blau calls unilateral transactions—the provision of important and needed services that could not be reciprocated—lead to a stable differentiation of power.[2] This power to command compliance is a form of credit that enables authority and organization to be extended. Time and again we saw that people did not perceive the services they received as obligating them. The lack of structure in the urban environment meant that people had many possible sources of services, and the complexity and mobility of urban life made the continuation of any services hazardous and difficult to predict. Those who provided services also became less committed to the relationship in face of the uncertainty of obtaining compliance in return. The conditions under which social transactions take place in Guatemala City thus not only inhibit the development

[2] Peter Blau, *Exchange and Power in Social Life*, pp. 21-22.

of mass political organization among the poor but are also likely to inhibit vertically integrated populist political parties. Populism is not an alternative to working-class political organization as a means of mobilizing the poor when these are insecurely integrated into urban life. Insecurity prevents the development of any stable political organization, whether vertically or horizontally based. As Hobsbawm points out, populism is more effective as a vehicle of an existing and sympathetic governing power than as a means of carrying a man or a movement to the top.[3]

The particular problems faced by these families are underlined by contrasting their situation to that of the two groups of Chilean workers studied by Di Tella.[4] Their work situations were taken to represent the two dominant modes of political mobilization among workers in Latin America. Miners, living and working under relatively primitive conditions, possess many of the characteristics of a solidary group. He contrasts them with workers in a nearby steel mill. The steelworkers are better paid, better educated, and have greater chances of job mobility. Compared to the miners, they are more moderate in their opposition to management, and their union is more likely to negotiate and cooperate with management. Di Tella shows that the steelworkers are to a degree integrated into the existing Chilean social structure through the impersonal mechanisms of education and the possibility of occupational mobility.[5] They are receptive to the ideologies handed down by management, because their education and work position enable them to perceive the individual economic advantages that they can secure. The miners have no such trust, and their position gives them no confidence in impersonal means of bettering their position. Their jobs and security depend on personal relationships and personal favors. Their integration is a personalistic one

[3] E. J. Hosbawm, "Peasants and Rural Migrants in Politics," in Claudio Véliz, ed., *The Politics of Conformity in Latin America*, pp. 43-63.

[4] Torcuato di Tella et al., *Syndicato y communidad*.

[5] Ibid., pp. 168-181.

and includes group solidarity and suspicion of other social classes. The transition from the type of political and social involvement represented by the miners to that represented by the steelworkers, as Di Tella points out, represents the major political change in Western Europe and the United States. The contrast between the miners and the steelworkers shows the significance of urban growth unaccompanied by industrialization, which places "working-class" families in Guatemala in a situation where they can benefit neither from group solidarity nor from impersonal mechanisms of social integration. In terms of education, these Guatemalan families show only a very slow improvement in educational standards from generation to generation. In both San Lorenzo and Planificada a large proportion of children legally obliged to attend school were not doing so. This proportion of non-attenders was greatest in the shantytown, San Lorenzo (38 percent of children compared to 27 percent in Planificada). Education appeared to have little meaning to these families as a means of obtaining steady jobs and occupational mobility. It was under these circumstances a highly ineffective mechanism of social control.

These families are thus neither integrated into urban life through cohesive relationships with others in like situation or through more impersonal mechanisms such as education and the possibility of occupational mobility. This gives to urban politics in Guatemala its peculiarly fluid and unstable character.

Dependence and Marginality

Following the above discussion, we need now to refine the concepts of dependence and marginality that have often been used to characterize the position of the poor in the cities of underdeveloped countries. It is clear that neither concept adequately expresses the basic dilemma of this group. We have noted that the incapacity of the poor to organize effectively is due to their overintegration into the city and not to their isolation from its political and social processes. Likewise, even this overintegration is not to be explained in terms of traditional patron-client relationships and the mentalities that accompany them. For one of the major dynamics in this integration is the active interest that other urban groups show in controlling the environment of the poor. The dependence that we have described is one produced by the attempts of city politicians, social workers, health workers, and many others outside these neighborhoods to understand the situation of the poor and to organize it in a way that fits both their particular model of urban life and their particular preoccupations.

The particular problem that the poor face is to define their boundaries so that they have greater control over their patterns of organization, excluding external interests from directly interfering. It is by delimiting an area of relationships that is their proper concern that a group has the opportunity to achieve some agreement on strategies of action and common goals. To the extent that a group cannot or does not wish to define its boundaries, it is unlikely to coherently organize as an interest group.

It is evident that these families stand to gain most when they are perceived by external interests as unknown quantities. Through informal organization, the shantytown dwellers extract significant concessions from urban administration partly because they are an unknown quantity and are seen as a possible threat. However, as external interests attempt to organize the shantytown and introduce formal associations into the milieu, the neighborhood becomes more fragmented internally. Consequently, they are less able to present a united front, and outside groups do not overestimate their potential.

The erosion of boundaries is, however, a product of the developments occurring in an informal urban environment. In such cities, the permeability of groups of poor families is a defining characteristic of their urban life. This means that we must interpret both marginality and dependence with caution, since they refer to states whose solution depends on the non-interference of external interests. Those who wish to alter the position of the poor must take care that the means they use to do it does not contribute to the permeability and greater dependence of this group. In this respect, formalization of organization, however desirable from our own view of participation and decision making, is inappropriate in environments where there is not the context of trust, public or private, to sustain it. The poor are, however, unlikely to develop in isolation in countries like Guatemala, because both those who are sympathetic to them and those who fear them are aware of the history of their political mobilization in communist and capitalist countries. Organizational techniques are imported both as a way of accelerating a development that has been achieved elsewhere and as a means of keeping it in check.

Order and Trust

This brings us to a more general consideration of the kinds of order that poor families maintain under the conditions we have described. One of the most important of these conditions is the growth of the city through a migration bringing active, competitive adults to participate in shaping the urban social order. Not only does the incorporation of these migrants disrupt the established bases for maintaining order, but their experiences have been to varying degrees discontinuous, making them inclined to an urban activity that helps them establish a social identity. The city becomes an arena within which diverse careers intersect and, in the various situations involving some degree of stable interaction, negotiate a basis for order. Since people are mobile from situation to situation, this basis for order must be flexible enough to permit transitions and not confine people to one group or location. Consequently, relationships are differentiated by the services they offer, and those involving greater intimacy are segregated from those involving specific and functional exchanges. In this manner people readily enter into relationships but rarely trust to them, thus facilitating short-term organization but not its continuity or development.

It is evident that families are successful in maintaining some kind of order so that their affairs, even the local ones, pass without too much that is unexpected or disruptive. One of the striking things to emerge from the account of organization in San Lorenzo is the degree of continuity in the opposing factions. This continuity is not only a continuity of leaders, but appears also to be a continuity in the perceptions that neighbors have of the issues with which they are confronted. In voting or even in casual street conversations or encounters, families in San Lorenzo have seen the distinction between the two factions as one of the major principles of organizing their local environment. Supporters of the committee faction talk of the Catholic Hermanidad with hostility and categorize those linked with it as untrustworthy, while members connected with the radical faction talk of the corruption and exploitation practiced by the committee that keeps neighbors in an improverished situation. This major distinction is complemented by lesser ones between Catholics and Protestants and between members of a friendship or regional group and those outside it.

The interesting thing about these means of ordering the environment is that they are basically fragmentary. No matter what the issue at hand, it does not serve to articulate the whole neighborhood through cross-cutting relationships that create trust and cohesion. Creating cohesion even within the major factions is a temporary matter and, once the confrontation is over, families related to the factions revert to the smaller groupings that serve the everyday needs of city life. The relationships people maintain outside the neighborhood insure that it never serves as an encompassing organizing principle for all its families. It is a local base in a city where locality is the major means of organizing people; but as a local base it is an artificial construct that bears little relation to the shape and importance of families' social relationships.

The neighborhood is, however, a necessary basis of organization for those categories without other relationships in the city. They form the most consistent supporters of locally based organization. Their relative isolation is accompanied by attributes that make them distinct in life style and in interests to families who maintain relationships throughout the city. There is unlikely to be any coincidence between the factors that promote trust among the locally based groups, such as the Protestants or the Hermanidad, and those that promote trust among the others. Even among locally based groups there are divisions of interest that make their cooperation problematic. The rewards these small interacting groups bring to their members depend in part on the extent to which they have access to local resources. Since these are regarded as scarce resources, this creates a further basis for mistrust between groups.

Under these conditions, the common denominator of discourse is provided by the public moralities to which families are constantly exposed by their urban life. It is a denominator of discourse that contributes to the fragmentation of those families by identifying others as wanting by the terms of that morality. For both factions, it is clear that they secure order by seeing themselves as poor but honest and as attempting to improve their situation despite a difficult environment. They point to others as exemplifying the dishonesties and corruption that attend this environment; they thus justify themselves to their external audience and make manageable the numbers of people in the locality whom they have to know and trust. In this sense, we cannot expect these slum dwellers to develop a particular morality of their own that contrasts with that of the urban groups living outside. To develop such morality would isolate them from relationships that are their main means of coping with urban life. It would also commit them too heavily to people upon whom they cannot depend, since job and residential mobility constantly threaten the stability of their local attachment.

I was in the ironic position of advocating personalistic moralities to people who uniformly preferred to adopt public ones and who, in spite of my sociological explanations, continued to categorize most of their neighbors as strangers who could well be guilty of corruption, vice, alcoholism, and prostitution.[6] In this respect, it is interesting to note that most reports that come from inhabitants of Latin American slums describe in detail the vice that surrounds them. This is also true of my own conversations with shantytown dwellers, who were always eager to tell me and other neighbors about the latest scandal and about the immorality of certain sections of the neighborhood. "He drinks too much," or "she is a prostitute," were common comments when I mentioned other neighborhood inhabitants. Undoubtedly, there is some truth in these remarks, but my overall impression of the shantytown is one of an ordered and "respectable" family environment.

The comments of shantytown dwellers reflect the ideology of their situation. The nature of their relationship with the city and the artificiality of their local base leads them to emphasize their own commitments to public morality. Despite their depiction of the neighborhood as full of vice, neighbors in San Lorenzo still manage to cooperate and to maintain relationships even with those they label as wanting in public morality. By not adopting a personalistic morality they do, however, contribute to the image that other urban groups have of them, and further contribute to their own fragmentation.[7]

Urban Growth and Social and Economic Development

The growth of Guatemala City and the increasing proportion of people living in urban places represents a trend that is often thought to be a necessary prelude to social and economic development.[8] Some of the data do indicate the possibility that the increasing urban population may eventually serve as an

[6] I am again using the term "personalistic moralities" to refer to moralities that take account of the particularities of the local situation.

[7] For example, see Oscar Lewis, *La Vida*, and Carolina María de Jesus, *Child of the Dark*.

[8] See Nathan Keyfitz, "Political-Economic Aspects of Urbanization in South and South-East Asia," in Philip Hauser and Leo Schnore, eds., *The Study of Urbanization*, pp. 265-309. Negative aspects are reported with a greater emphasis on the potential disorder of urban places in Shanti Tangri, "Urbanization, Political Stability, and Economic Growth," in Jason L. Finkle and Richard W. Gable, eds., *Political Development and Social Change*, pp. 305-321.

available resource for rapid industrial development in Guatemala. Migrants are more likely to obtain education in the city than they are in the provinces and they are less likely to live at a subsistence level or to consume a surplus in immediate social obligations. Instead, even among these very poor families, workers are energetic in seeking additional ways of making money and in using it to improve their diet and the material conditions of their life. In San Lorenzo a considerable amount of money has been invested over time in improving shacks and community facilities. In the three years of my acquaintance with this neighborhood, I would estimate that in actual expenditures and in labor time, these families invested close to 100,000 dollars in the improvement of housing and community facilities.

This provides the infrastructure that facilitates other and more economically productive investments—in education, in health, and in motivation to pursue a consistent job career. These are the positive aspects of the experience of urban life that have emerged from this account. Furthermore, it is certainly possible that migrants have made a further indirect contribution to their country's development by abandoning the subsistence farming or subsistence crafts of many provincial areas, thus facilitating the greater rationalization of enterprises through, for example, cooperatives.

The case of the consumers' co-op in San Lorenzo indicates another important dimension of urban social change, the learning experience that poor people obtain from dealing in a formal and organized context with other urban social groups. The co-op is a special type of organization because it is specifically concentrated on concrete objectives that could be realized by small and observable stages. The business of conducting the co-op gave members the opportunity to get to know each other and to develop exchanges among themselves, so that eventually there was some basis for the articulation and cohesion of the whole group. In these ways, the co-op is creating common interests that are identifiable in opposition to those of other, nonlocal groups.

Involvement with formal associations and with external groups and organizations provides a learning experience in which families see organization as a means to achieve an end rather than, as is the traditional case, as an end in itself. This change was one of the most significant processes I observed among families that mainly operated on the assumption that activity had only immediate relevance by rendering a specific service or expressing status. In the city, many came to recognize that their interactions and participation in different types of associations could be seen as but one stage in a long-term process that had been achieved elsewhere and might come about in Guatemala.

This does not mean that they came to recognize the importance of group action; often enough the change was to encourage individual planning and initiative. However, the beginnings of orientations that look to the future are apparent in their reactions to the co-op and even to the neighborhood's own attempts at organization. This means a further dynamic of change within the city; for although poor people might look at other social groups as their allies, it does mean that they take an increasingly active role in sponsoring politics in the city, encouraging politicians and interest groups to elaborate policies and attract their support. In this sense, families in San Lorenzo present a microcosm of the situation of the urban poor, providing a fertile field for the elaboration of politics and of associations that further change the potential of the urban political structure.

In all these respects my data show many similarities with those of studies of the urban poor elsewhere in Latin America.[9] One of the most complete documentations of their life styles in a Latin American city is that of Leeds' various studies of the *favelas* of Rio de Janeiro.[10] He demonstrates the manifold ways

[9] A useful bibliography is Denton R. Vaughan, *Urbanization in Twentieth Century Latin America: A Working Bibliography.*

[10] Anthony Leeds and Elizabeth Leeds, "Brazil and the Myth of Urban Rurality: Urban Experience, Work, and Values in 'Squatments' of Rio de Janeiro and Lima," a paper presented to the Conference on Work and Urbanization in Modernizing Societies, 1967.

in which *favela* dwellers are involved in urban life and institutions. They are shown to be resourceful manipulators of both the political and economic resources of the city; many of them have built up considerable businesses based on their *favela* residences. They are fully conscious of the subtleties of local and national politics and organize to take advantage of them. As in Guatemala, it is often the middle-class politicians who are subject to manipulation. Leeds points out that *favela* dwellers are not usually recent migrants and that they value work and initiative as much as the next man. Their relative disadvantages are the product of inequalities in power and wealth in their society and not of faulty adaption to modern urban life. Similarly, Mangin, in his reports on Lima, describes the considerable organizational capacity shown by the urban poor.[11] They organize land invasions, ensure their success, and, after the invasion, they demonstrate high levels of community organization and consciousness. So struck was Mangin by this phenomenon that he entitled one article "Latin American Squatter Settlements: A Problem and a Solution."[12]

All these accounts are agreed on the considerable resources present among the urban poor; they also indicate that these "marginal" people are highly politicized and capable of intervening in politics. On this point both their accounts and mine indicate that it is misleading to analyze the politics of the growing cities of Latin America in terms of a distinction between the marginal, nonpoliticized masses and the middle- and upper-status groups that compete for their votes.[13]

The level of organization that is usually reported is an individual one, and it rarely endures among the group for long periods. The poor in Lima or Rio may be resourceful, but they

[11] William P. Mangin, "Poverty and Politics in the Cities of Latin America," in W. Bloomberg, Jr., and H. J. Schmandt, eds., *Power, Poverty and Urban Policy*, Urban Affairs Annual Review 2, pp. 397-432.

[12] William P. Mangin, "Latin American Squatter Settlements: A Problem and a Solution," *Latin American Research Review* 2, no. 3(Summer 1967): 65-98.

[13] Compare Daniel Goldrich, "Toward the Comparative Study of Politicization in Latin America," in Dwight B. Heath and Richard N. Adams, eds., *Contemporary Cultures and Societies of Latin American*, pp. 361-378.

remain unorganized and contribute to the disorganization of urban politics. Their participation in urban politics is a learning experience that does not necessarily lead to their more effective group organization. It can, as Goldrich points out in respect to squatter settlements in Peru and Chile, lead to disenchantment with the efficacy of political involvement.[14] This appears to be happening in Guatemala also, though the types of relations that link these neighborhoods to the rest of the city ensure that their inhabitants will continue to be politically involved.

This account thus raises questions about the existence of a clear and positive relation between urban growth and social and economic development. Though migration reduces pressure on the land, the problems of the provinces are due less to land shortage and inefficient agriculture than to the particular distribution of economic and social power and to its impact on the "development" of the largest and most productive areas of Guatemala.

More basic are the questions raised about the types of social organization emerging in the city and their implications for consistently developing the society's resources. We have been watching people being incorporated into city life in a way that fosters competition for jobs and available space. This process of incorporation has the emergent property of weakening the development of groups that are organized around the pursuit of common interests.

This is not to argue that the poor are to "blame" for the slow development of their country, but to draw attention to the importance of their particular situation in assessing the possibilities of development. In assessing change, we must not look at the behavior and contribution of any single social group but instead assess the consequences of the general field of urban relationships. Decisions to invest in business, priorities in budget allocations, and the motivation to look ahead and plan careers are examples of crucial elements in the development process

[14] Daniel Goldrich, et al., "The Political Integration of Lower-Class Urban Settlements in Chile and Peru," *Studies in Comparative International Development* 3, no. 1 (1967): 1-22.

that are affected by contact with, and assessments of, the behavior of the poorer sections of the urban population.

In this sense, the type of urban development we have been discussing may have immediate, and lasting, negative effects on the process of development by pervasively weakening the individual capacity to rationally plan. Rapid and unplanned urban growth has meant that people form social relationships that, because of the disjointed nature of their life careers and because of their high mobility, are based on different situations. These relationships are consequently neither cohesive nor mutually consistent, and people are exposed to expectations of behavior that are often potentially conflicting.

What, then, is the likely development of Guatemala City's social and political structure in face of the difficulties of creating trust and a stable differentiation of power? First, we must situate the poor of Guatemala City within the general perspective of Latin American development. Using the typology developed by Di Tella to mark stages in the formation and political consciousness of a Latin American working class, it is clear that Guatemala presents none of the conditions for this development.[15] There are not the large-scale, if isolated, industrial complexes of countries such as Bolivia and Peru, nor is there the industrially based urban working class of countries such as Chile or Argentina. Guatemala does not have a substantial urban middle class that provides possibilites of occupational mobility for members of the working class and that is a possible ally in effecting nationalist policies of reform. There are not the social and economic underpinnings that shape ideology and organization and diffuse it among the working population. The Guatemalan case thus relates to what is one extreme of the political continuum in Latin America. This extreme has important implications, however, when in many Latin American countries the pace of urbanization continues to outrun the pace of industrialization creating competition and instability among all sectors of the urban population.

[15] Torcuato di Tella et al., *Sindicato y comunidad*, pp. 21-45.

Guatemala City has never experienced the type of economically based stratification that was long the basis for the politics of industrial Europe. Moreover, it appears that the absence of a working class conscious of its political interests is likely to be a permanent one. The trends we have noted suggest that the industrial sector of the economy is not proportionately expanding and that the increasing labor force disproportionately enters the service and commercial sectors.

The social relationships that develop in these sectors are predominantly those that articulate people vertically and not horizontally. In the service and commercial sectors, the work unit is often small and workers depend upon clients and superiors to a greater extent than in large industrial enterprises. Many of the jobs in these sectors involve self-employment, work in isolation, or minor clerical work—features that do not make apparent a position in common with the mass of the urban working population. It is because Guatemala, like many developing countries, is participating in industrialization at a late stage and under the influence of foreign capital and foreign technology that makes its industrialization process so different from that experienced in Europe and the United States, with very different implications for political development.

It is striking that the employment patterns that have been described earlier involve distinctive styles of work and distinctive social relationships. Craftsmen, factory workers, construction workers, and the self-employed have different prospects of participating in locally based activity, of voting, of being residentially and occupationally mobile, and of spending their leisure in different ways. These differences are not, however, associated with marked economic differences, when factors such as age are taken into account. This is similar to Jelín's discussion of occupational stratification in Monterrey.[16] Jelín's point is that under the conditions of rapid urbanization in Latin America, the distinctions between different classes of

---

[16] Elisabeth Jelín, "Trabajadores por cuenta propia y asalariados: distinción vertical u horizontal?" *Revista Latinoamerica de Sociología* 3 (1967): 388-410.

workers are no longer consistent in that, for example, economic dependence is also associated with lower pay and poorer working conditions. Instead, groups of workers are inconsistent in that their position on one dimension (such as dependence of independence) may give them interests opposed to social and economic superiors, whereas on another dimension (stability of work or wage) they are better off than other workers.

The working conditions of low-income people give them distinct interests that do not put them in common opposition to the more prosperous members of their society. These differences are, to some extent, expressed residentially, with some areas having higher concentrations of certain types of worker than others.

These differences make possible an emerging social stratification within this city based on occupational groups that work within the same sectors of the economy and are faced by similar conditions. This is more likely because the vagaries of political and economic development have a different impact on the various sectors of the urban economy. Some sectors absorb the increasing labor force, but at the cost of lower profits and underemployment. In contrast, other sectors benefit from the increasing consumption needs of the population and more easily regulate their intake. Some sectors profit from increasing foreign investment, which provides factories and offices, while others feel the increasing competition of cheaply made products, local and foreign. From this study, for example, it is clear that the transport sector of the economy has benefited, to the advantage of all within it, from the growth of the city, whereas craftsmen, traders, and certain types of service workers have felt a keener competition. Likewise, workers in semiskilled or skilled jobs in large-scale enterprises benefit along with their employers from economic prosperity, whereas unskilled and job laborers appear to have felt the increasing competition for available resources.

In describing this emerging system of stratification, we are also describing a basis for a political control imposed from above. In a city vertically divided by economic interests and by life styles there is an apparent identity of interests between those of different economic position. While most people in the two neighborhoods are ready to blame the rich and foreign exploitation for their own and their country's dilemmas, the interests they so identify are few and special in character. In fact, the poor are quite prepared to cooperate with professionals and middle-class politicians in an attempt to improve their position. An acceptable basis for political activity is thus presenting change as being in the common interest of different social groups and to which are opposed only the notoriously rich, the foreigner, or the general condition of underdevelopment. It helps to explain why so apparently conservative an interest group as the military and its allies can be voted to power by people of very different social positions on a platform stressing order, security, and a common endeavor to rescue Guatemala from underdevelopment and exploitation.

BIBLIOGRAPHY

Abu-Lughod, Janet. "Testing the Theory of Social Area Analysis: The Ecology of Cairo, Egypt." *American Sociological Review* 34, no. 2 (April 1969): 198-212.

Adams, Richard. *Crucifixion by Power*. Austin: University of Texas Press, 1970.

——————. "La Ladinzación en Guatemala." In *Integración Social en Guatemala*, edited by J. L. Arriola, Guatemala City: Seminario de Integración Social Guatemalteca, Publicación No. 3, 1956.

Arias B., Jorge, "Aspectos demográficos de la población indígena de Guatemala." In *Boletín Estadístico*, nos. 1-2. Guatemala: Dirreción General de Estadística, 1959.

Babchuk, Nicholas, and Alan Booth, "Voluntary Association Membership: A Longitudinal Analysis." *American Sociological Review* 34, no. 1 (February 1969): 31-45.

Balán, Jorge. "The Process of Stratification in an Industrializing Society: The Case of Monterrey, Mexico." Ph.D. Dissertation, University of Texas at Austin, 1968.

——————. "Migrant-Native Socioeconomic Differences in Latin American Cities: A Structural Analysis." *Latin American Research Review* 4, no. 1 (February 1969): 3-29.

——————; Harley L. Browning; Elisabeth Jelín; and Lee Litzler. Computerized Approach to the Processing and Analysis of Life Histories Obtained in Sample Surveys." *Behavioral Science* 14, no. 2 (March 1969): 105-120.

——————; Harley L. Browning; and Elisabeth Jelín. *Men in a Developing Society: Geographic and Social Mobility in Monterrey, Mexico*. Austin: University of Texas Press, 1973.

Bank of London and Montreal. *The Central American Common Market*. London: Bank of London and Montreal, 1966.

Banton, Michael. *The Policeman in the Community*. London: Tavistock, 1964.

Berry, Brian; J. L. Rees; and Philip H. Rees. "The Factorial Ecology of Calcutta." *American Journal of Sociology* 74, no. 5 (March 1969): 445-491.

Blau, Peter M. *Exchange and Power in Social Life*. New York: John Wiley, 1967.

Caplow, Theodore. The Social Ecology of Guatemala City." *Social Forces* 28 (December 1949): 113-135.

Chatterton, Michael. "Crimes of Violence and the Police." Manuscript, Department of Sociology, University of Manchester, 1970.

Chombart de Lauwe, Paul Henri; S. Antoine; L. Couvreur; and J. Gauthier. *Paris et l'agglomeration parisienne*. Bibliothéque de Sociologie Contemporaine, Serie B. Travaux du Centre d'Etudes Sociologigues. Paris: Presses Universitaires de France, 1952.

Cotler, Julio. "Actuales pautas de cambio en la sociedad rural del Peru." In *Dominación y Cambios en el Perú Rural*, edited by José Matos Mar et al. Lima: Instituto de Estudios Peruanos, 1969.

Dirección General de Estadística. *Sexto censo de población: El 18 de abril de 1950*. Guatemala City: Dirección General de Estadística, 1957.

——————. *Censos 1964: Población, resultados de tabulación por muestreo*. Guatemala City: Dirección General de Estadística, 1957.

Di Tella, Torcuato. "Populism and Reform in Latin America." In *Obstacles to Change in Latin America*, pp. 47-90. London: Oxford University Press, 1965.

——————; Lucien Brams; Jean-Daniel Reynaud; and Alain Touraine. *Sindicato y comunidad: Dos tipos de estructura sindical latino-americana*. Buenos Aires: Editoriál del Instituto, 1967.

Durkheim, Emile. *The Division of Labor in Society*, translated by George Simpson. New York: Free Press of Glencoe, 1960.

Epstein, A. L. *Politics in an Urban African Community*. Manchester: Manchester University Press, 1960.

Feldman, Arnold S., and Wilbert E. Moore, eds. *Labor Commitment and Social Change in Developing Areas*. New York: Social Science Research Council, 1960.

Foster, George. "The Dyadic Contract: A Model for the Social Structure of a Mexican Peasant Village." *American Anthropologist* 63 (December 1961): 1173-1192.

Gans, Herbert. "Urbanism and Suburbanism as Ways of Life: A Reevaluation of Definitions." In *Human Behavior and the Social Processes*, edited by Arnold Rose, pp. 625-648. Boston: Houghton Mifflin Company, 1962.

_____. *The Urban Villagers*. New York: The Free Press, 1962.

Garfinkel, Harold. *Studies in Ethnomethodology*. Englewood Cliffs, N. J.: Prentice-Hall, 1967.

Gluckman, Max. *An Analysis of a Social Situation in Modern Zululand*. Rhodes-Livingstone Paper No. 28. Manchester: Manchester University Press, 1958.

Goldrich, Daniel. "Toward the Comparative Study of Politicization in Latin America." In *Contemporary Cultures and Societies of Latin America*, edited by Dwight B. Heath and Richard N. Adams, pp. 361-378. New York: Random House, 1965.

_____; Raymond B. Pratt; and C. R. Schuller. "The Political Integration of Lower-Class Urban Settlements in Chile and Peru." *Studies in Comparative International Development* 3, no. 1, (1967): 1-22.

Gouldner, Alvin. "Cosmopolitans and Locals: Towards an Analysis of Latent Social Roles." *Administrative Science Quarterly* 2, no. 3 (December 1967): 281-306.

Hannerz, Ulf. *Soulside*. New York and London: Columbia University Press, 1969.

Hanson, Robert C., and Ozzie G. Simmons. "The Role Path: A Conceptual Procedure for Studying Migration in Urban Communities." *Human Organization* 27, no. 2 (Summer 1968): 152-158.

Hatt, Paul. "The Concept of Natural Area." *American Sociological Review* 11 (August 1946): 423-427.

Hawley, Amos. *Human Ecology*. New York: The Ronald Press, 1950.

Herrick, Bruce. *Urban Migration and Economic Development in Chile*. Cambridge: MIT Monographs in Economics, The MIT Press, 1965.

Hobsbawm, E. J. "Peasants and Rural Migrants in Politics." In *The Politics of Conformity in Latin America*, edited by Claudio Véliz, pp. 43-65. London: Oxford University Press, 1967.

Jelín, Elisabeth. "Trabajadores por cuenta propia y asalariados: distinción vertical u horizontal?" *Revista Latinoamericana de Sociología* 3 (1967): 388-410.

Johnson, Kenneth F. *The Guatemalan Presidential Election, 1966*.

Washington, D. C.: Institute for the Comparative Study of Political Systems, 1967.

Kapferer, Bruce. "Norms and the Manipulation of Relationships in a Work Context." In *Social Networks in Urban Situations*, edited by J. Clyde Mitchell. Manchester: Manchester University Press, 1969.

——————. *Strategy and Transaction*. Manchester: Manchester University Press, 1972.

Keyfitz, Nathan. "Political-Economic Aspects of Urbanization in South and South-East Asia." In *The Study of Urbanization*, edited by Philip Hauser and Leo Schnore, pp. 265-309. New York: John Wiley, 1965.

Leeds, Anthony, and Elisabeth Leeds. "Brazil and the Myth of Urban Rurality: Urban Experience, Work, and Values in 'Squatments' of Rio de Janeiro and Lima." A paper presented to the Conference on Work and Urbanization in Modernizing Societies, St. Thomas, V. I., 1967.

Lewis, Oscar. *Life in a Mexican Village: Tepoztlan Restudied*. Urbana: University of Illinois Press, 1963.

——————. "Urbanization without Breakdown," *Scientific Monthly* 75, no. 1 (1952): 31-41.

——————. *La Vida*. New York: Vintage Books, 1968.

Litwak, Eugene, and Ivan Szelenyi. "Primary Group Structures and Their Functions: Kin, Neighbors and Friends." *American Sociological Review* 34, no. 4 (August 1969): 465-481.

Long, Norman. *Social Change and the Individual: A Study of the Social and Religious Responses to Innovation in a Zambian Rural Community*. Manchester: Manchester University Press, 1968.

Long, Norton E. "The Local Community as an Ecology of Games." *American Journal of Sociology* 64 (November 1958): 251-261.

Mangin, William P. "Latin American Squatter Settlements: A Problem and a Solution." *Latin American Research Review* 2, no. 3 (Summer 1967): 65-98.

——————. "Poverty and Politics in the Cities of Latin America." In *Power, Poverty and Urban Policy*, edited by W. Bloomberg, Jr., and H. J. Schmandt, pp. 397-432. Urban Affairs Annual Review 2. Beverley Hills: Sage Publications, 1968.

María de Jesús, Carolina. *Child of the Dark: The Diary of Carolina María de Jesús*, translated by David St. Clair. New York: Signet Books, 1963.

Matos Mar, José. *Urbanización y barriadas en América del Sur*. Lima: Instituto de Estudios Peruanos, 1968.

Mendez, Alfredo. *Zaragoza*. Guatemala City: Seminario de Integración Social Guatemalteca, 1968.

Merton, Robert K. *Social Theory and Social Structure*. New York: Free Press of Glencoe. 1963.

Mintz, Sidney W., and Eric R. Wolf. "An Analysis of Ritual Co-Parenthood (Compadrazgo)." In *Peasant Society*, edited by Jack M. Potter, May N. Díaz, and George M. Foster. Boston: Little, Brown and Company, 1967.

Mitchell, J. Clyde. *The Kalela Dance: Aspects of Social Relationships among Urban Africans in Northern Rhodesia*. Rhodes Livingstone Paper No. 27. Manchester: Manchester University Press, 1957.

—————. "Labor Migration in Africa South of the Sahara: The Causes of Labor Migration." *Bulletin of the Inter-African Labour Institute* 6, no. 1 (1959): 12-46.

—————, ed. *Social Networks in Urban Situations*. Manchester: Manchester University Press, 1969.

—————. "Theoretical Orientations in African Urban Studies." In *The Social Anthropology of Complex Societies*, edited by Michael Banton, pp. 37-68. London: Tavistock, 1966.

Morse, Richard. "Trends and Issues in Latin American Urban Research, 1965-1970, Part One." *Latin American Research Review* 6, no. 1 (February 1971): 3-33.

Nash, Manning. *Machine Age Maya*. American Anthropological Association Memoir 87, 1958.

Nelson, Philip. "Migration, Real Income and Information." *Regional Science* 1, no. 2 (1959): 43-74.

Park, Robert. "The City: Suggestions for the Investigation of Human Behavior in the Urban Environment." In *The City*, edited by E. M. Burgess and R. E. Park. Chicago: University of Chicago Press, 1925.

Pons, Valdo. *Stanleyville*. London: Oxford University Press, 1969.

Redfield, Robert. *The Folk Culture of Yucatán*. Chicago: University of Chicago Press, 1941.

—————. *Tepoztlan: A Mexican Village*. Chicago: University of Chicago Press, 1930.

Reissman, Leonard. *The Urban Process*. New York: Free Press of Glencoe, 1964.

Roberts, Bryan. "Politics in a Neighborhood of Guatemala City," *Sociology* 2, no. 2 (May 1968): 185-203.

——————. "Protestant Groups and Coping with Urban Life in Guatemala City." *American Journal of Sociology* 73, no. 6 (May 1968): 753-767.

——————. "The Social Organization of Low-Income Urban Families." In *Crucifixion by Power*, by Richard N. Adams. Austin: University of Texas Press, 1970.

——————. "Urban Poverty and Political Behavior in Guatemala," *Human Organization* 29, no. 1 (Spring 1970): 20-28.

Rodríguez, Mario. *Central America.* Englewood Cliffs, N.J.: Prentice-Hall, 1965.

Schnore, Leo F. "On the Spatial Structure of Cities in the Two Americas." In *The Study of Urbanization*, edited by Philip M. Hauser and Leo F. Schnore, pp. 347-398. New York: John Wiley, 1965.

Slater, Philip E. "Role Differentiation in Small Groups." *American Sociological Review* 20, no. 3 (June 1955): 300-310.

Spicer, Edward. "Patrons of the Poor." *Human Organization* 29, no. 1 (Spring 1970): 12-19.

Stinchcombe, Arthur. "Social Structure and Organization." In *Handbook of Organizations*, edited by J. G. March. Chicago: Rand McNally, 1965.

Strauss, Anselm. *Images of the American City.* New York: Free Press of Glencoe, 1961.

——————; L. Schatzman; R. Bucher; D. Ehrlich; and M. Sabshin. *Psychiatric Ideologies and Institutions.* New York: Free Press of Glencoe, 1964.

Suttles, Gerald. *The Social Order of the Slum.* Chicago: University of Chicago Press, 1968.

Swartz, Marc J., ed. *Local-Level Politics.* London: University of London Press, 1968.

Tangri, Shanti. "Urbanization, Political Stability, and Economic Growth." In *Political Development and Social Change*, edited by Jason L. Finkle and Richard W. Gable. New York: John Wiley, 1966.

Tax, Sol., ed. *Heritage of Conquest.* Glencoe, Ill: Free Press, 1952.

Termini, Deanne. "Socio-Economic and Demographic Characteristics of the Population of Guatemala City with Special Reference to Migrant-Non-Migrant Differences." M. A. thesis, University of Texas at Austin, 1968.

Theodorsen, George, ed. *Studies in Human Ecology*. New York: Harper and Row, 1961.

Tumin, Melvin M. *Caste in a Peasant Society*. Princeton: Princeton University Press, 1952.

Valentine, Charles. *Culture and Poverty*. Chicago: University of Chicago Press, 1968.

Vaughan, Denton R. *Urbanization in Twentieth Century Latin America: A Working Bibliography*. Austin: Institute of Latin America Studies and Population Research Center, The University of Texas at Austin, 1969.

Véliz, Claudio, ed. *Obstacles to Change in Latin America*. London: Oxford University Press, 1966.

Weber, Max. "The Protestant Sects and the Spirit of Capitalism." In *From Max Weber: Essays in Sociology*, edited by H. H. Gerth and C. Wright Mills. Oxford: Oxford University Press, 1948.

Whetten, Nathan. *Guatemala: The Land and the People*. New Haven: Yale University Press, 1961.

White, Alistair. "The Social Structure of the Lower Classes in San Salvador, Central America." Ph. D. dissertation, Cambridge University, 1969.

Wingo, Lowdon. "Recent Patterns of Urbanization among Latin American Countries." *Urban Affairs Quarterly* 2, no. 3 (March 1967): 81-109.

Wirth, Louis. "Urbanism as a Way of Life." In *Cities and Societies*, edited by P. K. Hatt and A. J. Reiss. New York: Free Press, 1963.

Wolf, Eric. "Kinship, Friendship and Patron-Client Relations in Complex Societies." In *The Social Anthropology of Complex Society*, edited by Michael Banton. London: Tavistock, 1966.

Zachariah, K. C. "Bombay Migration Study." *Demography* 3, no. 2 (1966): 378-392.

Zárate, Alvan O. "Principales patrones de migración interna en Guatemala, 1964." *Estudios Centroamericanos No. 3*. Guatemala City: Seminario de Integración Social, 1967.

INDEX